Best wishes to
Larry
From an old smoke eater
Warren Yates
10/96

A smokechaser's outfit circa 1933.

WARREN YAHR

Smokechaser

University of Idaho Press
Moscow, Idaho
1995

Printed in the United States of America.

98 97 96 95 5 4 3 2 1

Photographs marked WY were provided by the author. All others are courtesy of the United States Forest Service, Clearwater National Forest Ranger District, Orofino, Idaho.

CONTENTS

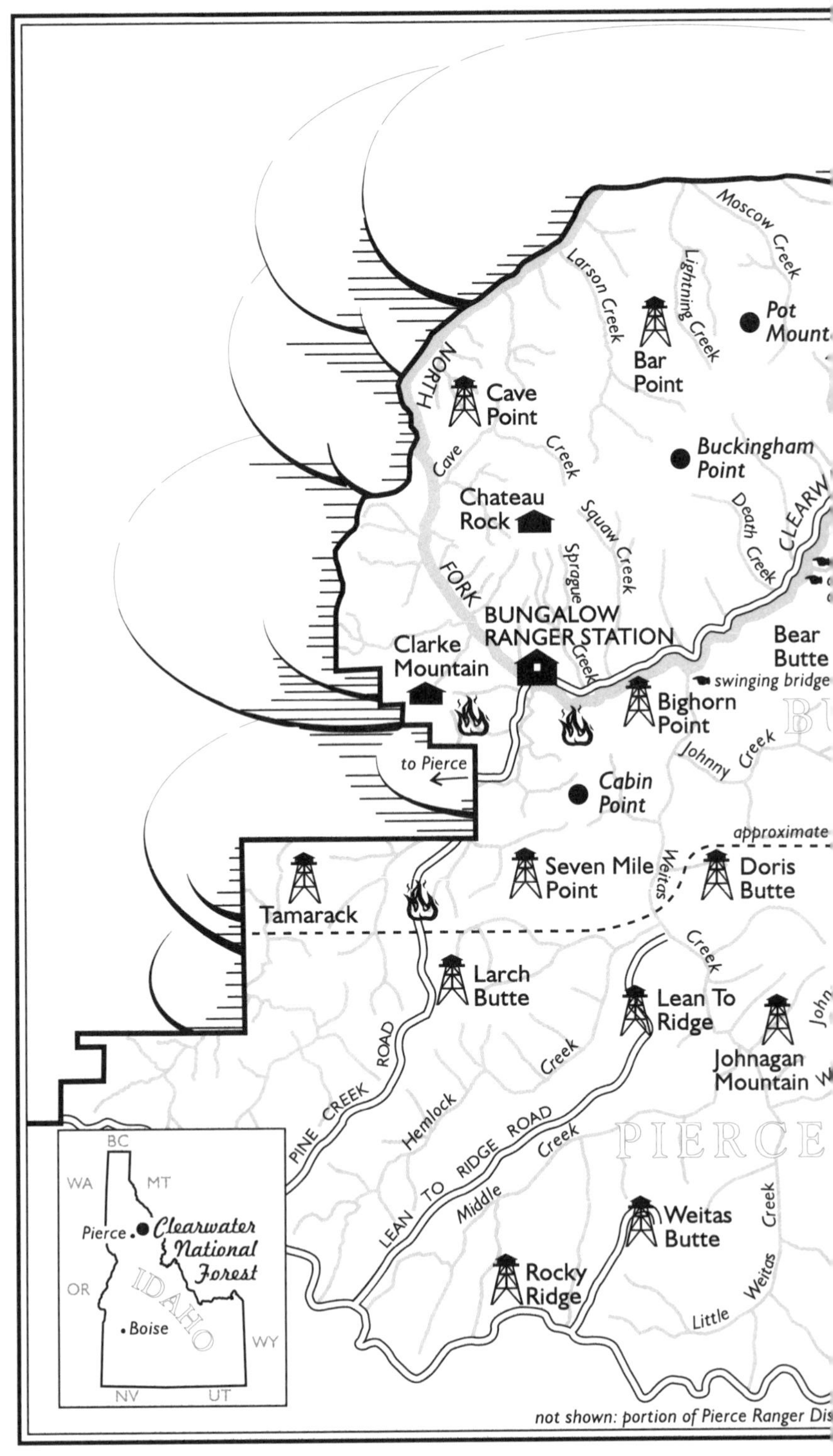

Moscow Creek
Larson Creek
Lightning Creek
Pot Mount
Bar Point
NORTH
Cave Point
Buckingham Point
Cave Creek
Chateau Rock
Squaw Creek
Death Creek
CLEARW
Sprague Creek
FORK
BUNGALOW RANGER STATION
Bear Butte
Clarke Mountain
swinging bridge
Bighorn Point
to Pierce
Johnny Creek
Cabin Point
approximate
Seven Mile Point
Weitas
Doris Butte
Tamarack
Creek
Larch Butte
Lean To Ridge
Johnagan Mountain
ROAD
PINE CREEK
Creek
Hemlock
LEAN TO RIDGE ROAD
Creek
Middle
PIERCE
Weitas Butte
Creek
Rocky Ridge
Weitas
Little
BC
WA
MT
Pierce
Clearwater National Forest
IDAHO
OR
Boise
WY
NV
UT
not shown: portion of Pierce Ranger Dis

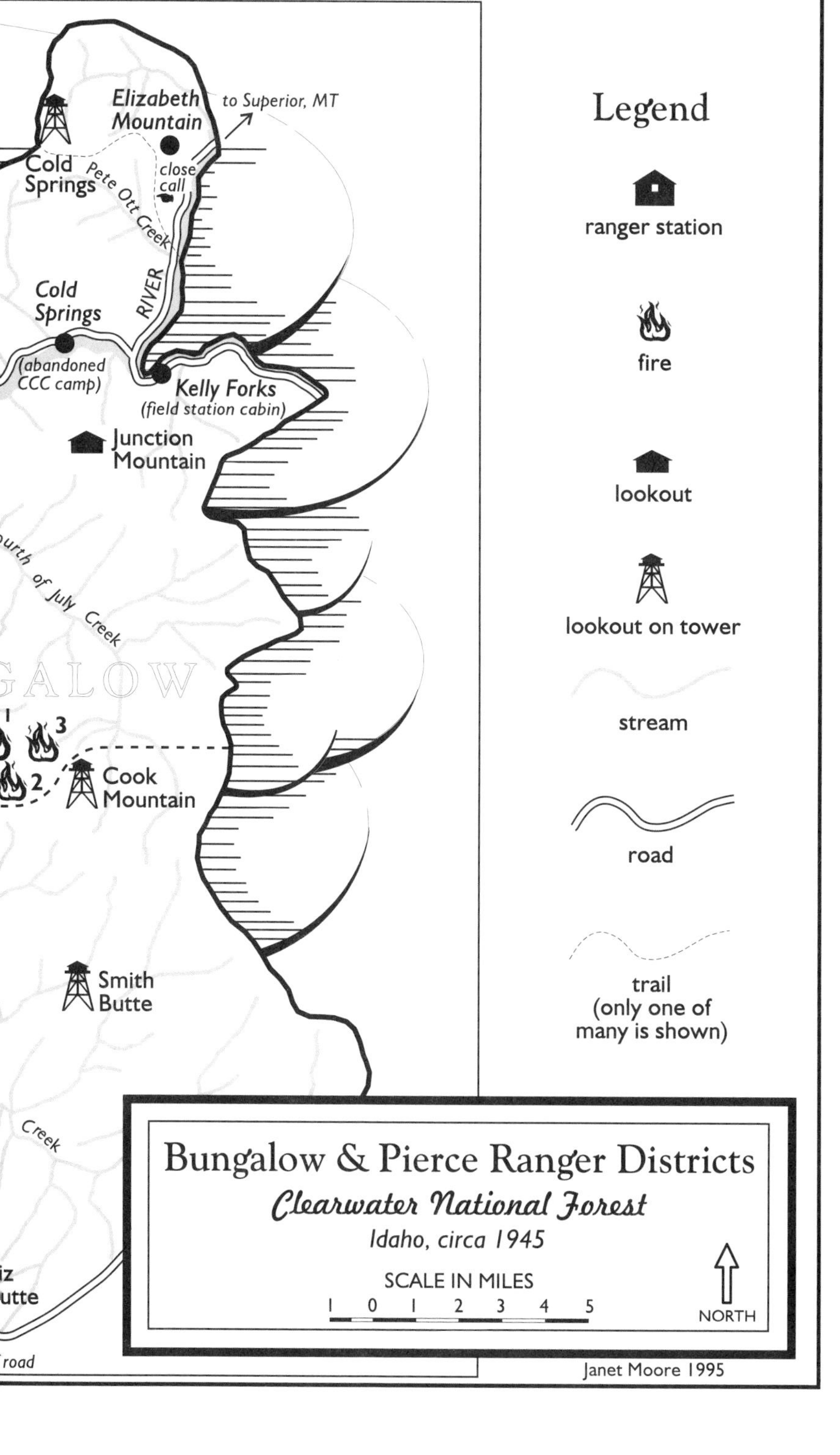

Bungalow & Pierce Ranger Districts

Clearwater National Forest

Idaho, circa 1945

SCALE IN MILES
1 0 1 2 3 4 5

NORTH

Janet Moore 1995

DEDICATION

To Doris, my sister, who insisted I start this book.
To my many friends who insisted I continue it.
To Carol, my wife, who somehow deciphered my handwriting and faithfully typed away.

Preface

These stories take place in the old Bungalow district of the Clearwater National Forest in northern Idaho during the 1940s. At that time only one road ran through the 105-mile stretch from Pierce, Idaho, to Superior, Montana. It was a treacherous road at best, as it still is today. Only narrow trails provided access to the lookouts and all supplies were brought up by foot, horseback, or pack mule—mainly the last.

In those days no commercial logging had been done in the district and probably not in the entire Clearwater, much of which had burned off in the fire of 1910 and was just now recovering. The burned-over areas were largely brush and small trees, which provided excellent feed for the deer and moose and elk in particular, since they were very numerous. In the unburned areas were large stands of virgin fir, pine, hemlock, cedar, and spruce. The lookouts were there to watch over these valuable trees.

It was an isolated, lonely life and not for everyone. Some thrived on it; others couldn't stand a week of it and came back in disgrace. It was a dangerous business, but being teen-age boys, we couldn't have cared less. Life always seemed a little sweeter when we risked it once in awhile—or at least that's the way we looked at it.

The lookout life has pretty much gone the way of the buffalo and pony express now. Of the hundreds, perhaps thousands, of lookout towers that once watched over our forests, only a few remain, and those are seldom occupied. So the wheels of progress keep turning. But then maybe it's progress and maybe it's not. Exposure to that kind of life for a few days might lure some of today's kids away from the television and VCR. That, in my humble opinion, would be progress.

The people in these stories are real, although some names have been changed. The places are real. The dialogue is as accurate as my memory permits after some fifty years. The Bungalow Ranger Station is gone now. Only a plaque commemorating old Jim Clarke, after whom Clarke Mountain is named, remains. But they can't take away the memories of those wonderful days when we went from boyhood to manhood in a few short months of the fire season. A few of those memories I would share with you.

One
How It Began

It was midnight when we stepped off the train in Spokane. Two more miserable sixteen-year-olds could hardly be imagined. For fifty hours we had been confined to hard, swaying, jolting seats. Sleep had been in short snatches no more than a half hour at a time.

Brian, my partner, had been here the previous year and knew where we were going even if I didn't. We were headed for an all-night theater—the only affordable lodging. As we shouldered our duffle bags, we were confronted by a friendly looking middle-age man.

"You boys looking for a place to stay?"

"Yeah."

"Why not come up to my place? I got a couple extra beds."

It sounded like a really good deal to me, but Brian had other ideas.

"Come on. Hurry up."

I followed but failed to understand why he refused the offer from this charitable gentleman.

"Hey, Brian, if we stayed with him we wouldn't have to spend anything."

"Don't you know what he is?"

"Just a friendly guy, I guess."

"Boy have you got a lot to learn."

Before we could go any farther, two young girls came up to us.

"Need a place to stay?"

I thought this had to be the friendliest town in the world, but Brian kept on walking, ignoring them. The girls kept pace with us.

"Really. We've got plenty of room. It wouldn't be any problem."

I lagged behind wondering how Brian could pass up a deal like this, but he kept going and I had to run to catch up.

"Brian, what's the matter with you? Don't you like girls any more or what?"

"Not that kind I don't."

"They seemed nice enough to me."

"Like I said before, you've got a lot to learn."

I had to admit that Brian was probably more worldly-wise than I was, but passing up that last offer was not what I would have called normal behavior on his part. I followed along anyway assuming he knew best, which undoubtedly he did.

Soon we came to the theater, paid our admission, and were treated to a double feature of Hedy LaMar steaming her way through "White Cargo" and a bevy of beauties in "Girls on Probation." Sleep did not come easily, but after the second time around even Hedy Lamar lost out to exhaustion and we fell into a fitful sleep.

When morning finally came, we looked and felt even worse than when we had staggered in. We went for a quick bite to eat and then took a bus to the edge of town hoping to hitchhike a ride to Lewiston, Idaho.

It was still early so most cars were heading into town. Eventually, though, a large truck filled to the top with household possessions came laboring up the road and pulled over and a lady rolled down the window.

"Where ya headin' boys?"

"Lewiston."

"This must be yer lucky day. If the truck don't break down, that's where we're headin'. Just climb on up and I'll hand yer bags up," she said, climbing out.

She was the first woman I had ever seen wearing cowboy boots. I was first up and was greeted by a ferocious dog that was chained to the front of the rack. I backed off.

"Just stay to the rear," the lady called. "He's mean but his chain ain't very long."

Brian came up and the lady handed us our duffle bags. We tied them onto the ropes that crisscrossed the load.

The truck struggled forward. We laid down behind our duffle bags to break the wind, and every time one of us stuck a head up, the dog snarled and lunged. Fortunately the chain was stout enough to hold a horse. Once up to speed the truck gave us something else to think about for it swayed ominously from side to side.

"Every time we turn a corner it feels like we're going over," Brian said.

"Maybe it's just cause we're up so high."

"Yeah, maybe. I sure hope so."

Mile after mile we swayed on through the beautiful Palouse country of eastern Washington. Rosalia, Colfax, and Pullman fell behind. Clouds began to form and up ahead we could see a full-blown thunderstorm in progress. When the first few raindrops spattered down, the truck ground to a halt and our cowboy-booted lady appeared.

"Sorry we can't fit you in the cab, boys, but there's just too much junk in there. What I will do is git this here cayoodle down so's you kin move up some," and with that she unhooked the dog's chain and removed our ill-tempered traveling companion. We moved forward into the hollow he had guarded, and once we got rolling again the raindrops sailed harmlessly overhead. Shortly afterward the road turned left and the storm went right. All we had to do was lay back and enjoy the ride and the fragrances after the rain. As the miles rolled by, Brian began looking ahead more often and at length he must have seen what he was looking for.

"I sure hope this truck's got good brakes."

"Why?"

"Look ahead."

"Holy cats! What's that?"

"The Lewiston Grade. Eleven miles of switchbacks, all downhill."

"Man, I never saw anything like this before. Look at the town down there. Can that be eleven miles away?"

I could feel the truck being downshifted. From our lofty perch we got a bird's-eye view of the grade with every swing and sway of the truck. Snaking our way downward, motor racing, we met cars and trucks laboring up toward us. Some of the occupants waved to the two of us clinging to the top of the load, but we were too busy hanging on to wave back. When we finally reached the bottom, we stopped and the driver stuck his head out.

"You wanta go on in to town or git off here?"

"We're headed to Orofino, so we'll get off now," said Brian.

"Okay. Throw yer stuff down, I'll ketch it."

So down we came and our driver, whom we had really not seen much of before, gave us a hearty handshake.

"You boys goin' to work for the Forest Service?"

"We hope to."

"Well, good luck to you."

"Thank you and thanks for the ride."

"Glad to be of help."

Over the raging of the dog, his wife called goodbye and blew us a kiss as they drove away.

"What nice people," I said.

"You'll find a lot of those out here," Brian answered. "I found that out last year."

We waved our thumbs at a dozen or so cars that never slowed down when Brian had an idea.

"Wait here. I'll be right back."

"Where are you going?"

"Across the street."

He disappeared into a roadside stand and came out carrying a large piece of cardboard with OROFINO printed on it.

"This'll help," he said, and sure enough the first car pulled over.

We hopped right in with our duffle bags and were greeted by a friendly middle-aged couple. The lady was most interested in where we'd come from and what our plans were. All in all it was an interesting ride until they let us off at the bridge that crosses the Clearwater near Spalding.

"Now for the last leg," Brian said. "If we're lucky maybe we'll get a ride all the way." He turned the cardboard over and printed PIERCE on the other side. We started thumbing again. Eventually a broken down '37 Chevy filled with a young couple and a half-dozen kids pulled over.

"Only goin' as far as Weippe, but if you want, we'll fit you in someplace."

"Great."

I wasn't so sure though. The tires were bald and the windows were either cracked or broken. Blue smoke issued ominously from the exhaust. What had once been a green car was now mostly red with rust. It had clearly seen better days, but a ride was a ride, so we accepted.

Obviously our duffle bags would not fit in the car, so our new driver stuck his finger in the hole in the trunk where there had once been a handle and lifted the lid. Pushing aside assorted junk, he made enough room to squeeze our bags in. Mine went into the spot formerly occupied by a spare tire.

Our carefree driver was a tall, slim man dressed in bib overalls. His wife sat beside a small child and held another on her lap. Four more children of various ages filled the back seat. There was no way to make room for us, so Brian's lap was occupied by a girl of perhaps three years, while I got a boy of about four. Two older ones sat between us, probably six or seven years old.

"Wait'll we hit the Greer Grade," Brian whispered to me as we lurched off. We could communicate without being overheard since the car had no muffler and the noise inside was deafening.

"Why?"

"You'll see."

Blue smoke seeped up through the floorboards. The road was visible between my feet and I kept my nose as close to the broken window as possible to avoid being asphyxiated and worried about the kids in the middle. I needn't have for they seemed totally unaffected by the fumes. After several miles the little boy on my lap turned and smiled at me. I felt something hot seeping through my trousers.

"He always does that when he's wetting his pants," the girl next to me shouted over the din.

She needn't have told me—I already knew. Next time he turned and smiled I was prepared and made him stand up and most of it went through the hole in the floor.

At last we crossed the bridge at Greer and I could see why Brian had been apprehensive. What loomed before us was another grade similar to the one at Lewiston, only gravel instead of pavement, and this time we were going up, not down. Sensing our doubts, the driver turned around.

"Don't you worry none—we'll make 'er."

With that we started up in high gear, then to second after the first switchback, and then to low shortly thereafter. With every downshift came a noticeable increase in not only the noise level but the fumes as well. We opened every window that still had a crank handle. I think there were two. About halfway up, with the temperature gauge against the top end and clouds of steam escaping from under the hood, we stopped. With his wife holding her foot on the brake, our driver produced a gallon jug of water and a towel and somehow got the radiator cap off without getting scalded and dumped in the gallon of water.

"That'll cool 'er off," he said as he let out the clutch and we started off once again.

It was a long, slow, painful climb, but miraculously we made it to the top—with the radiator boiling merrily away. If this was of any concern to our driver he showed no sign of it, nor did his wife. To the kids this was obviously an everyday affair. We chugged on to Weippe where it was announced, "End of the line, folks. This is as far as we go."

We pulled up to a small shack, which was apparently their home. Brian's lap rider had fallen asleep sucking her thumb—or had she succumbed to the fumes I wondered? She awoke still alive, however, as we all piled out. Shouldering our duffle bags once again we thanked our friends for the lift and started off down the road.

"I never thought we'd make it," said Brian.

"Neither did I."

"Why are you walking so funny?"

"Look at my pants."

"How'd they get so wet?"

"Didn't you know that kid wet while he was sitting on my lap?"

Brian thought it was hilarious. By the time Brian got over his laughing fit, we were out of town and an empty logging truck stopped for us.

We threw our duffle bags in back and climbed aboard.

"Going to Pierce?" Brian asked.

"Yup, that's where I live. I bet you're headed for the Ranger Station."

"Right you are."

It wasn't very long before we pulled into Pierce, and after saying our thanks we walked a couple blocks to the Ranger Station and signed in. The ranger looked us over.

"Either of you been here before?"

"Yes, I was here last year," Brian answered.

"What did you do?"

"Blister rust control."

"Is that what you want again?"

"You bet."

"Okay. There'll be a truck going out to Beaver Creek tomorrow. Just sign up in the hiring tent in the morning."

"Where do I go?" I asked.

"Go to the hiring tent and wait. You'll get on somewhere."

This came as a surprise. I had figured on Brian and me staying together, but now it looked like we would be split up. It was now late afternoon so we found a couple empty bunks and went to the cookhouse for our first decent meal in four days. There were several bunkhouses, all about half full of boys our age, and after supper we got acquainted with a few who were in nearby bunks. When the sun sank, though, the lack of sleep caught up with us, and even with the lights on and boys milling around, we slept right through it all.

Right after breakfast we went straight to the hiring tent, hoping to arrange something so we could stay together, but it was no use. Brian was the last one to go on the truck, which left shortly thereafter.

Now I was all alone and wondering where I would end up or if I would even get a job at all. The hiring tent was perhaps fifty by thirty feet, with benches all along the sides. In the middle sat a young fellow dressed in a Forest Service uniform at a typewriter. When someone came in wanting a certain number of boys, he'd select the ones he wanted and they'd report to have the necessary papers typed up and be on their way. As soon as one group left, more boys drifted in and the benches remained at least half occupied most of the time. At noon, everybody adjourned for an hour. Nobody as yet had expressed an interest in me.

The afternoon passed and the boys came and went and I was still passed over. It must be my size I thought. The ones selected always seemed to be the bigger, huskier boys. Just when the number began to dwindle and my hopes rose, more boys would come in and my hopes would grow dim again. I did, however, meet two other boys about my size, Jay and Dale, who were caught in the same predicament. We sat together for awhile, but then decided we'd have a better chance by splitting up. We did agree to eat our meals together, though.

The second day was a duplicate of the first. The bigger boys came in and were soon hired and the three of us sat and watched. How long this could go on, I didn't know, but what I did know was I was running up a bill at the dinner table and had little money to pay for it. I had to get a job—that's all there was to it.

Day number three, and things were not looking up. I resolved to start skipping the noon meal to keep expenses down. I'd just eat more at the other two meals. Jay and Dale agreed to do the same. At noon after all the others had filed out, a one-armed man came in and spoke to the young fellow in the Forest Service uniform.

"Shorty needs three boys at the Bungalow," the one-armed man said.

"You in a hurry, Frank?"

"Yeah, no time to waste."

"Everybody but these three are eating, right now."

Frank looked at us.

"How come you're not eating?"

"Can't afford it."

"I see. Well, he didn't say what size they had to be. Sign 'em up," Frank said.

The clerk inserted the first paper and then looked up.

"Any of you afraid of district work?"

"What is that?"

"Lookout duty—fire fighting and everything that goes with it."

We all shook our heads. As a matter of fact, I could scarcely believe my good fortune. This would be far more challenging and interesting than pulling out gooseberry bushes, which was what the blister rust control boys were doing. I was overjoyed. Hopefully, we'd get signed up and gone before the rest of the boys came back.

As soon as my papers were completed I made a mad dash to the bunkhouse for my duffle bag and climbed in the back of Frank's pickup. Nobody was going to dislodge me, no siree. Jay and Dale soon followed and we all breathed a sigh of relief as we rolled out of the yard. The other boys were just starting to come out of the cookhouse. We waved good-bye to them and sat back wondering where the Bungalow might be and what it was.

"I think it's another ranger station," said Dale. "Somebody said there's good fishing there."

Just what I wanted to hear. Jay was looking in through the back window.

"You should see this," he said. "Every time he shifts, he takes his hand off the wheel and holds it with his knee."

I had been wondering myself how Frank could drive these roads. Looking in I saw that when he grabbed the gear shift, his right knee would come up to hold the steering wheel steady until he got his hand back on it again. It was all done so smoothly that it was hardly noticeable.

The scenery was spectacular. In spots a few snowbanks still lingered between the towering evergreens. Sheer dropoffs of hundreds of feet passed by. A misjudgment here would surely be fatal, but our driver took it all in stride. Gradually we dropped lower and began to follow a beautiful stream. I could easily imagine the trout lurking there just waiting to be caught.

At last we rounded a bend, crossed a small bridge, and a barn appeared, and then a whole row of dark brown buildings with white trim. A flag flew from a tall flagpole. We pulled in front of what appeared to be the office and were greeted by a stocky man even shorter than myself.

Shorty's handshake was strong and his smile sincere and I liked him instantly—not only him, the whole place. It was nestled down at the foot of a mountain with the stream we'd been following—Orogrande Creek—running behind it. Beyond that was a large river—the North Fork of the Clearwater.

What a spot, I thought. I'll do anything that's asked of me, just so I get work here.

We signed a few more papers and then Shorty took us to the bunkhouse where we got settled.

"Have you eaten?" he asked.

I explained how it happened that we had not. He got a good laugh out of that and escorted us down to the cookhouse and introduced us to Bill Mitchell, who was washing dishes.

"Think you can fix these boys a little something to eat?"

"I'll think about it—while they're finishing the dishes."

Shorty winked at us. "When you're done get yourselves settled in the bunkhouse and I'll see you later."

With that I grabbed a dishrag and got to work. I was going to make a good impression no matter what. After eating I stayed and helped Bill clean up while the others went to the bunkhouse.

"You ain't hurtin' yourself none by pitchin' in," said Bill. "I see you ain't afraid to work. That's good. Too many boys come here and don't know how to work. They don't last long. Shorty is one good boss, but one thing he don't tolerate and that's laziness. Wade don't either."

"Who's Wade?"

"Alternate ranger. You'll meet him soon enough. I'll give you one little tip. Wade's a good boss and he's fair and square, but don't never talk back to him—that's my advice."

I took it and it served me well. Dishes done, I went to the bunkhouse. I had just opened my duffle bag when the door burst open and a huge, broad-shouldered man wearing cowboy boots and a hat to match strode in. He looked for all the world like John Wayne.

"Howdy son. I'm Wade Candler."

He extended his huge hand. Again, I liked this man right away. In fact, he treated me like a son. As long as I worked he and his wife, Buckshot, were like parents to me.

I was ready to embark on the most memorable and enjoyable time of my life. I would work at the Bungalow District over several fire seasons and at one point I hoped to make the Forest Service my career. I would be stationed at many of the lookouts and I would handle a wide range of jobs and different assignments. And I would meet some of the finest people I would ever know. Though many years have passed the memories are still vivid in my mind.

Two
A Night on the Town

As the three of us hiked down from the lookout called Chateau, I reflected back on the last few days and my initial training. Never before had I seen such mountains, or any mountains, as far as that went, except out of a train window. Nor had I ever been up in a lookout tower and stared in wonderment at the scene below. This was definitely the life for me—no doubt about it.

Jack (actually Richard) Johnson and Bill Fry had been superb companions, and were so capable, I could scarcely believe they were teenagers. Jack could scamper up a telephone pole like a monkey and Bill too. They even allowed me to put on the climbers and I made it to the top of a pole and down again. That was really something.

Now, as we hurried along, I realized that something would have to be done about my footwear. I was slogging along in my cousin's cast off work shoes, two sizes too large. Even with newspaper stuffed in the toes (a trick I'd learned from wearing cast offs most of my sixteen years), they still were too narrow and the smooth soles gave entirely too little traction on the mountain trails.

Those outlandish shoes hadn't gone unnoticed by Jack and Bill either. They referred to them as my "skis." Well, that matter would be taken care of when I got my first paycheck. Then I would get myself a pair of "cork boots" like the others wore. (These were actually caulked boots, but everyone called them corks. Caulked boots were heavy leather-soled boots with fifty or so protruding steel caulks—great for traction, especially on wet logs.)

It was going to take more than sore feet to dampen my enthusiasm, though. The mountains were already in my blood. Three days we had spent, two at Chateau and one at Cave Point. I had learned a lot in those few days, climbing, splicing, making insulators, hanging line, sawing logs and moving them out of the trail, and cooking. Oh, the cooking. Maybe it was just the fresh air and hard work, but those two boys surely knew how to put on a meal. Next time, they said, it would be my turn.

Another thing I learned was to play the game of Hearts. There was a deck of cards at Chateau and the last afternoon it had begun to snow after we got in, so we let down the shutters, lit a lantern, and, with a roaring fire in the stove, they taught me to play Hearts. We played to see who'd get water, cook supper, wash dishes, everything. Unfortunately for Jack, his run of cards was unusually bad and as a result he had a busy evening.

As we neared the ranger station we came first to the abandoned CCC Camp across the river. Taking a little time out we looked over the orderly rows of barracks, the various officers' homes, the generator building, library, pool hall with a pool table sitting there collecting dust, but no signs of cues or balls. They had probably been "liberated" long ago.

The library had no books that looked interesting, so we went on, thinking what it must have been like a few years ago when several hundred people lived here.

At the station, the rest of the boys were all excited about going to town.

"How're you gonna get there?" asked Jack.

"Shorty and Clyde are going out to get their families and they'll take a carful each, but we'll have to find our own way back, 'cause they'll be loaded down," replied Perk, one of the other rookies.

"How many are going?"

"Five, so far."

"Three more makes eight," said Jack looking at Bill and me. "How about it?"

"Suits me," Bill replied.

"Well, I'm down to a dollar and some change," I said, "but I need to get a fishing license, so I better not pass up this opportunity. I may not get another."

Actually, I had been fishing without a license and Shorty had warned me about it, so until I got one there was no more fishing and that was one thing I very much wanted to do. Bill ran into the office to see if there'd be room for us and came out grinning. "It's all set but we'll have to hurry. They'll be leaving in about an hour."

That meant a shower and supper right away, but we made it with time to spare, and then we all crowded in and were off to town. Pierce was quite a wild and wooly town in those days, as I was soon to discover.

Our first priority was to find a hotel room. There were two maybe three hotels in town at that time. Bill went into the Clearwater and reported back that they were full up. That didn't bode too well so we hurried on down to the Shamrock. Again, Bill went in while the rest of us waited outside.

"They've only got one room left, one single bed for two bucks, that's two bits apiece."

"We better take it," said Jack. "It's better than sleeping in the street."

Either way it didn't sound to me like we'd get much sleep with eight people and a single bed. How right I was.

All told there were Bill, Jack and myself, plus, Perk, Dale, Ival, and two boys named Bob.

Nobody bothered to look at the room. When it's the last one in town, there's no need to look. You are simply stuck with it. Next stop was a soda fountain across the street, bursting with boys from the blister rust control camps. There must have been a hundred of them all clamoring for the attention of one very pretty young lady who was frantically trying to turn out sundaes, sodas, floats, shakes, malts, and cones and somehow get them to whoever had ordered them. She was fighting a losing battle, though, for every time somebody succeeded in placing an order, he was promptly pushed to the rear and his sundae or whatever was usually eaten and paid for by somebody else.

All this made little difference to me. I had almost no money to buy anything with anyway. I did, however, feel sorry for the poor girl. Not only was she at her wit's end trying to please everybody, but half the boys were trying to date her and a few were making off-color remarks, which she tried to ignore.

Bill finally succeeded in getting her attention and ordered eight cones and we all sauntered down the street, cone in hand, headed for the dance hall.

Along the way stood a dry goods store and in the window were several pairs of cork boots. I looked at them longingly, but with no funds, they would have to stay there a bit longer. Meanwhile I would have to make do with my "skis."

As it turned out, Shorty took pity on me later and had the supply truck bring me a pair, the cost of which was deducted from my first check. I was surefooted from then on.

The dance hall was as crowded or perhaps even more crowded than the soda fountain. Every "blister buster" must have come to town. Boys outnumbered girls by a ratio of at least four to one. Girls could afford to be quite selective, and they were.

Our gang sort of drifted apart in groups of two or three. Bill and I stayed together and found a vacant spot on a bench from where we could look over the rather limited field. After much hesitation we finally decided to cut in on two rather plain looking girls who were dancing with each other.

The girls didn't impress either of us very favorably, and apparently the feeling was mutual, for when the music stopped they headed toward the far side of the hall and Bill and I returned to our spot on the sidelines. Just as we sat down I could hear from outside the sound of a fire siren.

"Must be a fire somewhere."

"No, that's just the curfew siren. All people under eighteen are supposed to be off the street in a half-hour."

"Do they enforce it?"

"Yeah, they're pretty strict about it."

"Maybe we should round the other guys up before long."

"I suppose so. In a little while."

The music had started up again and looking around for the rest of our gang, I noticed a couple of fellows making their way along our side of the floor. They were older appearing than most of the kids here, probably in their early twenties. They would stop briefly and talk to people on the benches and then move on. Probably looking for somebody, I thought.

Eventually they worked their way up to us. The taller one, a tough looking hombre, spoke to me, but with all the noise in the hall I couldn't understand him.

"What?"

Again he spoke, but I still couldn't make out what he wanted so I stood up to get closer.

"I said, do you want to fight?"

Now, I understood.

"What about?"

"To see who'll win." He grabbed me by the shoulders, "Come on, we'll git a drink first to kind a get you in the mood."

His hand was like a vise on my shoulder as he propelled me toward the front of the hall where he must have had a bottle stashed away.

"I bet yer a reg'lar little banty roaster, ain't you?"

"I don't back down from anybody," I foolishly replied, though the last thing I wanted was to tangle with this guy. He was a good half a head taller than myself and probably out weighed me by a good thirty or forty pounds. He could easily cripple me, and probably would, just for his own amusement. How did I ever get in a mess like this? I should never have stood up, but how did I know what he was up to?

Well, I would have to get out of it somehow, without losing too much face. If he busted me up I'd be unable to work and that meant no job and no pay and no money to get home on. I would have to think of something quick or it would be too late.

We had nearly reached the end of the hall, his hand still gripping my shoulder, when a blood-curdling scream erupted in the center of the dance floor, followed by pandemonium.

Girls started screaming and boys were yelling and converging on the scene. My captor momentarily relaxed his grip and I wasted no time in taking advantage of the opportunity, breaking away and making a beeline for the milling mob in the middle of the floor, where a pall of smoke hung over one still screaming girl.

I wanted to be of some help, if possible, but my chief motivation was self-preservation, so I worked my way into the densest part of the crowd where everyone stood around the hysterical girl.

"What happened?" I asked a bystander.

"That dumb jackass over there was dancin' with her and set her hair afire with his cigarette."

I looked where he pointed. That dumb jackass was Dale, still puffing nonchalantly away. Other people were glaring at him and it was plain that when things settled down he would answer for his carelessness. Best to get him out of here.

Suddenly there was a hand gripping my elbow. My heart sank, but it was only Bill.

"Let's get out of here."

"You said it, but we gotta get Dale out too. He's the one that set the girl's hair on fire."

"Holy cow, what next?"

Where were the rest of the boys? I looked around and there was Jack.

"Get the rest of the guys, we're leaving right now," I said.

"Already?"

"I'll explain later. Just hurry up."

Bill got Dale by the arm and started dragging him along. Dale seemed reluctant to go, but went anyway.

"What's all the fuss about? She only got singed a little."

"If you know what's good for you, you'll get out of here while the getting's good."

I had visions of a lynch mob organizing. Besides, I had reasons of my own for leaving. Furthermore, the curfew was by now past and we had to get back to the hotel before we got in more trouble.

"Why did you want to fight that guy?" Bill asked as we headed for the door.

"Man, that was the last thing I was inclined to do. All I did was stand up so I could hear what he was saying and the next thing you know I'm gonna be his victim of the week. I was lucky to get out of there in one piece."

"I'll say you were. That guy could have beat you up pretty bad."

"He was big enough alright. Guess I can thank Dale for getting me out of that one."

We stopped on the landing just outside the door to make sure everybody was with us. We were perhaps three feet above the sidewalk and several steps led down to it in either direction to the left and right. I noticed the girl from the soda fountain walking down the sidewalk on the other side of the street and apparently Dale did too, for from behind me came a loud wolf whistle.

"Who done that?" said someone directly in front of me.

"None of your business," said Dale directly behind me.

I looked down to see a big, mean-looking lumberjack, obnoxiously drunk and spoiling for a fight.

Just when we thought things were settling down, now this.

"Just come on down here and I'll teach you some manners, one, two, or the whole damn bunch, don't make no difference to me."

"Go soak yer head," came from Dale, as the war of words continued.

Obviously the man was not going to soak his head. As a matter of fact his disposition was not getting any better with Dale goading. It was a standoff as the two of them continued to trade insults. Obviously, he had us trapped. If we came down the stairs we were hemmed in by an iron railing and he could deal with us two at a time, which I had no doubt he was more than capable of doing.

From inside the hall, now, I could hear, "Where'd he go? Anybody seen him?"

Surely they were hunting for Dale and it was only a matter of time, until somebody discovered where he'd gone. Something had to be done to break the stalemate. I knew from past experience that a large tough man can knock the stuffing out of a whole group of kids like us if he is on his feet, but get him on the ground and it's an entirely different matter.

With that in mind, I said to the boy next to me, "Start down the stairs to your left, just enough to get his attention, but stay out of his reach. I'll run down the other way and tackle him around the knees and hang on till he's down, then we can make a break for the hotel. I don't think he can outrun us."

We had just begun to implement our plan when there was a new development.

"Some trouble here, John?" came a voice from my right.

"Nuthin' I can't handle."

I looked and there striding up the sidewalk came another big tough-looking gent, only this one had a star pinned to his shirt and a revolver on his right hip. In his left hand he carried a wicked looking billy club.

"Now you just run along, John, and let me handle this."

"Not 'till I teach these punks a few manners."

"I'll take care of that John, you just go about your business."

"I already told you, I ain't leavin' 'till I knock some manners into a few of them heads."

I saw the billy club switched from the left to the right hand ready for action.

"Now, John, I told you twice and I ain't about to tell you again. Git a move on—NOW."

John still stood there, defiant.

The club started up, "You gonna move or ain't you?"

John moved, probably for his own good, but turned to us.

"You ain't seen the last of me."

He walked slowly across the street glaring over his shoulder at us.

Our rescuer, however, didn't hold us in much higher esteem than the man he'd rescued us from.

"Come down here, all of you."

"Yes sir."

"You hear that siren awhile ago?"

"Yes sir."

"Know what that means?"

"Yes sir."

"You got a place to stay?"

"Yes, we do, at the Shamrock."

"Shut up and follow me."

"Yes sir."

So we got a police escort down the street to the hotel. Once there he stopped and looked us over. "Now if I see any one of you boys out on the street tonight I'll be puttin' you up in a place you ain't gonna like one little bit. You got that?"

"Yes sir."

"Now git in there and stay in there."

That pretty much settled things, at least for now. It was a rather subdued bunch of boys that started through the barroom and up the stairs. The lawman's voice must have carried inside for the people at the crowded bar looked at us and chuckled in amusement as we went through and up the stairs.

Bill had the room key and when he opened the door there was a mad scramble for the bed. Obviously, eight of us were never going to fit on it and it was a matter of first come, first served.

After much pushing and shoving it was decided that four was the absolute maximum capacity for the bed and that meant that the "lucky four" would have to be at an angle in order not to have head and feet hanging off, a most uncomfortable position indeed.

That left only the floor for the rest of us and there was very little of that. The room contained only the bed and a night stand at the foot end of it, there being scarcely room enough to move between the two. On either side of the bed, the walls were so close that there was just barely room for someone to squeeze in. That took care of two more, the other two (Bill and myself) would have to push ourselves under the bed, which we did. Any amount of bouncing on the bed (and there was plenty of it) brought the springs down on us plus the possibility that the whole thing might collapse. Never have I spent a worse night. While we were still arranging ourselves, somebody counted heads and noticed there were only seven of us.

"Whose missing?" Ival wondered.

The one small light bulb hanging down from a cord gave scarcely enough light to let you know who was who. That question was promptly solved by Jack, kicking at the door.

"Lemme in, will ya?"

"Open it yourself, it's not locked."

"I can't, I got my hands full."

I struggled out from under the bed and opened the door. There stood Jack with a case of beer, just what we needed.

"Thought you guys could use a little refreshment."

"Hey great. Who's got an opener?"

Somebody produced a Boy Scout knife with an opener and eight bottle caps hit the floor. When you turn eight teenage boys loose with three bottles of beer apiece, nobody is going to get much sleep, and nobody did. After the second round it was becoming understandably stuffy in the room, so the window had to be opened—only the window didn't open. It was nailed into the framework. That called for drastic measures, and out came the Boy Scout knife again. With some persuasion the nails were pulled out followed by the window, which we leaned against the wall.

"Now that's better," said Jack, who was occupying the spot next to the window. "All I want now is the pillow. You guys can have the bed, but I want that."

After some discussion it was decided that Jack was indeed entitled to the pillow, being as he had paid for the beer. Instead of handing it to him as he requested, with a shout of "here she comes," Perk threw it just beyond his reach and out the window it sailed. Everybody but Jack thought it was pretty funny.

"What'd you do that for?"

"What's the matter, can't you catch a big pillow?"

"Not if I can't reach it, I can't."

"Well, if you want it, you'll have to go get it."

"I oughta make you get it. You're the one that threw it out."

"Go get it yourself."

It began to look like we were headed for another confrontation, but Bill calmed things down.

"Stop your bickering, I'll go get the damn thing myself."

Before Bill could disengage himself from under the bed, Jack stepped over us and went out the door, obviously not happy. I couldn't say that I blamed him. From his spot on the bed, Ival watched out the window and gave us a progress report.

"He's down there. He's got the pillow. He's heading back."

Soon Jack burst through the door laughing.

"Boy, you shoulda seen the look on those faces in the bar, when I came back in carrying a pillow. One guy hollered at me to go back out and get one for him too."

The beer supply was starting to dwindle and, as might be expected, the trips to the bathroom at the end of the hall began to increase.

Whenever somebody got off the bed to take a trip, one of the floor dwellers would hasten to take his more comfortable spot, only to be displaced when he could hold it no longer and had to head down the hall himself. So the game of musical beds went on.

Bill and me being under the bed had no chance at all of getting a better spot. Jack was quite contented with his pillow, next to the window, so the exchanges were between the bed residents and the one on the floor next to the door. That being settled, it began to look like we might get some sleep, but it was not to be.

A drunk selected a fence post under our window and engaged in a rather one-sided conversation with it, very little of which was understandable. What we were able to gather was that his wife had run off and he was confiding to the fence post exactly what it was he intended to do about it. At first it was amusing, but after a quarter hour of it, Jack had had enough.

"Hey shut up down there. We're trying to get some sleep."

The drunk took no notice. Apparently he had found a good listener and had no intention of breaking off the conversation.

"Are you gonna shut up or do I have to come down there?"

"Don't you dare go down there," said Bill. "We've had enough trouble for one night."

"Okay, I won't. Just gimme one of those beer bottles, that'll fix him."

One of the Bobs handed him a bottle and it was soon on its way.

"Bombs away! Shucks, I missed. Gimme another."

That one didn't miss. There came a hollow "clunk" from down below.

Ival was looking out. "He's down."

Now everybody had to have a look.

"He's not moving."

"Maybe he's dead."

"Naw, I only grazed him a little—prob'ly just passed out."

"He's awful still."

"What're we gonna do?"

"Let's put the window back in. Nobody'll know where it came from."

Everybody agreed but Jack, who still insisted the man had only passed out. He was outvoted, however, and the window went back in. We were all pretty subdued temporarily at least. Ival would look out every few minutes and report.

"He's still down, not moving." That really quieted things down, and after half a dozen such ominous reports even Jack was a little less confident. After all, there were two bottles down below and two missing from our case. It shouldn't be too difficult to put two and two together. After a tense half hour, we got the all clear.

"He's gone."

We all breathed a sigh of relief.

"See, I told ya, he was ready to pass out and I only helped him along a little. I'm takin' the window back out."

By now we were out of beer, and everybody had taken their trip down the hall so it began to look like what little was left of the night might be spent in peaceful repose.

Again, fate took a hand. It began with angry voices in the hallway and soon escalated to boots scraping and fists flying right outside our door.

As a matter of fact, one of the participants was knocked so hard up against the door that it nearly gave way, prompting two of our boys to leap off the bed and put their backs against it, in hopes of keeping out any unwelcome guest. Had the fight spilled over into our crowded room, one can only imagine what could have happened. Fortunately for us though, it continued on down the hall, finally ending somewhere in the vicinity of the bathroom. Just how it ended or who won or lost, we were not in a position to determine.

Nobody was curious enough to go out and inquire, either. We were just thankful enough that they hadn't made it into our room to resolve their disagreement. When all was quiet for fifteen minutes, Perk looked out.

"Hall is empty, not a soul around."

"Good, now maybe we can get some sleep."

"Yeah," said Jack, "except it's getting light outside."

He was right. From where I lay I could see the sky beginning to brighten. Well, if the night had not been very restful, at least, it had not been boring either. I guess we were all too tired out to do any more roughhousing and too uncomfortable to sleep, so we just lay where we were and waited in silence for six o'clock when the first restaurant would open.

I couldn't have been more miserable, having spent the entire night on the hard floor under the bed with my jacket rolled up for a pillow. My neck hurt and my back and I guess everything else did too.

Besides that, I was ravenously hungry, having only had time for a few bites of supper. One or two of the boys had watches and at quarter to six everybody started out to head for breakfast, but Bill stopped me.

"Let 'em go, if you can wait awhile. The bed is gonna be empty and maybe we can get some shuteye. I have a feeling we'll be needing it."

"Okay. I'm hungry, but I can wait."

So we lay down and dozed off immediately only to be awakened by someone at the door an hour or two later. It turned out to be the cleaning lady.

"I thought you boys was all gone or I wouldn't of bothered you."

"Oh that's okay," I answered. "The rest went out, but we stayed to get some sleep. I didn't really get any last night."

"How come?"

"Well, with eight of us in here and one thing and another it wasn't overly restful, and then there was a big ruckus out in the hall that kept us awake for awhile."

"Know what you mean. I could hear all that racket myself. Say if you boys wanta sleep some more, I'll just mosey on down and do them other rooms first."

I looked at Bill and he shook his head.

"No we're about starved and it's time to get some grub anyway, so you go right ahead and we'll be on our way."

"Well, thanks boys, much obliged."

So we headed for the restaurant, feeling a bit refreshed, but not much.

The others had apparently eaten and left for we saw no sign of them. I was down to my last fifty cents plus the dollar I was saving for my fishing license, but in those days half a buck would get you a pretty substantial breakfast.

After having eaten we headed on down the street.

"How're you fixed for funds?" asked Bill.

"I've still got a dollar for a fishing license, but that's it."

"Need to borrow a little?"

"Not really."

"Well, then, I'm just gonna pick up a few magazines and candy bars to take on the lookout and then we can start thinking about how we're gonna get back to the Bungalow."

"I meant to ask about that. How do we plan to get there?"

"Hitchhike, I suppose, but there ain't too many cars on that road. We could wind up walking."

"That's a long way."

"I'll say it is—twenty-eight miles."

"Boy, I hope we get a ride."

"So do I. That's why I reckon we better get out there soon. Remember the other six guys will be needing to get back too."

"Let's get going."

So we picked up Bill's things at the soda fountain and then headed for the filling station where fishing licenses were sold.

Government employees were allowed to have a resident license, even though most of us were from out of state.

That taken care of, we walked on past the Ranger Station, where I'd spent several anxious days waiting for a job, and then proceeded out of town. A creek ran alongside the road and we could see a few trout rising, so we stopped to watch. Some sort of wooden structure sat rotting in a pond and we speculated as to what it might have been.

"Probably, had something to do with gold mining," said Bill. "You know gold was discovered here long ago and that's most likely what that thing was used for, whatever it is."

No cars came along so we walked at a leisurely pace, just talking and enjoying the scenery and the day. After several miles we came to another stream and watched the trout. I managed to catch a grasshopper and dropped it in the water. Instantly, there was a splash and it was gone.

"Hey, that was fun," said Bill, "Let's see if we can catch some more."

We spent the better part of an hour feeding the fish. Not a car passed during that time. As a matter of fact, we hadn't seen a car since leaving town. No cars, no ride.

It began to dawn on both of us that we'd better step up the pace or it would be dark before we made it to the Bungalow, unless we were fortunate enough to get a ride.

Finally an old man driving a model A Ford stopped, but he was going in the wrong direction.

"Howdy boys."

"Hi."

"Listen, I'm goin' into town and I'll be comin' back in an hour or so. I live maybe three, four miles down the road. If you feel like waitin', I'll pick you up on my way back."

"Okay. Thanks a lot."

"What do you think Bill?"

"It's tempting, but he may get in some bar and not come back for a long time."

"That's what I was thinking and after all, we'd only get a few miles out of the ride anyway."

"Good. Let's start hoofing it. You know the only traffic on this road is really Forest Service trucks and fishermen. The trucks don't run on Sundays unless there's a fire, which there isn't, and the fishermen are all coming back, not going in. That means our chances of getting a ride are mighty slim."

"I see what you mean, and it seems to me it must be well past noon, so we'd better get a move on."

Bill was in complete agreement and we started off at a brisk walk. Every mile there was a marker, so we always knew how far we had to go, though some miles seemed much longer than others, especially the uphill ones. The sun was already behind the trees when we hit the fourteen-mile marker, the halfway point. My feet were beginning to hurt. I noticed Bill starting to limp too, but neither of us mentioned our discomfort. As we walked or rather limped on, we talked of many things—hunting, fishing, our families, friends, girlfriends, school, anything and everything that came to mind. We found out a lot about each other on that long walk. At the eighteen-mile post there was a "jungle phone," so Bill rang Bungalow to see if there was anyone who might come and get us.

"No luck," he said, putting down the phone. "Nobody around but Bowlander and he doesn't have a car, so I guess that's that."

"Bill," I said, "my feet are hurting me so bad, I'm not sure I'll make it that far."

"What's the matter?"

"My shoes are too short. Wish I'd have worn my 'skis.'"

"What size are they?"

"Eight, why?"

"Mine are nines and they're plenty big on me, but there's a hole in the right sole and I've got a big blister where the gravel gets in."

"What say we try switching shoes. Maybe that'll help."

"Okay, let's try it."

So we tried on each other's shoes, but not before I found something to cover up the hole in Bill's right one. He had broken out two of his candy bars and offered one to me.

"Thanks a lot, Bill. This is great, but what I really need is the cardboard that's inside this wrapper."

"What for?"

"To cover the hole in your shoe."

That did the trick and my toes began to stretch out to their normal size again easing the pain. Bill, too, was happy to get something between his blisters and the road. All in all it worked out fine for both of us. By now it was pitch dark, but with the energy from the candy bars and the foot relief we were enjoying, the miles flew by. The road became more level as it began to follow the Orogrande Creek, and we settled down to a fast pace.

"There's Dee Dee cabin," said Bill, "four miles to go."

It took about an hour and the bridge and Bungalow were right ahead. We were now walking almost like robots, and we found it difficult to stop, nearly crashing into the building.

Stumbling through the door in the dark, we groped around looking for our bunks.

"Who's there?"

"Just us. We walked all the way."

"Hold on, I'll get a lantern lit."

It was Jay, who had wisely not gone to town, he and Mike were the only ones there.

"Boy, you guys look awful," he said squinting at us.

"We feel worse than we look."

"What time is it?"

"Twelve-thirty."

"Where are the rest of the guys?"

"Last we saw of them was about six o'clock this morning. They're out there somewhere. Let's get to bed."

Sleep didn't come right away, with all the aches and pains, but gradually I dropped off. The rest staggered in, one by one, two by two, at various times. Jay kindly got up and lit the lantern for all of them, but I didn't get up and neither did Bill. The cook would be banging away on his triangle soon enough.

The worst part was we would be starting three days of fire school in the morning. Nobody was overly alert that first day, myself included, but somehow I passed and I had my job. Some others were not so fortunate.

It would, however, be a long, long time before I had any desire for another night on the town.

Three
Lost

I was disgusted. Here I was on my first fire tower at Seven Mile Lookout, just where I wanted to be, and already I was feeling sorry for myself and only a week had gone by. Things were not going well. I was alone trying to do jobs that needed three or four hands, and as a result I was getting nowhere. At test call I poured out my frustration to George and he listened patiently.

"I'll talk to Shorty and see what he says."

"Thanks George, I'd appreciate that."

Later that evening Shorty called.

"Sounds like you could use some help."

"Could I ever."

"Well, I'll tell you what, Clyde is gonna come up with your mail tomorrow and he'll give you a hand for a couple of hours. We're supposed to get a new man in soon and then I'll send him up, too. Clyde should be there by mid-morning."

I was cutting brush, when Clyde rode up on Shorty's horse Stub the next morning.

"I brought your mail and some fresh meat," he said reaching in the saddlebag.

"Won't the meat spoil in this heat?"

"I doubt it. Mutton don't spoil that quick."

"How will I know if it's spoiled or not?"

"Can't really say. It smells so bad fresh, it's not easy to tell when it goes bad. Maybe you'd best boil it up soon if you get a chance."

"I'll do that."

We set to work right away. At noon we came in and started a fire to get the hunk of mutton boiling and there was ample time to have a lunch and look over my mail. At suppertime the mutton smelled so bad I threw it away. In the mid-afternoon, it was time for Clyde to head back to Bungalow.

"Thanks a lot Clyde," I said as he tightened the saddle girth.

"Glad to be of help. The new guy is due in tomorrow."

Two days later Bernie showed up and right away we hit it off. One day we were working on the trail to the Pine Creek Road and as we sat eating our lunch, I made an observation.

"Do you hear what I hear, Bernie?"

"Just what is it you want me to hear?"

"That creek down there."

"Yeah, now that you mention it, I do hear it. Why?"

"Sounds like it could be pretty fair size to me."

"It does at that."

"Do you suppose there might be trout in it?"

"Could be. I wouldn't be surprised if there were."

"How far down there would you guess it to be?"

"Can't be more'n a quarter mile, I'd say."

"That's what I was thinking. Let's take a look at the map when we get in."

"Okay. What you got in mind?"

"Well, with tomorrow being Sunday, maybe one of us could sneak away and give it a try."

"Sounds good to me. I'll do my washing if you'd like to go."

"It's a deal."

The map confirmed our estimate. Larch Creek was about a quarter mile off the trail, and I planned to head there soon as the breakfast dishes were done.

"Maybe you oughta ask permission," Bernie cautioned.

"What if they say no?"

"Then I guess it'd be off."

"That's why I'm not asking."

"I see what you mean. If anybody asks for you, I'll tell 'm you're getting water or something."

"Good. I'll hurry all I can."

"Take your time. I'll hold down the fort."

I knew I could count on Bernie, so I was out the door and on my way the next morning. It was only about a mile to the jumping-off place, and I covered that in under ten minutes. Time was important. If somebody called and insisted on talking to me, Bernie could only stall so long. If there were no fish, I'd just turn around and hurry back and if there were, well, we'd see. At any rate the stream had probably never been fished before, so if fish were there they'd be plentiful and dumb—the perfect combination.

At the point where the creek seemed closest to the trail I started downward through the heavy timber. It proved to be farther than I had anticipated. The map hadn't shown the additional four or five hundred feet downward that I'd failed to take into account. Soon I was at the stream looking for a likely pole to cut. In minutes I had a fly in the water.

Splash! I yanked back and out flew a trout only four inches long—too small. I threw it back. Another splash and another four incher and another and another. Are they all the same size I wondered? Maybe if I moved downstream there would be a pool and larger fish. I found a small pool, but the fish were all the same size.

How many of these would make a meal? A dozen, twenty, maybe more? And I'd forgotten to take a bag to put them in. I began stuffing fish in my shirt pockets, but they would only hold four or five apiece. Time was fleeting and I was worried about being gone too long. Best get going.

I began climbing back toward the trail. I hoped Bernie wouldn't laugh when he got a look at the minnows I was bringing back. As I climbed higher I began to watch for the trail, but even though it seemed I had gone far enough, there was no sign of it.

Going still higher, I was sure I had passed it, but I kept on in case I had underestimated the distance. Finally I came to a solid wall of brush, which we called chaparral. Whether or not it was I'm not sure, but it was some pretty awful stuff. Now I knew I had gone too far since I had not come through any brush on the way down. There was only one thing to do—just go slowly down again keeping both eyes open for the trail. The phone line alongside it would make it pretty hard to miss. I would just have to look more carefully.

Heading slowly downward and scrutinizing every inch of the way, I eventually arrived back at the creek again having seen no sign of a trail. How could that be? The trail and stream ran virtually parallel to each other, so if I went straight down in the first place and came straight back up, I had to come across that trail, and yet I hadn't.

Trails don't just get up and walk away. I was doing something wrong, but what? Maybe if I went to the exact spot where I had first hit the stream and went up I'd get lucky. Finding the spot was easy. My footprints were there in the soft earth and the stub was there where I'd cut the pole. Starting upward again, I kept a sharp eye out and before long found myself back at the line of chaparral.

What to do now? There seemed no point in going over the same ground another time. The trail was most certainly not between here and the stream, of that I was sure, but where in the world could it be? Looking upward I could see what appeared to be the top of the ridge several hundred feet above me. If I could just get up there, maybe I could see the lookout and walk straight to it cross country. It couldn't be much more than a mile away. That seemed like a good idea, but it would be tough going. The brush all pointed downhill and was so dense I had to climb on top of it to move ahead. The upper branches were alive, but underneath it was all dead wood and very brittle, so when I broke through it was difficult to get out and I got all scratched up in the process. In this fashion I fought my way up to what appeared to be the top of the ridge only to find it was just a small hump and the actual ridgetop was still much farther—twice as far as I had come. To attempt that was out of the question. I was already soaked with sweat and exhausted, and my legs were bleeding from a hundred scratches.

I stopped to get my breath and ponder my situation. Going higher was out. So was going back down. If I continued along the side of the ridge at least I would be heading in the general direction of the lookout, but this proved to be more easily said than done. The brush was almost as difficult to penetrate in this direction as it had been in a frontal assault. After a couple hundred yards I gave up and did the only thing I could do—started back downhill. Maybe I would stumble across the trail yet. This, however, did not happen, but at least I got clear of the brush and came to more open, level country and walked on for about an hour.

I had to admit to myself that I was absolutely and totally lost. I had no idea any more in which direction the lookout might be. I could only be fairly sure that it was not to the south. But whether it was north, east, or west, I hadn't a clue.

I was sure that Bernie had expected me back by now. I was worried sick that he'd call in and report me lost and that would surely be the end of my job, if not his. Why had I ever gone off like this and done such a stupid thing?

I caught a whiff of something that smelled pretty bad. Where could *that* be coming from? Then it dawned on me—right from my own shirt pocket! Those little trout had ripened in the heat. I threw them away, kicking myself for being such a fool. A very thirsty fool, too. I would have to find water soon. Thirst was not as important to me, though, as the nagging worry over how long Bernie would wait before calling in and reporting me missing. So far I hadn't really given any thought to the possibility that I might not make it back. I was still confident that somehow I'd find my way out of this mess. Whether I'd still have a job was an open question, however.

The sun was now well past its zenith giving me some sense of direction, but it was of little help since I had no idea where I was in relation to where I wanted to go. Finally I sat down on a fallen tree and resolved to think this thing out and come up with some sort of plan.

As I sat there my mind wandered back to a time when I'd been in another very tight spot. I was ten years old and had gone fishing with my cousin, Miles, at a place called the Sheboygan Marsh, which was nothing more than a series of man-made canals, the banks of which formed a floating bog. We had an old wooden rowboat with an equally old three-horsepower Neptune motor clamped to the stern.

We were anchored perhaps a mile from the only landing when what had started out as a beautiful, sunny day suddenly became cloudy and stormy. The wind began to churn the water into whitecaps, and we quickly pulled in our lines and prepared to head for shelter. The wind was so strong that our anchors failed to hold and we were blown against the overhanging bushes along the bank. I got the anchors out and attempted to row us to a safer spot, but the left oar only got tangled in the bushes and proved useless. The bushes simply sank under water when I vainly tried to push us away from them. There would be no bank to take refuge on—the boat was our only hope.

Meanwhile Miles was frantically trying to get the motor started and was having no success. As the wind increased, the boat began rocking more wildly and waves started coming over the side.

"Start bailing," Miles shouted at me over the howling wind.

I grabbed the bait can, threw the worms over the side, and bailed as fast as I could, but the waves were coming in faster than I could bail. The lower the boat sank, the faster the water came in. I looked at Miles, still winding the rope around the fly-wheel and pulling again and again. The motor refused even to give one pop. Scared stiff and seeing the water deepen in spite of my frantic bailing, I tried to think of what else I might do to save us. Only one thing came to mind.

I had been at best a rather infrequent attendee at Sunday School. If my mother insisted I would go, though reluctantly. One thing I did remember, however, was the Lord's Prayer, and now was certainly an excellent time to put it to use. We needed all the help we could get. So I said it silently with all the sincerity I could muster, which wasn't too difficult considering the circumstances.

When I came to the end and silently said "for ever and ever, amen," the motor started with a bang and ran perfectly all the way back to the landing. Some would think it was a coincidence, but I did not. In my mind I was sure what had made that motor start. I never did tell Miles, though. I was afraid he'd laugh at me.

The present situation was not dissimilar, so I supposed it might not be a bad idea to say it again. It surely couldn't hurt. I did and felt more confident for having done so. Somewhere I had read that to avoid going in circles when lost, a person must pick out an object, walk toward it, and then pick out another, and so on in a straight line. This is what I vowed to do. Looking around I spotted an old dead snag about a hundred yards away lined up with another a similar distance beyond. That looked to be as good a course as any, so I started off. Halfway to the second snag, I stepped right out onto a trail.

Talk about results. I couldn't have been more impressed, and I looked up and said a very audible thank you. I wanted to be sure He heard. Now that I had found a trail the question was which way to go—left or right. Not having any idea of where I was didn't make the decision any easier, but in the end I went to the left. This proved to be the right decision, for within a quarter mile I came upon a sign that said Seven Mile Lookout. That really straightened things out. I should be back in less than an hour if I really hurried. With luck, Bernie might not have panicked yet.

My thirst and exhaustion forgotten, I poured on all the speed I could muster until I came to an unmarked fork in the trail. Looking around for anything that would help me get my bearings, I found nothing and took the right fork simply because it looked to be more distinct. After a half hour, I topped a small rise and a lookout appeared several miles off. Only the house was visible, not the tower, but I figured this had to be Seven Mile. Greatly relieved, I descended into the next valley and stopped to drink from a stream that ran through it. The color of the water and its size made me think of Larch Creek, the one I'd been fishing in.

The next rise gave me a better view of the lookout ahead, much closer now. Part of the tower was visible. At the next rise, the lookout loomed up dead ahead, but something was wrong. I could see the bottom of the tower and to the right of it stood another building. Between the two was a car. My heart sank. For the first time I knew where I was—not at Seven Mile at all, but at Lean-to-Ridge, the only lookout around with a road to it.

My first thought was to turn right around and go back the way I'd come, but an idea popped into my head and I plunged on. When I came closer a boy my age came out on the catwalk.

"Come on up, whoever you are."

When I reached the top of the stairs he stuck out his hand. "Name is Jim, what's yours and where in the world did you come from? Holy Cow! You look like you bin dragged through a knothole. What's happened to you?"

"I'll explain everything in a minute, but first I need a favor. Would you get Bungalow on the phone and then ask to talk to the guy on Seven Mile? When you get him on the phone, make sure nobody's listening in and tell him I got lost and should be back in a couple hours."

"I'll get right to it."

It didn't take long and he gave me a thumbs up sign.

"Why hello there Seven Mile, this is Lean-to-Ridge, just makin' a social call. Is anybody else on the line? Good. Say listen, your partner got himself turned around somehow and ended up over here. Says he'll be homeward bound in a little bit, soon as I git him something to eat."

He and Bernie had a short conversation and he put the phone down.

"Now to git you fed. You like ham? I just opened a can."

"That would hit the spot."

While he busied himself with getting me a lunch, I spilled everything—except the prayer. I had no idea how he'd react to that, so I kept it to myself.

"My biggest worry was that Bernie might call in and spill the beans."

"Yeah, I see what you mean, but he didn't sound worried when I talked to him," Jim said handing me a huge slice of ham surrounded by two thick slices of homemade bread.

"Like some lemonade? I just made it."

"I'd love it. It was pretty dry out there."

"Reckon it must'a bin."

While I ate, he kept up a steady chatter and I tried my best to answer between bites. I hadn't been aware of being hungry, but now I was ravenous.

"How about some homemade cookies?" Jim asked when I'd finished the sandwich.

"That would be fine, but I'd better eat 'em on the way or it's gonna be late when I get back."

"Here, just stick 'em in yer pocket."

Anxious to be on my way, I thanked him again for his hospitality and hit the trail. At least now I knew where I was going. I had had one lesson that would not be soon forgotten.

When I came to the stream, I took another drink. I had little doubt now about what stream it was. I should have known when I crossed it the first time that I was going in the wrong direction. At last I came to the fork in the trail where I'd made the wrong choice, and from there it was only a short distance to the main trail. I had been within a twenty-minute hike of Seven Mile and had gone off on a ten-mile hike instead.

"Boy, do you look used up," Bernie remarked when I came up the stairs.

"I'm undoubtedly more used up than I look."

"We having fish for supper?"

"No, we're not."

"Catch any?"

"Yup. Musta caught a couple dozen."

"Where are they?"

"Some I threw back and some I threw away."

"Now that's a heck of a note. Why'd you do such a thing?"

I explained and then I asked, "Bernie, were you worried when it got so late?"

"Why no, I wasn't expecting you until suppertime or later."

"Man, I was afraid you'd call in and report me missing."

"Aw, I wouldn't do a thing like that. I figured you knew how to take care of yourself. Now you just park yourself on that bunk while I get some supper on. I can see you're pretty well done in."

"Thanks Bernie."

Later, after dishes were done, I told him what a day I'd had. Then I crawled into my sleeping bag and had no trouble at all getting to sleep.

Much refreshed the next morning, we were on the phone line, much of which had been pulled down by winter snows when we passed the spot where my ill-fated fishing expedition had begun. I called a halt.

"Look Bernie, here's where I went straight down to the creek and I thought I came straight back up. Can you see any reason why I didn't find this trail?"

"Not really, unless you didn't come up far enough."

"I'm sure I did. In fact, I got into that chaparral up above."

"I guess then you must have crossed it without seeing it."

"In that case, I crossed it three times and didn't see it. That just doesn't seem possible."

"No, it doesn't, but look back a way. The trail doesn't come straight on. It goes back at an angle to the creek, and if you veered to the right coming back up, you'd have to go a long way to get to it."

"You're right at that and there's a lot of chaparral below the trail back there."

"Sure there is, I'd bet anything that's how you got mixed up."

"Could be. Anyway, I'm not going back down to find out." Being good and lost once had been enough for me.

Four
First Fire

The nineteenth of July never passes that I don't recall that day, over fifty years ago, of my first fire. It's forever etched in my memory. Not that I haven't experienced storms that were just as harrowing or fires that were just as bad or even far worse, but for some reason it was just an unforgettable day.

It all happened on Bighorn Point, which was really Bob's lookout. The two of us had spent a few days working out of Seven Mile (my lookout) after my previous partner, Bernie, had been injured in a fall from a pole. So Bob came over to help me out, and after we finished, we went over to Bighorn to do what needed doing there.

The nineteenth happened to fall on a Sunday that year, the only non-working day of the week for us. The day before I had gotten up extra early and as a special treat had baked a peach pie—double crust and all. Bob wanted to sample it right away, but I laid down the law. This is for supper and don't you even think about touching it before then.

When we went out to work, we put the pie, along with a few other things, in our cooler, which was nothing more than a wooden box with a screen door set out of the sun on the north side of the house. Not very effective for keeping things cool, but under the circumstances about the best anyone could come up with. A few lookouts had snowbanks, which were ideal for keeping perishables, but not Bighorn.

As we were returning that evening Bob was the first to notice something wrong.

"Uh oh, we got trouble."

"What? I don't see anything."

"Look up at the chimney."

"Holy Cow! What the heck is that?"

"The flying ants have arrived."

I had heard about them but this was my first experience. They made a habit of swarming around the highest available spot by the tens of thousands. Naturally, a lookout being the highest point around, the chimney rated first choice when it came to swarming time. Apparently this was an annual ritual for them and they made life absolutely miserable for the other occupants of the building, namely people. As Jack so often put it, "they don't eat anything and they don't bite, but they'll drive you nuts."

When we entered the house I could see these were indeed words of experience. Flying ants an inch deep covered the floor. They crawled over the stove, on the table, on the bunks, along the window sill, in the cupboards—the place was literally covered with a buzzing, crawling mass. Bob had been through this before and he knew what to do.

"Get a fire going quickly. That'll get that big gob of 'em off the chimney. Most of 'em are getting in from there."

I opened the door to the firebox and hundreds came pouring out. A fire would stop that invasion, but other points of entry remained. Meanwhile Bob had the broom going in a vain effort to clear the floor of our unwelcome guests. Gradually we got the upper hand, but we only succeeded in thinning them out. They kept coming in under the door, alongside the windows, anywhere there was a small opening. They seemed to be particularly fond of crawling up our pant legs, and soon we were dancing around trying to rid ourselves of those wretched pests.

"Be patient," Bob said, "They'll stop when it gets dark."

"I don't know if I'll last that long."

Darkness was still two hours away.

"When do we eat?" asked Bob. He was always hungry. I hadn't even thought about it.

"You mean you want to eat with those ants crawling all over your food?"

"Why not? Just brush 'em off. We gotta eat sometime."

"I suppose so. If you're that hungry, I'll get started. Just keep on sweeping."

By the time we sat down to eat the ants had apparently decided to call it a day and only a few stragglers marched across our plates. When we finished, Bob got up.

"That was one great meal there, ole buddy, now how about that pie."

"I'll get it."

Fortunately, the cooler was tight enough that the ants hadn't been able to force their way in, though they undoubtedly had tried. The pie was in superb condition. Bob was delighted.

"O-O-O-O-O, does that look good, here lemme cut it."

"Bob," I said, "you go ahead. I simply must visit the outhouse before I dive into that pie."

"Okay, but you better hurry. I might get carried away."

"You better not."

A visit to the outhouse was nothing to be taken lightly. It entailed a trip down the tower and a walk of a good hundred yards one way and then back up. You could figure on fifteen minutes, minimum. I must have meditated awhile that day, because when I came back in Bob was in a dither.

"Look, I'm sorry, it was just so good I lost control."

"What are you talking about?"

"The pie, I ate the pie."

"Well, I didn't expect you to wait, after all. Just so you left some for me."

"That's what I mean. I ate it all."

"You did *what?*"

"The pie, I ate the whole thing. It was just so good, I couldn't stop."

"Bob, are you kidding me?"

"No, really, look. I'll do the dishes alone and get the water. I feel just awful about this."

"I still think you're kidding."

"I wish I was. Look, I'll do anything to make it up to you. If you're mad, I don't blame you. It was an awful thing to do, but it was just so good."

"You mean you didn't leave me even one crumb."

"No. I'm sorry."

"Bob, I could clobber you."

"Go ahead, I deserve it."

"Would it do any good?"

"Probably not."

"Then get the hell started on the dishes."

"Okay. I said I would and I will, but look, I'll make a deal with you."

"I'm not sure about making any deals with you, but let's hear it."

"Okay, tomorrow is Sunday right? If you make another pie I'll take care of everything else all day. You won't have to lift a finger. That's how bad I feel about this."

"Okay, but just one thing, I'm not gonna make one pie—it'll have to be two, so I stand a chance of getting some."

"Oh, that's great. You're not mad at me then?"

"I s'pose not. Just stick by your word."

"No need to worry. If the ants come back I'll even take care of 'em myself."

"Darn right you will."

Well, Bob turned out to be a man of his word. He even shook the flying ants out of my sleeping bag before we turned in. He was up early taking care of the test call.

"Wade says there's a storm coming. I'll get water and firewood in after breakfast."

"A bad storm?"

"That's what they're predicting."

"I better get those pies baked pronto, then. We could be busy later."

So after breakfast, we left the dishes where they were and I got right to work. Before the pies went in the oven, I made little designs in the crust, the way I'd seen my mother do, and then sprinkled sugar and cinnamon over the top. Give it a professional touch, I figured. They looked like masterpieces when I opened the oven door and Bob was the first to notice.

"Boy, oh, boy, just look at that. You have got to be the best chef in the Clearwater."

"Flattery will get you nowhere—just keep your paws off, 'till I tell you."

"Okay, okay. I can wait, I promise."

"This time you better or the fat'll be in the fire but good."

"Speaking of fires, take a look at the sky to the southwest."

"Kinda black and blue isn't it?"

"I guess so. Looks like the forecast was right for a change."

I took the pies out to the cooler and noticed the wind picking up. Just then the phone rang.

I looked at Bob, "It's all yours remember?"

He picked it up and didn't do much talking, just nodded his head and occasionally said "right" or "okay."

At last he hung up.

"That was Wade."

"What's he have to say?"

"Heavy thunderstorms headed our way, dangerous lightning, fire danger moderate to high, and he and Juanita are the only ones at the Bungalow."

"Oh, great. Where are the rest?"

"Shorty and Clyde went out last night, and George and Bowlander went along. Nobody expected any weather like this."

"If this is as bad as they expect, Wade will really have his hands full."

"I guess so. At least Juanita is there to handle the switchboard."

She was Wade's daughter and was a very capable girl, but with no ranger or dispatcher on hand, she could be hard pressed if things started getting hot. All we could do now was watch and wait. Bob made a hasty lunch at noon.

The sky continued to darken and lightning began to flash off in the distance.

"One good thing about a storm," Bob said, "the ants take a day off."

"By golly you're right. They must smell something coming."

"So do I. As a matter of fact, I can hear it too."

The rumble of thunder was plainly audible now, and the lightning strikes were marching straight in our direction. Bob handed me a pencil and paper and switched on the little battery-powered light over the mapboard.

"Here you mark 'em down as I call 'em off and keep track of the times."

"Right."

This was going to be exciting, my first real experience as a lookout. Thus far, there'd been no fires in the district and all I'd done was trail and telephone work. This, now, was what I hired out for. Let it come—I was ready.

First came the wind, with such ferocity that the tower rocked from side to side, causing dishes to rattle and cans to come rolling across the floor from the cupboard. The lightning came in one blinding flash following another and the accompanying thunder made it nearly impossible to make oneself understood.

In the midst of it all Bob grabbed a towel and ran out the door. I thought he had taken leave of his senses, but in a moment he was back in and from under the towel emerged our two peach pies, in pristine condition.

"I was afraid they'd get wet," he shouted as he stuck them in the now cold oven.

We had taken down only a few lightning strikes before the storm simply obscured everything. While it raged on, we could only stand in awe of it and wait until it passed. Then we would see what it had done.

Gradually it did pass, and visibility rose to a half mile, then a mile, and at last in late afternoon the sun peaked out and we began counting smokes. Most of them were fairly distant. The closest appeared to be about a mile and a half back alongside the trail that we had walked in on from Seven Mile. As we began the task of locating each fire, sometimes disagreeing about its whereabouts, the phone rang.

This time I took it.

"Bighorn."

"How do things look up there?"

"Well, Wade, we're still working on it, but off-hand there must be twenty or more smokes that we can see right now."

"Any close by?"

"Just one to the west near Cabin Point."

"How close to Cabin Point? There's a lot of green timber in there you know."

"Right. From here it looks to be just this side, not quite in the timber."

"Okay, we'll want to keep close watch on that one. How's the wind velocity up there?"

"We don't have the anemometer hooked up yet, but it's blowing hard, probably around twenty-five or thirty."

Wade sounded worried.

"That's what I was concerned about. Call me when you get a location on the rest of 'em and watch that one at Cabin Point like a hawk. We don't want that to get away on us."

"Okay. We'll call in as soon as we finish."

Meantime Bob had kept working on locations, but darkness came before we could finish. From then on it was pretty much guesswork, not being able to distinguish landmarks. Bob called in the information that we had and when he hung up he reported to me.

"Wade is plenty worried about that one fire up here, but he says to keep an eye on it for now. One of us may go after it later."

I was really anxious to go. After all that's what I'd gone to fire school for. Not that Bob hadn't, but he'd been on fires the year before and I was still a rookie, impatient to see what it was all about. But when the call came about ten o'clock it was Bob who got to go and I was left behind to man the phone. What a disappointment.

Bob wasn't the only one out there either. Wade called and said that he'd sent several of the other boys out too. There were more than enough fires to go around. His strategy was to go after the ones in or near standing timber, while everything was still wet from the rain. The rest we would tackle later. An hour after Bob left, Wade was on the phone again.

"How's she look?"

"Can't see much change. It's still blazing up pretty good, but not getting any bigger."

"Well, that's something. Let me know if there's any change."

"Right."

Another hour went by and I could feel footsteps on the stairs. Suddenly, Bob burst in.

"I gotta call Wade. The tree is just to hot to handle. Every time I chop at it, a bunch of burning stuff falls down on me. Look at my hat."

I could see what he meant. The hat had been burned through in a dozen places. While he explained the situation to Wade, I started getting my boots on, hoping I might get to go. I was almost ready when the conversation ended.

"Wade says we should both go and take a saw along. Once the tree is down, one of us is to come right back here."

"Did he say who?"

"No. We can decide that ourselves."

"Okay, let's go. I'm ready."

"Just as soon as I gas up this lantern. My batteries are just about finished and it's really dark out there."

He was right, of course. The night was pitch black and the wind was still blowing furiously. The burning tree, however, acted like a beacon and as we neared it I could see burning chunks fall off and land in a shower of sparks. Luckily the surrounding area was still wet from the rain so the fire wasn't spreading. That tree would have to come down, though, before things dried out or we'd have real problems. As it was we'd have enough.

The tree was aflame along its entire length. First, we'd have to cool down the lower section before even starting to saw it down. It was too hot to get near otherwise.

"See what I meant," shouted Bob over the roar of the flames. With the wind blowing and fanning the fire, the whole thing was burning like a torch.

"I'll say I do," I shouted back, starting to throw shovelfuls of dirts on the burning trunk.

When it was cool enough to start sawing, we began, one of us keeping an eye overhead for falling debris. We stayed on the windward side so the smaller pieces blew away from us, but every once in awhile somebody would shout look out and a burning chunk would come crashing down as we jumped aside. Smoke came pouring out of the saw cut and burst into flame as we cut deeper, and we had to stop and throw on more dirt to cool things down. At last the cut started to open up and Bob yelled timber and over it went in a shower of sparks and flaming chunks.

"Boy, what a sight," grinned Bob.

"You said it. I'll stay and put it out if you like."

"You want to?"

"Sure. I could use the practice."

"Well, okay, if you're sure that's what you want."

"Yup, just as long as you can be trusted alone with those pies."

"Heck, I'd forgotten all about 'em. I promise they'll be all there when you get back."

"Oh, go have a piece. You gotta be hungry."

"I am, but a promise is a promise."

"Whatever you say. Just take off now so I can get to work."

There was no way he could find his way back without the lantern, so I was left to work by what light there might be from the fire. Throwing dirt to cool things down consumed a couple hours, and when no flames remained I was left in total darkness.

Stumbling around I located a spot out of the wind that was fairly dry and I laid down to rest. I could do no more until daylight came.

I must have drifted off, because the next thing I knew, coyotes were howling far off in the first gray light of dawn—just enough light to start mopping up what remained of the fire. Stiff and cold at first but gradually loosening up, I bent to my task. The coyotes kept up their howling, sending chills down my spine. This was the first time I'd heard their mournful song and it was quite a thrill for me.

When the first rays of sunlight appeared I took off my gloves and, as we had been taught in fire school, felt every square inch of tree trunk to make certain no hot spots remained. Satisfied, I dug a trench around it and that was that. A final once over, and I shouldered the firepack and started for home.

The trail back to Bighorn followed a narrow ridgetop, affording me a good view of the valleys on either side. Clouds lay along the bottoms of each one, making it seem as if I were walking along on an island. The wind had dropped during the night and overhead the clouds were rapidly thinning out promising a beautiful day.

About a mile out, I could see Bob start down the stairs. He must have been watching for me. As we neared each other he put one hand behind his back as if to hide something. Indeed he was, for when we met he produced two pieces of peach pie wrapped in waxed paper with a big grin.

"You must be hungry. Just thought this might hit the spot."

"Well, I can't think of anything that could possibly be any better."

With that we sat right down on a handy rock and wolfed down those two pieces of pie.

Bob looked at me, licking his fingers, "Best I ever ate."

I had to agree. I've never had any better before or since.

Five
The Pole Shy Ballet

The Bungalow District was bisected by the North Fork of the Clearwater River. Six lookouts were on the south side and four more lay on the north side. Big Horn lookout was eight miles to the west of Bear Butte, where I was located, and Junction lookout was nine miles to the east. Some of the lookouts had towers as high as fifty-five feet while others had no tower at all. I was manning Bear Butte, a forty-five foot structure; Junction, on the other hand, was an eight-foot high log structure. All of us lived inside the lookout itself in rooms approximately fourteen feet square with a circular map board and range finder in the center and a stove, table, cupboards, bunks, and washstand along the outside walls. There was about a three-foot catwalk all the way around the outside of the building.

The lookouts were situated so they had the best possible view of the surrounding country, and no thought was given about how close or how far away they were from the nearest water. It seemed as if they put the lookouts up first and then went looking for a spring, so it might be anywhere from 250 yards away, as it was at Junction, to 1500 yards away, as it was at Big Horn. Since a mile is 1760 yards, you can see no one wasted any water. We carried water in two five-gallon canvas water bags, all of which leaked like sieves. I usually hung one on my back and one in front for a total of 80 pounds when full. However, with water gushing out and soaking into boots and clothes, there was little incentive to stop and rest. You would come struggling up the last step lucky to have half the water you started out with and fill every metal container in the place before it all ran away. Of course, the farther you had to haul water, the less you had when you got there. As George down at Bungalow put it, "I know what you boys are a doin' with water up there. First you wash your clothes in it, then you do dishes in it, then you take a bath in it, and then you make coffee out of it."

Big Horn, Bear Butte, and Junction were all on the same phone line and this vital communication link consisted of connecting wires strung between any poles that could be cut nearby or a handy tree that happened to be in the right place. Most of the cut poles were knotty, small, and wiggly and were barely supported by rocks piled around their base.

Climbing the treacherous poles was risky business, but a large tree with three inches of bark could also be a real adventure. Since I was the only one on the south side of the river with a set of climbers and climbing experience, I was in for trouble. To those of you who have never strapped on a pair of climbers and gone up a pole or tree, it may look easy, but believe me it's not—especially when you have to alternate between toothpick-size poles that threaten to tip over and trees with bark thicker than your spurs are long.

Guessing the length of the safety belt is also tricky. If it's too short, your chin is jammed up against the pole and your spurs pry out and down you come. If it's too long, your spurs are safely sunk in but you can't reach the pole. In both cases you come down and readjust the belt and go back up. Not me, though. I really liked the challenge of hanging on with one hand and trying to adjust the belt with the other, with the result that I made many dramatic descents. Falling properly took real knack. My first fall I clutched the knotty pole to my chest and got burned all the way down with slivers from forehead to navel. You also tried to avoid coming down with one of your spurs embedded in the other leg, as one friend of mine did.

I was not fond of climbing, and one morning I couldn't get a call through to Junction without going through the switchboard at the Bungalow—an ominous sign indicating the line was down. A broken line on a mountainside will take off downhill like a scalded cat when it snaps through the insulators, which were no more than ceramic letter o's. It won't stop until it snags in some brush or runs out of steam in a tangle at the bottom of the hill.

Sure enough, at six p.m. test call, Norma acknowledged my call with the grim news that Shorty wanted to talk to me.

"How'd you like to head over to Junction for a few days?"

"What for?" I said, as if I didn't know.

"Well, we know there's a broken line and you've got the equipment to fix it, so why don't you head over there tomorrow. See if you can locate the break on the way. Charlie is on at Junction now, so he can give you a hand, and Bowlander is down at Kelly Forks, and he can bring up any wire you need and help out for a day or two."

Charlie was a good hand, and Bowlander, the mule packer, was a huge bear of a man. Bowlander had no teeth, but he could eat steak just as fast as the rest of us, though I never figured out how. However, neither of them would have anything to do with climbing. That would be my department, and I wasn't looking forward to it.

Next morning dawned bright and sunny, and I left for Junction with a few clothes and the line equipment in my backpack. The trail ran a mile along a ridge and then there was two miles of switchback and it went straight on down from there to Fourth of July Creek. The line kept getting tighter and tighter the farther I went.

At the creek it was clear where the trouble lay. The line had somehow gotten into the water and been caught in some logs headed downstream. These had piled up on some rocks a good distance from the crossing with the line tangled hopelessly in the midst of it all. I worked my way down to the log jam since it gave me a place to cross without getting my feet wet, and salvaged enough line to make it to the first pole on the opposite bank. Then I headed on to Junction six miles away hoping not to find more trouble. Most of the way the line lay away from the trail, but at a point where it rejoined the trail there were quite a few hangs down from some miserable, skinny, knotted, leaning poles.

Charlie seemed overjoyed to see me, as well he might. After all, he would be on the ground while I was risking life and limb.

When we gave Shorty a call with the news, he said he'd have Bowlander on his way up first thing the next morning. That meant he would be on horseback towing a mule packing the wire. He had about ten miles to cover and wouldn't arrive until sometime in the afternoon.

The next day dawned bright and sunny and Charlie and I took off on a six-mile hike to the break in the line to see if we could get things in order before Bowlander arrived. At midafternoon we were just getting the wire up as close to the break as we could when we heard someone singing "Back in the Saddle Again." There came Bowlander astride a horse named Ellick with the mule behind packing what appeared to be about a mile of coiled-up wire.

"What mule is that?" I asked suspiciously.

"Take a guess," said Bowlander.

"Adolph!?"

"None other, but I hung sacks of rocks on his other side to calm him down a bit."

"Why in the world did you bring him?" I asked.

"Shorty sent him to Kelly Forks by himself so he don't teach the other mules bad habits."

This made some sense. Adolph had plenty of bad habits without spreading them around. I had already had one experience with Adolph when Bowlander had packed into the lookout called Bar Point. At the time, I had not received any perishables or mail for two weeks and was anxious to get some news from home. When a packer arrived at his destination, it was customary for him to untie all his mules and let them stand "tied" to the ground by their own lead ropes. Usually they were cooperative and anxious to be relieved of their burdens so they could have some oats and a good roll. The mule bearing my mail had, however, maneuvered himself into a patch of brush and was devouring it at a rapid rate. He seemed reluctant to come out. The lead rope was somewhere down between his feet, so I made a grab for his halter instead—a bad mistake. Being quicker than me, he wound up with the right sleeve and half the back of one of my better shirts in his mouth. Still determined to get my mail, I got a long stick and fished out the lead rope so I could get him away from his brush fortress. Once he was out, he stood subdued and I began to untie the pack from the front ring of his packsaddle. His head swung around like a wrecking ball and with enough force to render an elephant senseless, but I was keeping an eye on him and jumped back in time to avoid having my head hammered. Unfortunately, however, I was also far enough back to have my toes crushed by his left rear hoof.

The commotion finally caught Bowlander's attention up in the tower, and he came down the stairs two at a time with a large chunk of firewood in his huge fist hollering his lungs out. The tide of battle swung in my favor. My foot came loose, and I grabbed the lead rope and hung on until Bowlander arrived. I was hoping he would bash the miserable critter's head in, but instead he pulled him up nose to nose and launched into an unprintable description of what he would do to him should he misbehave again. I really doubt that any human male could accomplish what Bowlander threatened, but that mule was taking no chances. He stood like a statue.

"I see you and Adolph has met," said Bowlander.

"Is that Adolph?" I replied. I had heard horror stories about him.

"Hell, yes! Didn't you know?"

"No, I didn't, but I sure wish I had. All mules look alike to me."

"Sorry I didn't warn you," said Bowlander, "but you're not likely to forget what he looks like now. Better go get a different shirt on."

Later I was to learn that Adolph had left a trail of victims along the Clearwater and a few at his winter quarters near Missoula. Apparently the only thing that kept him off the poodle menu was the fact that he was a mountain of strength. It was said he could carry a piano or a pickup truck right up the side of Mount Everest and never miss a step. Another of his talents was getting through a narrow opening without damaging his packs. Most mules were pretty good at this, but Adolph was a master. Even where the clearance was only the thickness of a piece of paper, he'd slip through and never touch bark. He always got to carry the eggs.

Well, that was Adolph and we were stuck with him. Anyway, since I was elected to do the climbing someone else had to manage that assassin, not me.

To get the wire off Adolph, Bowlander had to do a rerun of his nose-to-nose routine, but Adolph knew when he had to behave. It didn't take long to splice in a new piece of wire and get it all back up on the poles, which were of climbable size and fairly well anchored. Charlie volunteered to follow the line up the mountain while I went on ahead on the switchbacks, well away from Adolph, who brought up the rear behind Bowlander and Ellick. We'd gone about two miles with no word from Charlie when we rounded a bend and there he sat on a log beside the trail.

"Trouble?" I asked.

"Yup. Big log over the line about seven or eight hangs down."

We got our equipment together and started down. Bowlander followed with a crosscut saw. The log was a huge red cedar about four feet in diameter with the line buried beneath it so tightly we couldn't slip it out.

"Boys," said Bowlander, "let's think this one over a bit. What do you say to cutting the line and resplicing it?" This was not an approved practice, but cutting the log would take close to an hour and then the hangs would take another hour, and we still had to walk back to lookout in time for the six p.m. test call.

Now in such a case, somebody hangs onto each end of the line while the third party cuts it. Then you bring the ends together into a sleeve and crimp them with a special tool. Even though it sounds pretty simple, there is a lot of weight on the downhill side, so that person (in this case Bowlander) had better be braced and ready when you make the cut. We got ready and snipped the line. Smooth as silk Charlie pulled his end out and I quickly slipped the sleeve on and crimped it. All we had to do was pull the other end up and get it in the sleeve. Bowlander had the line around his arms and was moving forward and Charlie was pulling from the uphill side while I tried to get the two ends together. Suddenly Bowlander went over backwards skidding through the brush yelling, "That damned elk! That damned elk!" All we could do was stand there and watch him go, wondering what was happening. He kept pointing downhill as he went, and down below was a cow elk that had run into the line and that was just then backing up to have another try at it.

We started yelling and waving our hats and the cow elk took off. Poor Bowlander was all scratched up and bruised and his back was hurting to boot. By luck he had hung on or the damned elk would have pulled the whole works apart and we would have had to restring the wire through all the insulators. This time Charlie and I pulled the ends together and Bowlander did the crimping.

After we got the line back on the poles again, we went back up to the trail and started for the lookout. Since the line followed the trail and I had checked it the day before and found no problems, we could head on in. About two miles from the lookout Bowlander said, "Boys, let's take a peek over the hill and see what's going on at Junction Lake. Might be we could get done early tomorrow and have a little time for fishing."

I had heard about the lake, but this was the first time I had seen it. What I saw made my eyes bug—a beautiful jewel of a mountain lake with trout raising all over. It was down in a hollow about 500 feet below us. Several snowbanks were still on the mountainside, but in the sunny areas there were grasshoppers all around, and apparently that was what the trout were feeding on.

We headed back to the lookout for supper and cranked up the phone. Big Horn answered right away and that meant there were no more breaks, just the hangs on the awful poles remained to be fixed. At six p.m. test call Shorty was pleased we had made such good progress. He was optimistic we could complete the work in the morning in time for Bowlander to return to Kelly Forks and for me to get back to Bear Butte. There was a storm building and he wanted us in position in case we were needed. We talked about it and decided we'd see how it looked in the morning and then make up our minds about fishing.

Morning again looked sunny and bright with no hint of a cloud. That rolled the dice in favor of Junction Lake, depending on how the work went. We left early, Bowlander in the lead on Ellick with the equipment hanging from the saddle horn. We left Adolph with his front feet trussed in a pair of hobbles. He managed to hop along after us as far as the horse bars—a rail fence about thirty feet long on either side of trail with a couple of poles across the trail itself. Horses and mules accustomed to walking only on a trail will seldom stray far enough to one side or the other to go around the bars. In addition, Bowlander hung a bell on Adolph to make him easier to find if he should escape.

We got to the hangs and the first pole I had to go up was a miserable, knotty, spindly thing with rocks piled around the base. Once I got up it started to tip, and even with Bowlander and Charlie trying to hold it up, it slowly came down leaving me hanging by my safety belt. After we got it up again, I said, "Bowlander, how good a horse is Ellick?"

"None better," he replied.

"Do you suppose he'd hold still for me while I stand on his rump to fix the hangs if you get him up against the pole and hold him?"

"Well, he's a good steady horse, but he ain't never been in no circus."

"I think it's worth a try," I said. Nothing could be worse than those toothpick poles. "Besides, it would be a lot faster and leave time for fishing."

With some misgivings, Bowlander agreed and I took off my boots and swung up into the saddle as we headed for the next pole. Ellick stood like a rock, and I grabbed the pole and stood on his rump. Charlie slid the insulator up to me with a forked stick and we were in business. We went from pole to pole that way and Ellick seemed to get in the spirit of the thing and hardly had to be led. He knew his job.

Things were going so smoothly that none of us thought of the serious flaw in our method. Every morning, promptly at eleven o'clock, Norma would call all the lookouts with the weather report. Now, this may not seem to have been a hazard, but ask anybody who has been on the receiving end when someone cranks one of those mean little generators that makes the phone ring, and he will tell you that he has received one hell of surprise. Add to that the fact that when Norma gave the thing a crank she really put some muscle into it, and the harder you cranked the more juice you generated. Everything would have been fine if we had been between poles when Norma laid into the crank, but as luck would have it Bowlander was standing with one hand on Ellick's steel bit and the other on the saddlehorn. Ellick was standing with his steel horseshoes embedded in damp ground and Charlie was just passing the insulator up the wire, which I held solidly in one hand with the other holding the pole. My damp socks were firmly planted on Ellick's equally damp rump. A disaster in the making if there ever was one.

All hell broke loose at eleven o'clock. I felt like I was being electrocuted and shot out of a cannon at the same time. Ellick, of course, became completely unstrung and sent me flying high enough to get a good look at the top of the pole and a bird's-eye-view of Charlie standing on the ground with his mouth agape, apparently ignorant of what had caused this sudden explosion.

Bowlander, who knew exactly what had happened, was hollering "Whoa son! Whoa son!" as he was being dragged through the brush for the second time in two days. I was fortunate enough to land in a clump of bear grass, and aside from a scratch or two, was none the worse for the experience. Bowlander was limping around and holding his back again by the time he got Ellick under control.

"Well," I said, "at least we know what time it is."

Charlie, still puzzled by the occurrence, asked "What's that supposed to mean?"

"It's eleven o'clock. What happens at eleven o'clock."

"Norma always calls in the . . . oh! I see! So that's what this is all about."

"Yes. This is all Norma's doing. I wish she wouldn't turn that crank so hard!"

By that time Bowlander had limped over to join us.

"How'd you survive?" I asked.

"Well, I can recall having felt better a time or two, but I guess I'll make it."

"Good. Do you think you can get that horse up to the next pole so we can try to get some fishing in?"

"Now listen," said Bowlander, "I got elk drug yesterday and horse drug today and I ain't havin' any more of it. Besides, this horse is so pole shy now I'll be lucky not to get bucked off every time he passes one for the next six months. You got any more good ideas to keep from climbin' them poles?"

About this time we heard the sound of a bell coming down the trail. Adolph had come to join us.

"Looks like we got company," said Charlie.

"Just what we need," I replied. "How are we ever going to do any fishing or even get any work done with him around?"

"I best take him back so he don't bother us no more," said Bowlander.

"While you're there," I said, "pick up a dozen or so good-sized spikes and a hammer. By the time you get back I'll have all the pieces cut for a ladder and I can put one together and use that instead."

Off they went to the strains of "Back in the Saddle Again" with Ellick crowhopping at every pole and Adolph braying his head off. Charlie and I set to work cutting and peeling the pieces for our ladder.

When Bowlander came back he said, "That was some ride I had. The next guy that rides this horse better take a good seat before he gets to the first pole."

The ladder went together in short order and we got the rest of the downed line back up without a hitch. We had time to spare for our fishing trip. To get there, we had to go over a rise and then slide down several hundred feet to the bowl that held the crystal-clear waters of Junction Lake. Bowlander insisted on riding, and Ellick plunged down over the side with his hind legs tucked beneath him and his hooves sending down an avalanche of rocks and pine cones. At the lake there were so many grasshoppers it was hard to decide which one to chase. We ran around slapping our hats down and then grabbing underneath with our hands. We put the grasshoppers in the Prince Albert cans Bowlander had brought along, cut some poles, and rigged up to get supper.

To say it was easy to catch those trout would be an understatement. Every time an impaled grasshopper hit the water, a trout would dash up after it. The trick was to get on the side of the lake with a ripple on the water so they didn't see you too easily. Once we figured that out, we really made saps out of those cutthroat trout. In a short time we filled a cut open two-gallon water bag with fourteen- to sixteen-inch-long trout and packed in some snow around the top.

I wondered how Ellick was going to get back over the hill carrying Bowlander, who weighed over 200 pounds, but he made it with a couple of rest stops on the way. The weather had turned cloudy and cooled off, so it felt nice and cozy in the lookout after we got the fire going in the cookstove. I took the rest of the trout we weren't going to eat right away out to the snowbank nearby that served as Charlie's refrigerator. That gave me an idea.

"Boys," I said, "if somebody else puts on the rest of the meal, I'll make us a special treat."

"What you got in mind?" asked Charlie.

"Well," I said, "we've got condensed milk, sugar, cocoa, and salt and there's plenty of snow out there. Need I say more?"

"Sounds like you're talking about making ice cream, and if you are, you've got a deal."

After all the ingredients were mixed together in a small kettle, I put it into a larger one and packed in snow and salt. With the aid of a butcher knife to cut the frozen cream away from the sides, it wasn't too long before we had what would pass as ice cream. Coupled with fresh trout, canned peas, and mashed potatoes, we had a meal fit for a king.

When Shorty checked in at test time, he warned again of the impending storm and asked if I'd be ready to go back to Bear Butte first thing in the morning.

"Sure thing," I replied.

After the dishes were done, I went to the spring for water, and the temperature had dropped, and dark, ominous clouds were gathered on the horizon. Ellick and Adolph had come closer to the lookout sensing something and wanting to be near us.

Once the woodbox was filled and a fire started, somebody suggested a card game, but we were pretty well worn out and too full of food to stay awake. After the livestock were fed and hobbled, we curled up in our sleeping bags.

I awoke at dawn feeling cold and clammy. The fire was out and I could see we were fogged in. First thing to do was get a fire going to heat the place up. A lookout is really drafty, what with all the windows. When the wind blows cold it's downright uncomfortable. A fire helps, but on such days one tends not to stray too far from the stove. I've spent many days sitting on a chair with my feet inside the oven reading a book, getting up only to put more wood on the fire. It was customary to make a pot of hot cocoa and a kettle of chili or maybe Spanish rice, get three or four of the lookouts on the phone at once, and spend the day in conversation. It helped to relieve the loneliness a great deal.

"It don't look good out there," said Bowlander. "Best I get the stock ready to travel. I'm glad they stayed close. I'd have a time finding them in this fog."

By the time Bowlander got back in, Charlie and I had coffee, pancakes, bacon, and eggs ready. Then Shorty called.

"I know it's early," he said, "but I'm anxious for both of you to get going. How far along are you?"

"About half done with breakfast," I replied.

"O.k.," he said. "Just as soon as you're done you both take off. Looks like we could get some snow on the higher points, and I'd just as soon see you back the sooner the better. How's it look up there?"

"Fog's lifting and it looks like it's starting to drizzle with a flake or two of snow mixed in."

"Don't forget to call in as soon as you get to Bear Butte."

"I'll do that."

We gulped down the rest of our breakfast and got ready to leave. I noticed Adolph was nuzzling Bowlander's arm as he was adjusting the cinch. "What's he up to?" I asked.

"Don't know what's got in to him," Bowlander replied. "Never done anything like that before. Must be he doesn't want to be left up here."

"Serve him right if he was," I said.

We said goodbye to Charlie and I took the lead. We would travel together for a mile and then Bowlander would take the trail down to Kelly Forks while I would be going the eight miles to Bear Butte. By the time we had covered half a mile the rain had changed to snow and was already starting to cling to branches and tufts of grass along the way. When we got to our parting point, our tracks were quite plain in the snow already building up on the trail. We stopped and Bowlander said, "Son, you better get a jacket on."

"This flannel shirt is all I brought along," I replied. "I sure didn't figure on getting caught in a snowstorm. I don't see you wearing one either."

"That's true," he said, "but I'll be going downhill all the way on horseback. Now listen, son, if it gets bad and that trail gets hard to follow, you'd best go back and hole up at Junction for a day or so. If Shorty says anything, I'll back you up."

"Well," I said, "I've been in lots of snow before, and besides, this'll probably turn to rain again when I get down lower."

"Could be it will," he said, "but don't count on it. I know Shorty said to make tracks for Bear Butte, but he don't want you lost in no snowstorm, either, so if the trail starts to close up with brush and ferns hanging in it, turn your tail around and head back to Junction."

"Don't worry," I said, "I'll be careful and I'll talk to you from Bear Butte."

"Alright," he replied, "but keep in mind what I told you. I hardly want to come lookin' for you any time soon."

With that we parted, Bowlander singing his favorite song, now muffled by the heavy snow. The last I saw of them was Adolph's rapidly whitening back disappearing down the trail. Bear Butte lay eight miles away and I was determined to be there in record time. I was getting wet on my shoulders and my feet were starting to get damp and cold. I was wearing "cork" boots, as most of us did at the time. There is nothing that will conduct heat away from your feet faster than the fifty or so steel caulks in them in snow. The only answer to that was to keep moving fast.

The next two miles were along a ridge following the phone line we had just put up the day before and the trail was easy to follow. But when the line left the trail and I came on the switchbacks, I could see what Bowlander meant about the trail closing up. Brush and ferns had begun to bend over onto the trail under the weight of the snow. I could see that there could be trouble ahead if the snow didn't let up. But at this point I was still confident that it would.

I continued on, but it slowly began to dawn on me that the time was at hand when I would have to decide whether to go forward or turn back. My tracks were rapidly filling in behind me. However, I still had hopes that the snow would change to rain as I continued downward since Bear Butte was about a thousand feet lower than Junction.

I plunged ahead to the crossing of Fourth of July Creek, the lowest point on the trail, snow still swirling down in heavy, wet flakes and standing now at a depth of eight or ten inches. I was completely soaked except for the small spot under my pack. To add to my problems, snow kept balling up under my boots making travel difficult. I had to stop frequently and clean the snow off with a stick, go a short distance, and then have to do it all over again. To make matters worse, my hands were so stiff with cold I could hardly close them around the stick anymore.

As I stood on the creek bank trying to decide if I should go downstream and cross at the log jam or just wade right through, it occurred to me that I was in very serious trouble and I would have to be extremely lucky to get out of it. Since my feet were thoroughly wet and numb already, I decided to wade, and the water would at least melt the snow off the soles of my boots. In I went up to my hips, the water feeling almost warm. I crawled out on the opposite shore and started up again. The phone line would guide me for a quarter of a mile, but then it would make the ascent straight up the mountainside completely away from the switchback trail. To follow the line was out of the question. I had become much too exhausted for such a steep climb, which would require me to use my hands as well as my feet. The trail was now completely closed in by overloaded vegetation with only the phone line along the side to give a hint I was headed in the right direction. As I slogged ahead, I thought back to the two times when I'd been in real trouble before, and it seemed that on both occassions I had been guided by what must have been my guardian angel. My only hope was that he or she was on duty today and not too busy rescuing somebody else, because I was going to need help real soon. As I neared the point where the phone line and the trail parted, I noticed what appeared to be a track of some kind angling into the trail ahead. As I came up to it, I could see that it was the track of a large elk and he was following the trail, at least for the time being. Many of the larger game animals, such as elk and deer, had a habit of using the man-made trails mainly, I suppose, because they were kept free of logs and offered the easiest way of getting from one place to another. When the trail and the line separated, the elk tracks made an abrupt left turn, indicating he was starting into the first switchback. The end of a sawed-off log protruding from the snow confirmed I was indeed on the trail. "So far so good," I thought.

Then the track made a right turn at the next switchback. My main concern was not to get so far behind that the snow filled in the elk tracks and not to get so close that he would smell or see me and go crashing off to Lord knew where leaving me completely lost. Visibility was down to a couple of hundred feet, but it was imperative for me to keep a sharp eye out ahead. I was also concerned that he would simply take off down any one of the dozens of game trails that crisscrossed the area, and I, of course, would follow.

As the elk tracks wound upward, the snow came down even more heavily making the going even harder. As the altitude increased, the temperature kept dropping, adding to my misery. The snow continued to build up on the bottoms of my boots and I had to scrape it off. I had to be careful not to make too much noise doing it. The last thing I wanted was to spook the elk leading me home.

Finally the grade seemed to be leveling out and there hadn't been a switchback for quite awhile. That meant that we were near the end of the climb and on the ridge that would lead straight to Bear Butte. Soon the phone line would rejoin the trail, and that would again serve as my guide.

As I plodded along I couldn't help but wonder why this particular elk had chosen to head for high country in a snowstorm, defying logic. The mountain animals almost always headed for low country to escape the snow, yet here he was doing just the opposite. I could only conclude that my guardian angel was definitely on duty today and had sent me a rescue party of one elk. I began to watch for the line that would confirm I was where I thought I was, and after a short distance I saw it. Only one more mile to go.

About a quarter of a mile ahead the trail split with one path going to the right down to the river. At that point the elk track swung sharply to the right away from the line and I stopped, peering through the falling snow and saw him there, perhaps fifty yards away, a magnificent bull, his huge antlers still in velvet, his back all white with snow. He was just standing looking over his shoulder at me as if to make sure I had come through all right. I called to him, "Thank you, my friend," and with that he trotted off into the swirling snow. I turned my face upward and said another thank you to whoever sent him.

With the line to guide me, my spirits lifted and though I was cold, wet, and tired, at least the possibility of getting lost was now behind me. Finally through the snow I could make out the tower ahead. A few steps more and I was at the stairs. Nothing ever looked so good. I kicked the ice off my boots one last time and started up. At the second landing I simply had to rest. My legs wouldn't go any more. After a minute or two I got up and made it to the top. Now I could see inside—my stove, my table, my bunk, my sleeping bag, everything as I had left it. All I had to do was turn the knob and I would be in, but my useless hands wouldn't cooperate. The fingers were so stiff they simply would not bend. I tried squeezing the knob between both hands to no avail. I kicked the door, but it wouldn't budge. In desperation I put my left hand on the knob and with my right elbow I forced the fingers to bend around it, keeping the pressure on with my elbow until the knob finally turned. I stumbled in. My boots were still so iced up I skated across the hardwood floor and didn't stop until I banged into the stove, bruising my shins, but I was so numb with cold I scarcely felt it. I had to get my pack off and then get the door shut. Since I couldn't stand on my icy boots, I crawled to the door, but there was too much snow wedged in for it to close all the way, so I simply pushed a chair against it for the time being. I wanted to start a fire, but there was no way my fingers could be made to strike a match. I wanted to take my boots off, but the leather laces resisted my futile efforts to pull them open. I absolutley had to call the ranger station and let them know I was o.k., but my fingers could not grasp the crank on the phone. That problem was solved when I heard the long, short, long ring that meant somebody was calling Junction. I crawled to the phone, which was on the post under the center map board, and managed to squeeze it between my hands and lay it on the floor. The first voice I heard was Bowlander saying, "Last I seen, he was headed for Bear Butte, and the way he talked he was a-goin' there come hell or high water."

"He sure didn't come back here," said Charlie, "and it's still snowing to beat the band. Must be over a foot on the ground and getting deeper every minute."

"I know," said Shorty, "there's even a few flakes down here. If we don't hear from him pretty soon, we're going to have to do something, but at this point I don't know what."

"It's me," I cut in, "I'm here."

"Who is where?" somebody said.

"I'm here at Bear Butte. I made it."

Then all three started talking at once and I couldn't make sense of any of it. Finally Shorty restored order. "I'm so glad to hear your voice," he said. "You had us worried."

"I figured as much," I said. "I was a bit worried myself."

"I know how those trails are when it snows like this," Shorty said, "how were you able to find your way?"

"That's what I'd like to know," said Bowlander. "I was even afraid old Ellick was a-gonna get lost."

"Boys," I said, "it's a long story and you're just gonna have to wait. If I'm not froze to the floor, I'm crawling into my sleeping bag, wet clothes and all, and thaw out enough to get a fire going. I'll pull the phone next to the bunk and if you want me just ring and I'll holler into it, o.k.?"

"You just do that," said Shorty. "We'll talk later when you're thawed out."

Well, I got into that sleeping bag and crawled down until only my nose stuck out and shivered myself to sleep. Later I awoke, still cold, but my hands were flexible enough to hold a match. It wasn't easy, but once a fire was going and the door was shut, the world began to look a little brighter. With the oven door open and my feet inside, I got my boots off and got into some dry clothes. I remembered Charlie had given me a nice fat trout before I left from the ones we'd caught at Junction Lake, and I put it in the frying pan. After the dishes were cleared up, I called the boys and told them exactly what happened to me.

"You're a mighty lucky young fella," said Bowlander. "It ain't like an elk to head higher in a snowstorm."

Later in the evening the other lookouts called to hear my story and talk about the storm. When I went to bed that night, I reflected on what had happened over the last four days. Certainly they had been the most eventful of my life up to that time, and as I went to sleep I said another thank you to whatever power it was that sent that bull elk to lead me home.

Six
Man Overboard

The test calls that we made at six a.m. and six p.m. were a very important part of lookout life, not only from the standpoint of making sure that everybody was alive and kicking, but also because that's where we got our weather reports, fire danger reports, and, at morning call, our orders for the day. The evening call was always followed by time for socializing. Whoever was at the switchboard would plug us all in together and all the lookouts would carry on conversations. What little social life there was for a lookout consisted of these evening phone visits.

When it turned dark somebody would light his lantern and everybody would have to acknowledge having seen it, and then one by one little pinpoints of light would appear on the high peaks, each one dutifully noted by everyone else. Technically, each of us was required to call in on an individual basis, but in reality it didn't work out quite that way. There were usually three lookouts on one line, so when we heard somebody ring the short and long for Bungalow the sequence went like this.

"Bungalow."

"Bighorn test call."

"Okay."

"Bear Butte here."

"Junction here."

"Okay. Here's the weather and fire danger report."

If Shorty answered, however, we all called in separately and then he would call back with the reports. That way he was sure that our rings were coming through and so were his.

Gene was on Bear Butte with me and the weather was clear and the fire danger moderate at our morning call—no storms in the forecast. We were working on the trail down to the river, taking turns at lookout duty and trail work. This day happened to be Gene's day on the trail, so I spent the day baking sourdough bread and getting some washing taken care of. I lit a fire around four o'clock and took my time getting a good meal on so that when Gene came in at five we could sit right down and be all cleaned up in time for the post-test call social hour.

When nobody rang at six o'clock, I grabbed the crank and gave it a spin.

"Bungalow." It was Norma.

"Bear Butte test call."

"Okay."

"Big Horn here."

"Okay."

We waited for Junction to come on for a minute.

"Is Junction on?"

Silence

"I'll ring him," I said.

Long, short, long. No response.

"Let me try," said Norma.

Again a long, short, long. Nothing.

"Is my ring coming through?" asked Norma.

"Real good."

"Let me see if I can raise him," said Bob on Big Horn.

Long, short, long. Still nothing.

"Maybe his phone isn't working or the line is down," said Bob.

"That's probably what's wrong," said Norma, "but I'm going to report this to Shorty. I expect he'll be calling you."

"I'll get my boots on and be ready to travel, just in case," I replied.

We all hung up.

"What's going on?" asked Gene.

"Don doesn't answer and I'm the closest one to him, so I might be elected to go over and check," I answered.

Once my boots were on, I got a few things together and threw them in a pack. Then I studied the map board. I had never been to Junction before and wanted to be sure I didn't go off on any false trails. Meanwhile, the ringing for Junction continued. Gene was listening in, and he shook his head and hung up. It rang several more times and then came the short, short, long.

I picked it up. "Bear Butte."

"Are you ready to go?" It was Shorty.

"Yes, anytime."

"I just got a hold of Don. He's hurt pretty bad."

"What happened?"

"I'm not too sure because he passed out while he was talking, but near as I can tell, he went up to fix the chimney sometime this morning and the shutter he was standing on gave way. He must have fallen ten or twelve feet and it's all rock down below. Apparently he's been unconscious all day and just made it back to the phone now."

"What do you want me to do?" I asked.

"Well," he said, "Wade and Bowlander are catching the horses now and we'll take a mule along to pack him out, if we possibly can. There's an ambulance coming from Orofino that'll be at the horse bridge to meet us when we get down. Now, you'll be the first one there, so it's up to you to do whatever is necessary."

"I understand," I said, "but I'm not all that much of a doctor."

"None of us are," he said, "but you'll have to do the best you can."

"I will."

"Do you know how to make a splint?"

"I've seen pictures."

"Okay. There are some old packing crates under the house. Just pry them apart—they'll do for a splint if you need one. If you don't, just make him as comfortable as possible and we'll be along as quick as we can."

"Okay," I said, "I'm off."

Gene had my pack ready to slip on when I hung up the phone.

"Good luck," he said, as I headed out the door.

About a hundred yards down the trail I turned to look back and he was at the rail waving. I waved back and took off. As I hurried along, I did some mental calculating. If Shorty and the boys were able to catch the livestock and get them loaded in half an hour and then drive to the horse bridge, a distance of twenty miles, they should be there in about an hour and a half. Then they would have to unload, saddle up, and ride up another seven miles. That would take another two hours, so at the earliest they couldn't make it before ten o'clock. By trail from Bear Butte to Junction was nine miles. However, if I followed the phone line down to Fourth of July Creek instead of taking the trail, I could cut off about a mile and a half, and that's exactly what I planned to do.

The line went right straight down the mountain side—steep, but manageable. It zigzagged a bit as it went from tree to tree, but I had been over it before and knew that it was a considerable shortcut. There was a salt lick about a hundred yards downhill from where the line left the trail, and as I approached it I was going at top speed, barely under control. Due to the zigzagging of the path, visibility ahead was limited to ten yards at best and at the speed I was traveling that was covered in about one or two seconds. When I came around a bend and saw a cow elk looming up ahead crosswise in the path with her head down, licking at the salty ground, I realized a collision was inevitable.

All I had time to do was throw up my hands in an attempt to lessen the impact, but that had little effect. Evidentally, she had recently rolled in the dust, because a lot of it flew out when my hands hit the top of her back.

Which one of us was more surprised is hard to say, but that elk let out a woof like a dog and lit out of there like her rear end was afire, mowing down all the saplings in her path. Why she ever let me get that close, I'll never know. Either she was deaf or, more likely, thought I was another elk approaching.

Just how many people have shared the experience of running bodily into a live, wild elk I can't imagine, but they must be few indeed. At the time, I didn't give it much thought. I simply plunged on, just hitting the ground often enough to steer. Normally, I would have taken off my boots to cross Fourth of July Creek, but not today. I splashed across in about four bounds, scarcely getting damp. It would be an unfamiliar trail from here on.

The valley was deep in shade, but up above I could see the sun shining on the mountaintops. I wanted to get to Junction in daylight if possible. A strange trail in the dark with no flashlight was something to be avoided at all cost. With all the speed I could muster, I started the six-mile climb to Junction. Just thinking of Don's situation and what I would encounter when I got to him really got the adrenalin flowing.

The sunlight kept advancing up the mountainside faster than I could move, despite my frantic pace. It was always just a few hundred feet above me, providing me with an opponent in the race. Just as I came to more level ground the sun cast its last rays on the treetops and sank out of sight.

Twilight tends to linger on the high points and this was a factor in my favor. I passed the trail to Twin Peaks. Another mile and the trail down to the river and the horse bridge flew by. Shorty and the rest should be there soon. I was in heavy timber now, and level going. The elk were coming out at dusk to feed. I never saw so many before. Daylight was fading fast as I passed the spring where Don got his water. It wouldn't be long now.

Suddenly, the timber ended and there was the lookout two hundred yards ahead. A shutter hung from one hinge and below it was a mass of sharp rocks. I was just hoping Don was alive as I bounded up the short stairway and opened the door.

In the fading light, I could see Don lying face down on the floor, the telephone just beyond his outstretched hand. Dried blood was matted in his long, blond hair and appeared to have run out of the one ear.

"Don?"

No response. When I put my hand in front of his nose I could feel his warm breath. The place was nearly dark now but there was a lantern on the table. I shook it, and it had fuel in it. A few pumps got pressure up and I lit it off. These things can be tricky, but this one sprang to life right away. Now, at least I could see. Don hadn't stirred, so I touched him gently on the shoulder.

"Don."

One eye opened, horribly bloodshot, the iris barely discernible.

"You got here," he whispered.

"Yes, how are you?'

"Not so good."

"What can I do for you?" I asked.

"I'm so cold."

"Okay. I'll get a mattress off the bed and see if we can get you onto it and then I'll cover you with a sleeping bag. First, let me hang that phone up."

No sooner is that done than it rang long, short, long.

When I picked it up, I heard Shorty's voice. "Did we bring some gas for that lantern?"

Somebody said something but I couldn't hear what it was.

"Shorty?" I asked.

"Don?"

"No, this is Warren."

"Warren?"

"Yes."

He was instantly angry. "Why in the world haven't you left, yet?"

"I did. I'm at Junction."

"You can't be."

"Well, I am. Got here five minutes ago. Don is right here beside me."

"Well," he said, "if you say you're there, I guess you are. How does Don look?"

"I just got here," I said, "so there hasn't been time to look him over yet. Right now he says he's cold, so I'm going to try to get him on a mattress and then cover him up. Soon as I can, I'll get a fire going."

"Does he have any compound fractures?" he asked. "The kind where the broken bone pierces the skin?"

"I really don't think so," I said, "but he has all his clothes on so it's hard to say. He doesn't appear to be bleeding now and there's not too much blood on his clothes, so I don't think that he has any compounds."

"Can I talk to him?" he asked.

"Do you feel able to talk to Shorty?"

"You talk," Don whispered.

"I don't think he's quite up to it," I said. "He's still pretty groggy."

"Okay," Shorty said. "We're ready to go now anyway. Just make him as comfortable as possible and we'll be there in a couple hours—but be careful getting him on that mattress, he may be hurt inside."

"I'll be careful," I said and we hung up.

"Okay, Don," I said, "before we try to get you on the mattress, let's see what's wrong with you so we don't hurt you more than you are already. Can you tell me if anything is broken that you know for sure?"

He was beginning to look more alert now, which I took to be a good sign. His head was badly swollen and dry blood was caked around both ears and his eyes were terrible looking, bright red, probably not a good sign. He thought awhile and when he spoke it was with obvious difficulty.

"I can hardly hear, my ears are ringing so loud, and it hurts to breathe."

Must have broken ribs, I guessed, and a concussion for sure—maybe worse. He paused to get his breath then started to speak again.

"My right wrist is broken and two fingers on that hand."

When I looked I could see he was right. From the elbow down that arm was terribly swollen and discolored, white bone showing too close to the skin for comfort. Again he took a short rest, then continued.

"My collarbone is broken on that side. I can feel it when I try to move, but that's it I think."

"Can you move your legs?"

"Yeah. It hurts too much to move 'em now, but they moved okay when I crawled back up here."

"Alright," I said. "If I get the mattress right beside you, do you think we can get you on it without hurting you?"

"Let's try," he said.

When the mattress was right up against him, I said, "What's going to be the easiest way for you to get on here?"

"I don't know," he said, "maybe just roll me over onto it."

He was still face down, so if I rolled him over gently, that should put him on the mattress face up.

"Are you ready?" I asked.

"Yes. Let's give it a try."

Slowly I got my hands under him and with his help we were able to roll him over onto the mattress. He winced with pain, but all in all it hadn't gone too badly. I opened up a sleeping bag and put it over him. He looked so pathetic. Now to get a fire going and warm the place up. It was full dark and getting chilly.

As soon as the fire was going nicely I said, "Don, I'm going down below with the lantern to break up some crates, so Shorty can splint you up. I'll leave a candle going up here for you. Is there anything I can do for you before I go down there?"

"Yes," he said. "Just bring me up a bucket and put it beside me. I haven't gone all day and I think I better."

"Will you need me?"

"No, I'll be okay."

So I did what he asked and when I came back with the crating the bucket sat beside him containing some very dark liquid. At first I was going to take it and throw it away, but thought better of it. I just set it outside. Shorty ought to have a look at it. I didn't say anything to Don about it, but what was in the bucket, no doubt, contained more blood. I hoped it was less serious than it looked.

"Would you like something to eat?" I asked.

"Not really."

"How about some hot chocolate?"

"That would hit the spot."

So I rummaged around until I found what I needed and set it to heating on the stove.

"Anything else?"

"Yes," he said "could you please clean up the dishes and get my clothes put away for me?"

The poor guy, as busted up as he was, he was worried about Shorty seeing his messy house. And the place was a bit of a mess. His clothes were strewn around and I put them all in a pack. If they took him out tonight, he surely wouldn't be back for a long time. He might as well take all his possessions along. Then there were the dishes—a pan full of dirty ones on the stove and more on the table. He must have been about ready to wash dishes when he fell.

When the hot chocolate was ready, I propped him up the best I could and held the cup so he could take a little at a time. His spirits improved when he got some nourishment. After all, he'd been without any for about fourteen hours now. We chatted as I got the dishes cleaned up and put away, his voice getting stronger the more he talked.

When I was finished he said, "Thanks for doing that for me. I didn't want Shorty to see the place the way it was."

"Glad to do it," I said. Actually I was—there seemed so little I *could* do for him, that I felt a little guilty about not being able to do more.

At last I could see a lantern at the edge of the timber, and then horses and riders began to appear. George was walking out front with the lantern, followed by Shorty, Wade, and Bowlander on horseback with old Ned, our gentlest mule, following along behind.

As they dismounted Shorty asked, "Well, how's the patient?"

"As far as I know," I said, "he has a broken collarbone, wrist, several fingers, and ribs, and a head injury, just how serious, I don't know, and I saved this for you to look at," and showed him the contents of the bucket.

"I suppose that's to be expected," he said, "after taking a fall like that. Let's go have a look at him."

We all trooped in and Don greeted everybody rather feebly, trying to be cheerful, but fooling nobody. While Shorty examined him, George looked at me and shook his head.

"Come on out and give me a hand gittin' the firstaid stuff," he said looking at me.

Once outside, I asked, "Does Shorty still figure on packing him out tonight?"

"If he's not too bad off he does. There really ain't a lot of choice in the matter—the doctor won't come up here and there ain't too much he could do if he did. We'll just have to see what Shorty says. I'm glad I ain't in his shoes."

We brought in a large firstaid kit that had been packed in on old Ned. Shorty was still carefully looking Don over.

"Do you think you could stand?" he asked.

"Maybe."

"Let's try it. Your legs seem to be okay." With the help of Wade and Bowlander, Don got to his feet unsteadily.

"I don't feel so good," he said.

"Are you going to throw up?"

"I don't think so. Just let me get used to being up for a minute." He leaned his head against Wade's chest.

"Just take your time," said Shorty.

After a minute he said, "That's better."

"Okay," Shorty said, "now let's get that shirt off so I can tape those ribs."

I looked in the firstaid kit and found a wide roll of adhesive tape. Trying to get the shirt off proved too much for Don, however, and his knees started to buckle. I quickly slid a chair under him. After a minute he started looking a little better.

"Maybe we better get him splinted up first," said Shorty.

So we got some crating taped to his right forearm and then placed it across his chest and taped it tight. The splint extended just past the damaged fingers so Shorty put one turn of tape over their tips and declared that job done. It looked real professional to me. Now, we had to get him on his feet again to get the ribs taped up. It went a little better this time. When we pulled his shirt up, there was an ugly bruise covering his whole right side.

"This won't feel too good," said Shorty, "but it's gotta be done, so just hang on a couple minutes and we'll have you fixed up and ready to travel. Sweat poured off Don's face, but he gritted his teeth until the taping was done. We set him back in the chair.

"What the heck is this in the coffee pot?" yelled Wade. He was at the stove sniffing it, a look of disgust on his face.

"I made some hot chocolate for Don," I said.

"It's a wonder he's alive after drinking that stuff," said Wade. "What that boy needs is good strong coffee."

"Well," I said, defending myself, "it's what he asked for and I made it for him." Wade was teasing me, of course. So we poured the rest of it in a pan to keep warm and Wade started making a pot of coffee. While waiting for it to heat up, Shorty asked me how I had managed to get over here so fast.

"I cheated a little," I said. "I followed the line down to Fourth of July Creek."

"So that's how you did it. Even at that, you must have done some fast moving," he said.

"S'pose I did," I said.

Then I told about running into the elk. Everyone expressed their amazement except George.

"She prob'ly smelt you a comin' and figgered you was just another elk. They don't take a bath too often either, you know."

"I'll have you know I took a shower last time I was at the Bungalow —six weeks ago," I said.

Don was relaxing a little now, enjoying the fun.

"Well," George said, "in that case maybe you done like Bowlander does. He always rolls in a pile of elk turds 'fore he goes huntin'. That way he can walk right up on 'em."

Now, it was Bowlander's turn. "If I'd roll in some of that stuff you made for supper last night, I don't doubt I could climb right aboard one of 'em."

And so it went, on and on. At last the coffee was ready and everyone had a cup, except Don, who finished off the chocolate. He was looking better now, more cheerful. Downing the last of his coffee, Shorty put his cup down and looked at Don.

"Think you can ride?"

"I'll try anything."

"Best we go then."

Wade and Bowlander helped Don down the stairs. Shorty went ahead and began tightening the cinch on his saddle. George brought old Ned around and we made sure the packsaddle was on good and tight. This type of saddle had a ring on the front and rear so Don could be tied on. It would be safer but less comfortable.

"Are you ready, Don?" Shorty asked.

"Whenever you are."

"Okay, boys, let's get him aboard."

With that Wade and Bowlander picked Don up and set him on old Ned.

"How is it?"

"Not too bad."

Bowlander tied him loosely to the rings on the saddle, while Wade rigged up some rope stirrups and got Don's feet secured in them. Shorty was about to mount up, but I stopped him.

"When you called from the horse bridge, I heard you ask somebody if there was enough gas for the lantern. Is there?"

"George," he called, "how much gas is there in the lantern?"

George gave it a shake. "Just about empty. I'll go fill it."

"Glad you thought of that," said Shorty. "I'd rather not travel in the dark, especially tonight."

"One other thing," I said, "would you give me a call when you get to the horse bridge? I'd like to know how things went."

"I surely will," he said.

Pretty soon George came out with a full lantern and they were ready to go. George went ahead leading Ned and Wade and Bowlander walked alongside keeping an eye on Don. Then came Shorty, riding his horse Stub and leading Badger and Ellick, the other horses. I walked along for a few minutes and then wished everybody good luck and went back to the lookout. I sat down for a while and then called Bungalow. Norma answered right away and I told her that they were on their way. I was about to hang up when Gene came on.

"I'm on at Bear Butte."

"Big Horn too," I heard Bob say.

"How's he doing?" Gene asked.

So I told them about all that had happened and after answering their questions we all hung up and went to bed. I lay awake a long time, thinking about Don and what he must be going through on the way down. I must have drifted off just before the phone rang. It was starting to get light.

"Junction."

"Well, good morning." It was Shorty.

"How's Don?"

"He made it pretty well. The ambulance was here when we got in and they pulled out with him about five minutes ago."

"That must have been some trip down."

"It was. I hope I never have to make another like it, and while I have you on the phone, after you get cleaned up this morning I'd like you to get back to Bear Butte and have Gene take over on Junction."

"I'm on, Shorty," said Gene.

"Oh fine. You got the word then, to head for Junction after you get squared away?"

"Yup. I'll take off as soon as I get my dishes cleaned up."

"So will I," I added.

"Good. Oh, and Warren, this time you can take your time," he said laughing.

"I'll do just that," I said.

And after a good breakfast and the dishes were cleaned up, that's exactly what I did.

Sometime later we heard that Don's mother came from North Dakota to get him when he recovered enough to travel. That's the last we ever heard.

Hopefully, he made a full recovery.

Seven
The Blue Grouse

There are several species of grouse that call the western mountains their home, the largest of which is the blue. Compared to the others he is truly a giant, tipping the scales at a mighty three or even four pounds—easily as large as the domestic chickens one finds in the supermarket these days. Blues have a habit of sitting far up in some pretty tall trees, well out of range of the missiles that I had been throwing at their lesser cousins, which seemed to prefer the ground under their feet.

This was my first year on the job, and I hadn't yet acquired a revolver, so my only weapons were sticks and stones. I had played considerable baseball and was known to have an accurate throwing arm, my peg from short to first being consistently within reach of the first baseman. Now, however, my arm deserted me. Try as I might, after perhaps two dozen or more attempts I had yet to draw a feather. Nearly a month had passed since I had been posted at Bar Point Lookout, and after that many days of Spam, corned beef, and Vienna sausage, my mouth began to water every time one of these delicious feathered creatures strutted anywhere near me.

Around this time a boy named Marvin, from my home state of Wisconsin, was sent up to spend a week or so giving me a hand on a couple of jobs that required more than one person. He proved to be a great companion and willing worker, but in one respect we had a serious difference of opinion.

It came to light the first time a grouse strode out into the trail ahead and I quickly picked up a rock and fired, missing the bird, of course.

"Why'd you do that?"

"Why? Because I'm getting sick of canned meat, that's why. I thought maybe we could have something fresh for supper tonight."

"Corned beef isn't so bad. I kind of like it actually."

"Well you have it for a month straight. Maybe you won't like it so much."

"Probably, but I don't think I'd ever get to the point where I'd want to harm one of those nice birds."

"Well, I'm already at that point, and if I'm lucky we'll be having chicken dinner one of these days."

"I still don't think it's right to kill innocent creatures."

"Look, Marvin, do you think the cow that went in that corned-beef can just walked up and asked somebody to boil him up and stick him in there?"

"No, but they're raised for that."

"To me it's no different."

The argument went on and on and neither of us gave an inch. In spite of this we got on well enough, and I even made a few points one day when a hen grouse with a bunch of chicks appeared and I made no move to molest her while she stood her ground in front of us and her young ones scampered off into the brush. This puzzled Marvin.

"How come you didn't throw something at that one?"

"Marvin, I may be somewhat of a savage in your eyes, but when it comes to a mother with babies, that's where I draw the line."

"Well, I'm glad to hear that." At least we had found something we could agree on.

So the days went by. I kept throwing anything that came to hand at potential dinners and missing, of course, and Marvin kept scolding me. After a week or so, our time together was drawing to a close, and Marvin would move on to his own lookout at Cold Springs.

We had just come in off the trail after a hard day's work and I went up the tower to start supper. Marvin said he would first visit the outhouse before coming up. I had just begun to peel a few potatoes, trying to decide what can of meat to open for supper, when I heard Marvin shouting from below. Running to the window I looked down on a truly amazing sight. A blue grouse was running for its life dragging one wing and close behind ran Marvin, of all people, waving a club. I could think of no plausible explanation for his behavior. By the time I got down the stairs to join in the chase, the two of them had covered quite a distance, so I had to run full out for five minutes just to catch up.

The bird had the makings of a great broken-field runner. Every time we cornered him, he somehow managed to give us the slip. We were relentless, though, and eventually he zigged when he should have zagged, and I caught him with a lucky swing of the stick I was carrying. What a bird he was—a good four pounds, maybe even more. Plenty for supper and possibly a sandwich for lunch tomorrow, but first I had to hear from Marvin, the bird lover, how this ever came about.

Both of us were still too out of breath to do much talking, but I could see by the way his head hung down that it wasn't just exhaustion. The pangs of remorse were already setting in.

"Marvin, how did this happen?"

"I didn't mean to do it."

"You didn't! Are you kidding me?"

"No, really."

"If you didn't mean to do it, what *did* you do?"

"Well, I was just walking back to the tower when I saw this bird, so I picked up a stick like I've seen you do a hundred times and threw it. I didn't really want to hit him at all. I just sort of threw it without thinking, I guess."

"So you plunked him dead center and broke his wing."

"I must have. Next thing I knew I was after him and you know the rest."

"Well, I'll be darned. From now on I'll try to miss 'em and maybe that'll bring me better luck."

As we walked back, I was already plucking our prize, leaving a trail of feathers behind.

"Marvin," I said, "if you finish peeling the potatoes and get a fire going, I'll get the bird ready and then we'll have us a meal you'll never forget."

Before long I had the bird dressed and Marvin had everything else under control. When I singed the bird over a candle Marvin looked amazed.

"Where'd you learn how to do that?"

"Marvin, I grew up on a farm. This is old stuff to me. I've done it dozens of times," I said as I proceeded to cut the bird up.

We had only two quarter-pound sticks of butter left, but I put a whole one in the frying pan. Might as well splurge on a meal like this. You only live once. I mashed the potatoes and made creamed peas and carrots, and when the "chicken" turned a golden brown, I made a nice thick gravy and brought it all to the table for Marvin's inspection.

"There, what do you think of that? Did your mother ever put on a more appetizing meal than this?"

"I guess not, and it sure smells good, too. Let's eat."

I started loading my plate with the potatoes and vegetables, giving Marvin first choice of the bird. After all, he was the one who was really responsible for getting it. He was trying to get a drumstick but was running into trouble.

"What's the matter?"

"Can't seem to get my fork into it."

"Grab it with your fingers."

"Okay, but it seems awful tough to me."

"Lemme see."

I grabbed a thigh, thinking it might be more tender, but it wasn't. Marvin had managed to saw a small piece from his drumstick and was chewing away. Finally he spit it out.

"I can't swallow this. It's just too tough."

I was busy chewing away and finally had to give up.

"Maybe the breast is better. Let's try that."

We did and the result was worse.

"Marvin," I said, "let's boil this thing for awhile—that ought to soften it up."

So we got out a kettle and threw the pieces in and put a huge rock on the cover to make our own brand of pressure cooker. With a good fire roaring away, the kettle was soon rocking back and forth as the steam lifted the cover on one side and then the other. The sun had set by now, so we lit a lantern. The potatoes were starting to crust over on the back of the stove, and the vegetables didn't look any better, but I was determined to eat that bird no matter what. After an hour of checking every ten minutes, Marvin felt that he could wait no longer.

"It's got to be more tender now. I'm starved. Let's try it anyway."

I agreed, so we fished the pieces out and they did seem to be somewhat more tender.

"Let's try a little before we load our plates again."

"Good idea."

I let Marvin go first. He chewed and chewed and finally had to give up.

"Not yet, huh?"

"Nope."

"Should we stick it back in the kettle or do you think maybe once more in the pan might do it?"

"Maybe we should just heave it out and forget it."

"After all this—not on your life. I'm gonna give it another try in the frying pan and that should do it."

So back in the pan it went. It was getting later, we were both getting hungrier, and the rest of the food was looking worse and worse. Besides, we were using our last stick of butter and the packer wasn't coming for another week. Things were not looking too bright. Twenty minutes went by and it was now or never. The pieces were considerably smaller than they had been two hours before.

"You try it Marvin, I don't have the nerve."

He tried to stick a fork into one of the pieces and shook his head.

"No good?"

"Nope, not a chance."

He dropped the fork and went over to the cupboard, and held up a can of Fray Bentos corned beef for my inspection.

"Should I?"

"Might as well. The pan's still hot."

While Marvin opened the can I dumped the contents of the frying pan off the tower. What remained of our supper was eaten in glum silence. When we crawled into our sleeping bags, Marvin had one last comment.

"I wish I'd never thrown that stick."

"You and me both."

I saw many blue grouse after that. They gazed down at me from their lofty perches in complete safety. Even though in later years when I carried a revolver I could easily have bagged one, for some reason I just didn't feel inclined to.

As for Marvin, we were to run into each other a year or so later in New Orleans when we were both in the Navy.

Some years later, when I'd settled down to my life's work, one of my co-workers came up to me and asked, "Did you ever cook a blue grouse?"

"Yes, I did, but how did you know?"

"I had a dream."

"Not about that!"

The truth was he had a daughter attending the University of Wisconsin and she was dating Marvin. In fact, he had spent the weekend at their home. In the course of conversation my name had come up and the story of the blue grouse followed.

I had hoped to contact Marvin again, but apparently his relationship with the girl was of short duration and I never got to see him. But wherever he may be, I know our one unforgettable meal together is forever imprinted in his memory.

Eight
The Campground Caper

For some reason or other I had grown quite fond of Bar Point, now that summer was winding down. Perhaps it was being on the same phone line with Jack and Mike or maybe I was just beginning to appreciate the life of a lookout. That's why I had some regrets when Shorty asked if I still had my walking shoes.

"Yes, I do."

"How'd you like to head down to Kelly Forks in the morning?"

"I guess so, sure."

"Fine you might as well get rid of any perishables. There won't likely be anybody up there any more this year."

"Okay."

"Better leave at first light and take a lunch along. That'll be pretty close to eighteen, twenty miles by the time you get there."

"We'll skip morning test call, then."

"Right. Just call in as soon as you get to Kelly Forks. Old Bill Mitchell will be there so you won't need to do any cooking. I'll be coming up the next day with another old-timer you haven't met yet and then we'll get started on that trail up Flat Mountain."

So that was that. It didn't take long to get my things packed and throw out the food I wouldn't need for breakfast and a lunch. I sat out on the catwalk until it was too dark to see, thinking back over all the pleasant times I had spent here. Most people regarded Bar Point as one of the least desirable lookouts in the district, but somehow it fit me like a glove.

I guess it didn't matter anyway. In less than two weeks school would be starting and I would be on my way home, so maybe the time at Kelly Forks would be pleasant enough.

I set the alarm plenty early but needn't have. I woke up and shut it off just as the first hint of dawn appeared in the sky. After a hasty breakfast and getting a lunch together it was time to clean the place up and fill the woodbox—a must before leaving. Then I took one final check and it was time to go.

When I got a short distance down the trail I turned around and gave a last look back at my "home away from home," wondering if I would ever see it again. I never did.

The walk to Kelly Forks would take me over some very interesting country. Pot Mountain, reputed to be the highest point in the Clearwater, was right on my route, and I was looking forward to making a little side trip up to the old abandoned cabin there. It was plainly visible from Bar Point, and none of the other boys had ever been there. I intended to be the first.

Elk were out feeding and I must have seen dozens of them as I strode along. The scenery, as always, was nothing short of spectacular. So my sadness at leaving soon vanished and I settled down to enjoy the walk.

The trail followed along the side of Pot Mountain and at a point where I felt the cabin was directly above, I started straight up. Before long I came upon the old dilapidated cabin that had served as a lookout long ago. Some folks said it had been the first lookout in all of Region One. It was high up, all right, like being on top of the world. Bar Point stood out plainly to the west and Chateau still farther on. In fact, most of the lookouts in the district could be spotted from up there. I spent some time marveling at the view and then it was time to move on.

Around noon I came to a small stream and sat down beside it to eat my lunch. No need to carry drinking water along—every stream held cold, clear, perfectly safe water. By early afternoon I began to cross and recross Cold Springs Creek, just as the map had shown, and soon the abandoned Cold Springs CCC Camp came into view. The barracks still stood in orderly rows, the gravel paths between them now going into weeds. Across the road, the ball diamond with its rusting backstop, the base paths still faintly visible, looked as if it had seen happier days. The whole place seemed sad to me, like a ghost-town. Leaving it behind I covered the couple of miles to Kelly Forks in short order and spotted Old Bill sitting on the porch waiting for me.

"Howdy son. I see you made it."

"Yup, and a mighty pretty hike it was. Just let me unpack and call in and I'll bring out another chair and relax with you."

I had a few reservations about Bill. First of all, he was not the most ambitious guy in the world, possibly due to the fact that he was in his sixties and not what one would call very robust physically. Then, too, he always wore a Forest Service uniform, creating the impression that he was a man of some authority when in reality he was only a cook and general handyman. I guess he thought that the uniform gave him the right to order people around, a practice he engaged in all too often. If, with the uniform and all, someone happened to mistake him for the district ranger, he was not apt to change their opinion.

Well, that was Bill, and despite his obvious shortcomings he was, if little else, a good conversationalist, or as much of it as you could believe anyway.

So we sat and talked until the sun went behind the treetops then, true to form, Bill ordered me to start a fire and get the table set. We seemed to be about out of water and the woodbox needed filling too. I knew better than to argue and besides I didn't mind. I was accustomed to doing these things anyway.

Bill did put on a good spread, I'll say that for him, but as expected, when we got up from the table he retired to his chair out on the porch while I did the dishes. When I came out to join him he gave me the once over.

"Git yer hair combed—you look like a grizzly bear—and hurry up. We're goin' over and check the campground."

"I didn't even know there was one around here."

"Hell yes, not a half mile up the road. Git a move on so's we git back 'fore dark."

Well, this was news to me. I thought I might do a little fishing, but there was no use arguing with Bill. His mind was made up. He was rolling a cigarette when I came back out.

"Took you long enough. C'mon let's get goin'."

It wasn't like Bill to be in a hurry about anything, but maybe Shorty had ordered him to do this. It didn't seem likely, but what the heck, there might be something interesting at the campground. So off we went down the road and before long I could see a column of smoke rising from where I guessed the campground must be.

"Must be somebody there."

"We ain't there yet—how kin ya tell?"

"Smoke's going up."

"Can't see it yet. My eyes ain't' what they used to be. Is there only one smoke?"

"Yup, and one pickup parked close to it. That's all there is."

"Shucks. Thought there'd be more. Well, I'll check 'em out, anyway."

What it was he intended to check out or had the authority to I couldn't imagine, but we were closing in and I would soon find out.

Two elderly men in bib overalls were hunched over the fire tending frying pans, one with some nice trout and the other with potatoes. We walked right up and Bill went into his act.

"Well, howdy there gents. I see you had some luck fishing."

"Howdy, ranger. Yes we did as a matter of fact."

"I see you have Washington plates on your pickup. I reckon you took the time to git yourselves an out-of-state license."

"Yes sir, we did. Got 'em right in Pierce on the way in."

So they dug out their licenses and Bill scrutinized them carefully. With his poor eyesight, he probably couldn't see past the end of his nose anyway. He proved that by asking them if they were from Spokane. Their addresses were right there in front of him.

"No, we're just dirt farmers from the Palouse Country."

Bill was looking the camp over.

"That's a right honorable occupation if you ask me, and I see you boys are also good judges of fine whiskey."

He spotted a quart bottle of Four Roses.

"Why, yes. Would you care to try a sample?"

Now I knew why we were here.

"Oh, I suppose maybe a little drop or two."

One of the men, the spokesman, handed Bill the bottle and he tipped it up. Bubbles began to rise.

"By golly that does a man good," he said as he handed it back.

Now the bottle holder looked at me.

"How about you, son, care for a little nip?"

"Well, I, uh, no—no thanks."

My experience with alcoholic beverages up to this point had been limited to perhaps six bottles of beer in sixteen years.

"Here, go ahead. Don't be bashful. It'll do you good, put hair on your chest."

"I don't know, I uh," suddenly he thrust the bottle at me.

"Go on, yer among friends."

"Well, okay."

There was no way out. I tried to take just a little but wound up with a whole mouthful, about three good swallows worth. Coughing and sputtering, my eyes watering, I handed the bottle back.

Everybody got a good laugh out of it. The man who'd been quiet up until now, came over and slapped me on the back.

"You'll git used to it. Hell my boys was takin' a nip or two when they was still in the high chair."

This seemed highly unlikely to me, but I wasn't about to doubt him. By now the bottle was back in Bill's hands, and it had been sampled by both campers on the way.

I pretended to be interested in something down by the river, so as to be absent when it came my turn with the bottle again, but Bill called me back.

"These gents want to pick some huckleberries but don't have nuthin' to pick in. So you just hustle on back and git a couple of them water buckets. We got plenty of 'em."

"You mean those with USFS stenciled on the side?"

"Those're the ones."

"Bill, those are government property. Are you sure you want to give those away?"

"Course I'm sure," then turning to his new friends, "you gentlemen pay taxes don't you?"

"You bet we do."

"Then them buckets belong to you just as much as anybody else—ain't that right?"

Both agreed that this was so.

"Why don't we just lend 'em the buckets," I said. "They can return 'em when they leave."

Both the men nodded in agreement, but Bill would have none of it.

"They pay taxes and they're entitled to 'em. Now skedaddle back there and get 'em. Hell, we don't have no use for half of what we got anyway."

I could see there was no point in trying to talk him out of it, so with some foreboding I started off. It seemed to me we were being overly generous with government property. People could get in trouble doing that sort of thing. It was dark by the time I got back to Kelly Forks, so I lit a lantern and looked around for the buckets with the least legible markings. Even those were plainly marked USFS in large black letters. Nobody could doubt where they came from. As I neared the campground again, all three were silhouetted against the fire, which was flaming up a lot higher than when I left. Somebody must have dumped quite a bit of wood on it in my absence. There was a lot of loud talk and backslapping going on combined with quite a bit of bottle passing. The Four Roses bottle, now empty, had been replaced by one with Paul Jones on the label. Everybody was on a first-name basis. Ed and Herb, I soon found out, were the campers' names.

"Here, have a drink Sonny," shouted Ed shoving the bottle at me.

There was no refusing now. The party had developed a momentum of its own. Taking as little as possible, I passed the bottle on.

The two frying pans were empty, and three dirty plates sat on a rock beside them. Apparently Bill had shared their supper. When the bottle came to me again I took a small swallow and said, "Bill, it's time we got back to Kelly Forks."

"What's yer hurry? We're just gettin' started, ain't we?"

I had just enough booze in me to get defiant.

"Stay as long as you like, then, but I'm going."

"Now you ain't gonna be a wet blanket, are you? How'm I gonna find my way back in the dark?"

"You can have the lantern. I'll get back without it."

Bill was in no mood to leave but finally caved in.

"Okay, let's give that bottle a once around and then we'll go."

Reluctantly, I agreed.

At last we bid our new friends good night and staggered out of the campground. I was a little tipsy, but Bill had to hang onto my shoulders to keep upright.

"Legs ain't what they used to be," as he put it.

Somehow, we managed to make it to Kelly Forks without any major mishap, and I gave Bill the lantern to take into his bedroom so he wouldn't fall over something and break his neck. In spite of a splitting headache, sleep came easily. The phone woke me up.

"Kelly Forks."

"Time for test call, young fella. You still all tired out from that long hike yesterday?"

"Must have been, Shorty. I slept like a log."

"Well, good, then you'll be ready for a little work today."

"Sure will."

"I won't be able to get up there much before noon, so you stick around this morning. You can saw up and split some firewood. Don't have to stack it up. We'll be loading it in the pickup."

"Okay, see you later."

Now I began to realize just how lousy I felt. My head hurt and my stomach didn't feel any too good either. Thinking that Bill might be up any minute, I started a fire and got dressed. I set the table and got the frying pans out, but Bill didn't make an appearance, so I opened the bedroom door and peeked in. Bill was snoring away, out like a light. Should I wake him? Maybe, maybe not. Either way he was likely to bite my head off.

Well, I would have to try.

"Bill, I got a fire going. You want breakfast?"

"Get the hell outa here."

That answered any questions I might have on that matter. As far as I was concerned he could just stay put until Shorty came and found him. I'd done my duty. After a light breakfast I went out and started making firewood. Around half-past ten, Bill came out, blinking in the bright sunlight, suspenders hanging down to his knees.

"What the hell you makin' all that firewood for?"

"Shorty told me to."

"We got plenty here. What's he want with more?"

"He didn't say, just said not to stack it up. We'll be loading it in the pickup."

"Now, what would he wanta do that for?" Bill grumbled as he went back in.

In a minute he came hurrying out.

"Hell's afire! Now I know what he wants with that wood. Hurry up we gotta—oh, shoot, here he comes."

Sure enough, Shorty was just coming down the driveway. He turned the pickup around and backed up to my wood pile.

"Hey, looks like you been busy."

"Bet your boots."

He waited for his passenger to disembark then called us over.

"Boys, I want you to meet Don Rorke. He'll be working with us for awhile."

We shook hands with Don, who gave us a big, toothless grin. Shorty took him in to get settled while Bill helped me load the firewood.

"What were you saying when they drove in?" I asked him.

"Never mind. I just hope it ain't what I'm thinkin'."

Bill looked mighty worried, but I couldn't figure out why. It must have something to do with the firewood, but what? When we finished loading, Shorty stuck his head out.

"Come on Bill, let's get some food on the table."

"Hold yer horses. I'll be right there."

He limped on into the house. Something was troubling Bill, that was for sure. Maybe a guilty conscience, if he had one. Then it struck me—those buckets. I bet he's worried about those buckets. Well, if that's it, he should have thought about it last night. It's a little late for that now. Besides, he probably has a hangover.

Over lunch Don was the center of attention. When he found out I was from Wisconsin he started right in.

"You ever been to Ashland?"

"No, I haven't."

"Now there is one town you don't never wanta go near."

"Why is that?"

"Last time I seen Ashland there was waves sixty feet high comin' in off a Lake Whatsitsname and rollin' right down Main Street."

"Is that right?"

I had seen waves on Lake Michigan get to five or six feet, but sixty had to be laying it on a mite thick.

"Yes sir, an that's when I packed my duffle and took the first train West. Bin here ever since."

"Looks like you picked a good time to leave there."

"That is a fact, an I ain't been sorry neither—no sir, not fer a minute."

Shorty was getting quite a kick out of the conversation, but Bill looked pretty subdued. He liked to be the center of attention, but Don was upstaging him today. He just wasn't himself, there was no doubt about that. After lunch, Don volunteered to help me clean up and after we'd finished Shorty said, "You and Don might as well get started brushing out that Flat Mountain trail. I'm taking Bill along to check the campgrounds and drop half this firewood at each one. By the time we get up to Pete Ott Campground and back it'll be time for supper, so we won't be joining you on the trail."

I looked at Bill. His face was ashen. Now I knew for sure why he was so edgy. If Shorty spotted those buckets there'd be hell to pay. He was a swell boss, but I doubted he'd approve of giving away government property, and if it came out that Bill was letting on that he was the district ranger, he wouldn't be too pleased with that either. Not that Bill actually said he was, he just never said he wasn't. My main concern was that if it came down to it, would Bill and the campers tell the truth about my reluctant role in the matter?

It was a short walk to the trail, and as we worked, Don kept up a steady stream of chatter about all the places he'd been and the things he'd seen. I seldom got a word in edgeways, but I didn't mind. It took my mind off of what might be going on at the campgrounds.

We were in full view of Kelly Forks all afternoon, and about half-past four we saw the pickup drive in and smoke come out of the chimney, so we started down. I couldn't wait to see Bill. When I did he was his usual cocky self.

"What happened?" I asked when I got him aside.

"Whaddya mean, what happened?"

"You know, at the campground."

"Nuthin' happened at no campground."

"I mean were the campers there, the ones that you gave those buckets to?"

"No. There wasn't nobody at neither campground."

"Nobody at all?"

"Not a soul."

"That's a relief. I was afraid Shorty might see those buckets."

"Is that what's got you all strung out? Hell, them boys had a right to them buckets. They's taxpayers ain't they?"

"If you say so."

That was our Bill.

Nine
Fire on Clarke Mountain

It had been one of those days. Jerry and I had been opening the trail from the ranger station toward Big Horn Point and had run into all sorts of trouble. Every bend in the trail seemed to reveal more downed logs, sometimes even two and three in a group. Moreover, we were unusually inept at guessing where the balance point on the log lay and managed to get our saw pinched more often than not.

At one point, in fact, we had gotten the saw bound up so badly that wedging it out proved to be futile and we had to take turns chopping it out with an axe, wasting an hour in the process.

Well, that was all behind us now, and we were back at Bungalow taking out our frustrations on some meat and potatoes in the dining hall with perhaps six or so other boys. About halfway through the meal, Shorty strode in and looked us over carefully.

"Old John and two of the boys left for Chateau this afternoon," he said, "and on the way up they spotted an old burn still smoking about a half mile off the trail. Pretty good size—maybe an acre or more." Looking at me, he said, "I'd like you, Jack, Jerry, and Don to take off for there at first light. You should arrive about the same time as the boys from Chateau. Wade and Bowlander will ride up with you and take a couple mules so you won't have to pack any equipment, just a lunch. I'll get you up early enough for a good breakfast before you go." No doubt he would.

"Well, that's that," said Jerry, grinning. "Maybe somebody else can get their saw pinched on that Big Horn Trail."

"I wouldn't count on it," said Jack. "You two will probably be pinching away again soon as we get the fire out."

We all hit the hay a bit early knowing it would be a short night and a long day of dirty, smoky work ahead. It was still pitch dark when Shorty's lantern lit up the bunkhouse and the four of us rolled out, sleepy-eyed, and headed down for breakfast. You had to go through the kitchen to get into the dining hall and the smoke was so thick in there that you couldn't see across the room. Somewhere in that haze, George was frying something.

"Are you okay in there, George?" somebody hollered.

"If I ain't you won't be a gettin' much to eat," came a reply.

"What in the world is all that smoke for?" somebody else yelled.

"Never you mind—when they're smokin' they're cookin'—when they're black, they're done." George was a real comedian as well as one whale of a good cook.

After we groped our way to the table we found it already heaped up with sourdough pancakes, bacon, eggs, and some fried trout that somebody, probably George, had caught the evening before.

Finally George appeared, eyes watering, and sat down to dine with us.

"Now you boys, if you work real hard and git back in time for supper, there's gonna be a real surprise here for you."

"You gonna make a real special treat for us?"

"No, I ain't, cause I won't be doin' the cookin'."

"Who is?"

"The new cook, of course." A new cook. This was serious.

"Not just a new cook, but she's got a flunky too."

"She?" This sounded good. "Who's the flunky?"

"Her daughter." This sounded better.

"How old?"

"'Bout your age." Still better.

"What's she look like?"

"Better'n Bowlander."

"Much better?"

"Yup."

"How much better?"

"Like I said, if you don't loaf around like you usually do, and git back in time for supper, you can see for yourselves."

If ever there was an incentive for hard work, this was it. Breakfast was finished in no time flat and we were all out the door raring to go. Wade and Bowlander were already saddled up and putting packs on the mules. It was just getting light enough to see a little. Our caravan started off in the half light, slowly making its way up the trail.

As the sun was just about to peek over the horizon we spotted the boys from Chateau silhouetted against the brightening sky coming down a ridge to the east of us. Now, we could look across a deep valley and see the burned area on the other side, perhaps a half-mile away. So we unpacked the mules and shouldered the fire packs and saws and started making our way downward and then back up to the ridgetop where the Chateau crew was already at work.

The fire, what there was of it, proved to be nothing more than a bunch of smoldering logs and a few stumps that had burned down into the roots—nothing serious, just a lot of hard, dirty work. By mid-afternoon, things were pretty well over and with nine of us digging a trench around the perimeter, it wasn't long before Wade declared the fire officially out and we began the descent and then the climb back to the stock.

Everybody pitched in to load up the mules again and then we took the downhill trail back home. About halfway back, Jack suggested that as long as we had been on a fire, we might as well look the part and began smearing some black junk on his face from an old burned stump. Jerry and Don did likewise, but I figured I was dirty enough without making things worse. All that blackening didn't look very authentic anyway. Apparently, I wasn't the only one who thought so, because when we arrived at the ranger station, Clyde, the dispatcher took one look at us and doubled over laughing.

"Just look at those guys," he yelled. "Smeared charcoal all over their faces so they'd look like they've been on a fire."

Of course, Shorty, George, and the new cook and her very pretty daughter turned out to witness their embarrassment as they slunk away to the washhouse. I stayed awhile talking to Clyde about the fire, when suddenly a voice behind me said, "Hi, I'm Dorothy."

I introduced myself and we chatted, and then she said, "After supper if you'd pick enough huckleberries, I'd be glad to bake a pie for you boys."

"That's a great idea," I said. "But how'd it be if I helped you clean up the dishes and you can help me pick the berries?"

She thought this would be lots of fun, so I dashed off to take a shower. How could I be so lucky? Girls out here in the boondocks were indeed a rarity and a pretty one rarer still, and here I was going berry picking with one I'd only met ten minutes ago.

The other boys had a good fire going in the oil drum stove when I arrived at the washhouse. There was a really unique system for running water at the ranger station. A small stream was dammed up several hundred feet above and a pipe ran down from there to provide water for the entire place. There was plenty pressure because of the height involved, and hot water was provided by a series of pipes in the oil drum stove. The only trouble was no fire in the stove, no hot water.

"What are you grinning about?" somebody asked.

"You'll never guess," I said.

"Does it have something to do with the new flunky?"

"Could be."

"What?"

"Oh, nothing much," I said, trying to be as casual as possible."

"She's really a doll," said Don. "Come on, what happened?"

"Nothing really, I'm just going to help her with the dishes so we can go picking huckleberries, that's all."

"That's enough," he said. "What do you plan to do with the berries?"

"She's going to bake a pie for you ungrateful people."

"Now ain't that sweet. Do we get to go along?"

"You sure as hell do not."

"How about the pie—we get some of that, right?"

"Oh, I suppose, but don't hang around all night."

Now Jack had an idea.

"I'm gonna ask Norma if she'd like to go along. Maybe we can pick enough for two pies." Norma was the office girl who had a room in the main building. She was Wade's niece and apparently took her meals there, because I never saw her in the dining hall.

After supper was over, true to my word, I grabbed a towel and dried all the dishes and then the four of us went up the mountain in search of berries. Having been on the trail to Bighorn only two days before, I knew ripe berries would be in extremely short supply since it was still too early in the season. But I wasn't going to risk losing my chance at an outing with a pretty female companion by letting on that I knew our efforts would be wasted, berrywise at least. And of course, it wasn't an all wasted effort. Several times we encountered difficult spots in the trail, and I would offer my hand to fair Dorothy, assistance which she was quite capable of doing without, but she would take my hand willingly and each time give it a squeeze, which I would answer with another one, thereby staking my claim.

The hated work on the Bighorn Trail now took on an entirely different dimension. If I could somehow prolong work on that trail, I could return to the ranger station every evening and who could tell what might develop? The lonely life of a lookout had suddenly lost its appeal.

As we climbed higher, we came upon Jack and Norma staring down toward the river and the road running alongside. Jack motioned us forward, pointing down at the road.

"Look what's going on down there," he said.

There was, indeed, something going on. A truck was parked beside the road bearing what seemed to be a large log raft. Several men were standing around the truck and the ranger station was emptying out fast. Everybody headed down the road in their direction.

"Let's go see," said Norma, and off we went.

On the way down all the difficult spots were negotiated with the same hand holding, which seemed to last a bit longer each time—a very good sign.

Quite a crowd had gathered at the truck by the time we arrived. Everyone was examining the raft and mountain of equipment piled around it and upon it. Three rather elderly men were talking to Shorty, who was taking a dim view of their plans.

"I don't believe it can be done," I heard him say.

"We're gonna do 'er just the same," one of them answered.

"There's plenty of bad rapids between here and Kamiah." Shorty cautioned. I wasn't too sure where Kamiah was, but I knew it was a long way down river.

"I know that, but this here raft kin take anything that river kin throw at us," answered the man.

"Well," said Shorty, "it's a free country and if I can't talk you out of it, then I guess you'll have to try it, but remember I strongly advise against it."

Shorty never said much, but what he said usually made sense. These guys clearly didn't stand much of a chance of floating that raft down to Kamiah.

Disregarding Shorty's advice, one of the men, a rather stout, white-haired gent looked toward the spectators and said, "How about a hand with this here raft."

I guess we were all anxious to see them off, so everyone joined in sliding the raft down some heavy planks to the water where, once it was floating, it was tied to a rock. We all lined up on the bank and passed the equipment down to the raft while two of the party stowed it. The other one was handing it down from the truck, which he was apparently going to drive back to Kamiah. As the different pieces of equipment were passed along, I was surprised to see two high-powered rifles with telescopic sights. I asked what they intended to do with these.

"We won't be able to take fresh meat, so we're gonna shoot a bear on the way," one of the men responded.

That answered my question, but only raised another as to how they intended to keep the bear meat from spoiling, but I let it go, figuring their minds were made up anyway. Finally, everything was loaded and the two would-be explorers were ready to cast off. They shook hands with all of us and hollered "See you in Kamiah," to the truck driver and pushed away from the bank. Everybody waved and cheered them on as the current caught the raft and sent it downstream.

When the raft reached the point where the Orogrande Creek emptied into the main river, it began to head for the middle of the river and then go upstream, despite the frantic efforts of its occupants to make it head in the opposite direction. All they had for propulsion were two long poles. Long, but not long enough, it turned out, for the river was quite deep at that point. It was all quite humorous to the people on the bank, and the raft was soon coming right back to the starting point, caught in an eddy that refused to release it. As they passed, everybody waved and cheered again, much to the embarrassment of the rafters. After the third time around, with much flailing, they finally broke free and were last seen headed around a bend as daylight rapidly faded. The show over, everybody drifted back to the ranger station.

Jack and I fell in step with the girls.

"Well," Jack said, "I guess we won't be getting any pie, so what'll we do?"

"Come on to the cookhouse," said Dorothy. "The supply truck was here today and brought something just for us."

"What is it?" I asked.

"You'll see," she replied.

What it turned out to be was a crate of the most delicious Bing cherries I have ever tasted. Jack lit a lantern and the four of us sat and talked and ate those delectable cherries until all that remained was a mountain of pits. All this time, of course, the clock had been ticking away and by now it was close to midnight. So we parted, with some more hand holding—no need to rush things. The summer was still young and that trail to Bighorn was going to take a long time if I had anything to say about it. Lady luck was really smiling on me now.

After finding my bunk in the dark and crawling in, I lay awake for a long time chuckling over my amazing good fortune. I had always enjoyed the lookout's life, but, of course, I missed having the occasional company of a pretty girl. Now I was on the verge of having the best of both worlds.

Suddenly, I woke to a hand on my shoulder shaking me, a gasoline lantern hissing beside my bunk.

It was Shorty.

"Are you awake?"

"Yeah, what time is it?"

"About three o'clock."

"What's happened?"

"Bear Butte called in a little while ago. He spotted a fire on Clarke Mountain. I want you and Al to handle it. I'm going to wake him now. The cook is making some breakfast for you, so after you've eaten, stop by the office. There's a few things I'd like to go over with you before you leave."

After he left I fumbled around in the dark for my boots, still too sleepy to realize my luck was running out. I could hear Al scraping around getting dressed, and when he finally clumped toward the door, I joined him and we headed for the light in the cookhouse.

Al was a new boy from North Dakota. I didn't know him well, but he seemed a capable, pleasant sort. This was undoubtedly going to be his first fire.

The new cook was a very nice lady—all smiles when we came in to have breakfast. Dorothy was nowhere to be seen. I was kind of hoping she would be there, but she wasn't. After downing a huge breakfast, we headed back to the office, where Shorty was waiting for us.

"Boys," he said, "from what we can guess in the dark, this one's in green timber and flaming up pretty good. Must have been caused by the same storm that caused the fire you were on yesterday."

"You won't have to take any equipment. Everything you'll need is in the lookout at Clarke. The phone has been disconnected so you'll have to get that working and then call in. You'll be looking right down at that fire and can give me a good idea of what it's like. If it looks too bad we'll get some more people up there to you, or I'll get you some jumpers from Missoula. Just be sure you call in before you head for the fire. I want to know exactly what it looks like before you go."

"I'll do that," I said, and with that in mind we stepped out into the near darkness and turned up the trail to Clarke. I had never been to Clarke before, but the trail was quite easy to follow and the light increased as we went higher. The birds were just starting to awaken and give out their first morning songs, a small herd of elk went crashing off, and the fog was starting to lift off the river below as we zigzagged up the switchback trail. We would be five miles getting to our destination and about halfway the sun peeped over the horizon and showed us a cloudless sky, a promise of a hot day—not a good prospect for fighting a fire. At last we could see the lookout ahead, a small cabin set on a rocky mountaintop with a tiny cupola above. When we drew closer we could see down to our left and what we saw was not good.

Smoke was boiling out from a large stand of timber perhaps a mile away and a thousand or fifteen-hundred feet below us. Every firefighter fears a crown fire, which is one that gets into the treetops and leaps from tree to tree, gathering momentum as it creates its own draft. There was no way to tell whether this one had the potential to become a crown fire, but the ingredients were present, so there was no time to waste. When we came in the door the place was almost dark, the shutters still being closed, but a little light came down from the cupola above, which had no shutters and was where the phone was located, fortunately. At least I could work on that with some light to see by. The lower cabin was littered with packing crates containing the season's food supplies, several fire packs, a crosscut saw, sleeping bags, etc.

As I went up the ladder to the cupola, I said, "Al, would you stuff all the K rations you can into the best fire pack while I try to get this phone hooked up?"

Whoever had disconnected the phone had done a very thorough job of it. I had no idea there were so many wires in a phone and every one hanging loose. There were at least a dozen different possible wiring combinations and the only way to proceed was by time-consuming trial and error, and time was something we didn't have a lot of. After several unsuccessful tries to raise the ranger station, in desperation I sent Al out to hold the wire away from some brush that was touching it, with the excuse that it might be causing a ground. I knew better, of course. There were probably a hundred or more branches touching the line between there and Bungalow, but time was awasting and if Al held the wire while I turned the crank a lot of time could be saved. I would try a combination of wires, turn the crank and watch Al. Then I would move the wires and try again. Finally, I knew I hit the right combination when Al jumped about a foot and looked up at me, grinning. He knew he'd been had.

I cranked the short and then a long for Bungalow. Shorty answered right away.

"I'm at Clarke, Shorty. Sorry it took so long, but I had trouble getting the phone to work."

"That's okay. I should have given you a diagram anyway. How's the fire look?"

"Well, it's in green timber alright, smoking up pretty good, maybe a mile straight down a ridge from here."

"Can you see any flames?"

"No, just a lot of smoke."

"That's what Jim says from Bear Butte, but you're going to have to be mighty careful if that ever starts crowning. Just get out of there fast—don't even worry about your equipment."

"I understand."

"One more thing. Jim is keeping an eye on it, and if the smoke doesn't start to die down by around noon, I'm going to get you some help from Missoula. If that's the case, you'll be hearing an airplane by one o'clock."

"Okay. I've got that. We'll be on our way then."

"Fine, and good luck, and please be careful."

"We'll see you later." I checked the fire pack. Al had squeezed enough K rations in to last the two of us two days. Everything else was there. I robbed some extra flashlight batteries out of the other pack, stuffed them in, and we were on our way.

I took the pack while Al took the crosscut saw and a two-gallon water bag, which we would fill on the way. A water sign pointed down a trail that headed down toward the fire, so we wouldn't have to detour to get water. The sign said eleven hundred yards to the spring, and it wound steeply down through rock outcroppings mixed with large fir trees. We used an old coffee pot that someone had left at the spring to fill our two canteens and the water bag. We headed downward once more toward the smoke, which was still at least three-fourths of a mile away. By luck, we came across an old trail down the ridgetop where logs had been cut out showing that it had been used at one time. The trail stayed next to the ridgetop, but the fire seemed to be about halfway down the ridge on the left side. Just as we came to the point directly above the fire, there was a tremendous crash and smoke billowed out from down below.

"What in the world was that?" asked Al.

"I'm not sure," I said, "but I'd guess a tree just went down. We'll know shortly."

Sure enough, when we arrived at the scene, there lay a huge cedar tree, the trunk as thick as I was tall, probably one-hundred and fifty feet long, and all afire. When it fell many branches and other pieces had flown off and were setting fire to the carpet of needles and twigs on the forest floor. The first priority was to get these taken care of to keep the fire from spreading. Both of us immediately set to work stamping out the smaller fires and throwing dirt on the ones we couldn't stamp out. Some pieces had to be dragged to the burning tree to be taken care of later. We worked like demons for about an hour before we were sure the blaze was confined to the huge tree. Next we threw shovelful after shovelful of dirt over the tree trunk to cool it down, and when at last the flames were down we took a break.

It was about noon by now, and we felt the smoke had diminished enough so that we wouldn't be likely to have smokejumpers for company. We each opened a carton of rations and caught our breath while we ate. Both of us were already sweated up and pretty smoky to say nothing of a bit exhausted from the morning's exertion. I was beginning to wish I had gone to bed earlier, but maybe it would be worth it, after all. Time would tell. As we rested I said, "Al, you know when I was working on that phone, I was really cussing the guy who disconnected all those wires, but right now I'd like to shake his hand and say thanks."

"How come?"

"Just think a minute," I said. "If we'd been ten or fifteen minutes earlier, where would we have been when that tree burned through and came down?"

"I never thought about that," he said, "but you're right. Even if we could have gotten out of the way, there would have been an awful lot of stuff flying around."

"And all of it burning," I said. "We were lucky. Let's hope our luck holds."

Now the real work began. Though the tree was no longer flaming, there was still fire in the cracks and fissures that went deep into the heart of the trunk. To get at all the smoldering coals was going to be a tough job. By now our water supply was almost used up so in the hope of finding a stream or spring close by, I started downhill. We would need drinking water soon, so I would just have to go until I found some. Our luck still held. Not a hundred yards from the tree was a small stream where I used the canteen to fill the water bag. I reported our good fortune back to Al. We held a conference and decided the best way to deal with our problem was to saw the tree into pieces of manageable size and roll them down into the stream.

The first one, of course, was on the upper, thinner end of the tree so the cutting only took ten or fifteen minutes. When the log hit the water there was a lot of steam and hissing, so we knew that there was fire deep inside. When we rolled the second section to the stream, we discovered that there would be no room for a third one. Both floated in a small pool. The stream above and below was nothing but a trickle filled with rocks and boulders.

Al suggested that we saw off one more section and then think of a solution while we ate our evening meal. I looked at my watch, surprised to see that it was already five o'clock. Time had slipped away. I readily agreed. We both needed a rest badly and I was beginning to regret frittering my time away the evening before when I could have been in my bunk sleeping.

After thinking it over we came up with the idea of damming up the outlet of our little pond with rocks, thereby creating a larger pond. The sections that were in there now were simply too heavy to remove, so we'd have to make more room. So, after we'd eaten and rested a bit, we went to the stream and began gathering rocks and other material to see if we could raise the water level. Surprisingly, it worked quite well. Not only did the water level rise, but the pool widened enough to allow us to turn the logs and float them against the dam, holding back still more water, making the pond even larger. Now, we had room for several more sections, but that would be tomorrow. Daylight was fading fast and we would have to find a place to spend the night.

We began by trying to find a fairly level spot close to the smoldering log, which could afford us a little warmth. Unfortunately the log was on a steep incline, so with the shovel we dug out a depression, lined it with evergreen boughs and put on the light jackets that we had brought along. Darkness had overtaken us as we tried to arrange the boughs for maximum comfort, but no matter how we tried there was always something poking somebody somewhere. Finally, overcome by exhaustion, we lay down back to back and tried to sleep.

Suddenly Al sat up. "What was that?" he said.

"What was what?" I answered.

"That noise—didn't you hear it?"

"No, I didn't hear anything."

"Sounded like something was walking around."

"Prob'ly a deer or elk. Nothing to worry about."

"Are there bears around here?"

"Sure."

"Ever see any?"

"Maybe ten or a dozen last year—none so far this year."

"Oh. Any grizzlies?"

"Nope, just blacks."

Silence for a couple minutes.

"How about cougars?"

"Never saw one."

"But they are around here, right?"

"I guess so."

Silence again.

"Know what I wish we'd have brought?"

"What?"

"Sleeping bags."

"There's a couple at Clarke and a flashlight in the pack. If you want you can go get 'em."

"No. I just wish we had some, that's all."

"So do I, but if we get nice and quiet, maybe we can get some sleep without one, okay?" All was peaceful for awhile, then I felt Al tugging at one of the evergreen boughs. "What are you doing?"

"I'm cold. I thought I'd get a branch out from under and cover up with it."

"Not a bad idea," I said. "As a matter of fact, let's cut a whole bunch and lay 'em over us. I'm cold already and it's still early." So we got up and Al held the light while I chopped a pile of evergreens. We lay down and pulled them over us.

Pretty soon Al was stirring again.

"What is it?" I asked.

"Where are my gloves?"

"Should be right here by the pack. You want 'em?"

"Yeah, anything to conserve heat."

"Okay, I'll get mine too."

We lay the rest of the night shivering away, our backs pressed together for what little heat there was. Neither of us could have possibly slept for more than an hour before the first birds started chirping and the outlines of the trees began to appear. Gradually, shapes became more distinct and we crawled out of our frigid quarters about as miserable as two creatures could be. We were both shivering so badly that there was no thought of having something to eat, so we grabbed the crosscut saw and cut off another section of log and that brought some heat back into our frozen bodies.

When we rolled the section down, we were amazed to find the water backed up enough to accommodate everything we needed to put in there. One problem solved. As we ate our breakfast the sun peeped through the trees and began to warm things up a bit. In a little while we would be sweating away, wishing for some of that cold night air. We spent the morning sawing off sections of log and rolling them down to the water, where they hissed and sputtered as the fire inside went out. While we sat eating our noon meal I said, "Al, we're never going to finish this before dark, and that means spending another night here. Let's look around and see if we can't find something to cover up with. I don't relish going through another night like last night."

Al readily agreed, so we scouted around until we found an old dead tree with the bark pretty well loosened up. By carefully chopping a long cut up the trunk we were able to peel off two strips of bark large enough to easily cover both of us. We carried them back, one at a time, being extra careful not to break them since they were dry and brittle. Just how much of an improvement this would be we would soon find out, but nothing could be worse than the night we had just endured.

By late afternoon we reached a point where the saw was not long enough to be of any further use—the tree trunk was just too thick. We would have to think of some other method, so we began hauling water—two gallons in the water bag and two canteens full at a time. This worked fine for the top of the remaining log, probably thirty or forty feet, but the water simply ran off and left the bottom half of the log dry and still smoldering away. Darkness overtook us before we came up with a solution. Now it was time to try out our new beds. All the evergreen boughs could go under us, so that would be more comfortable, and by piling loose dirt along the edges of the bark we were able to seal ourselves in fairly well.

Once inside our little cocoon, the improvement was so great that we marveled at the comfort we were enjoying. We both dropped off immediately, never stirring until the sun woke us next morning. We were down to our last rations now, so we would have to finish up today.

The problem remained of how to deal with the underside of the log, which was still smoldering. Some smoke still drifted out, and, as the saying goes, where there's smoke, there's fire. After some experimenting we came up with the idea of filling the water bag, then one of us would hold his thumb over the spout while the other one squeezed the bag. By using this method we could shoot a stream of water perhaps six or eight feet. So the work began. While one of use went for water, the other would dig out under the log to get water all the way down in where there was any chance of fire.

I had forgotten to wind my watch so we had to guess at the time, but when the sun was directly overhead we reached the end of the huge log and were satisfied that it was completely out. Now all we had to do was dig a trench around it and that should finish it off. I used the grub hoe end of the Pulaski, which is a tool with an axe on one side of the head and a grub hoe on the other, while Al followed with the shovel. At last we were done, and were hungry as could be, having missed our noon meal. I shouldered the pack, much lighter now without the food, while Al took the saw. We could stop at the spring below Clarke and pick up water on the way back.

After we had gone perhaps halfway, I stopped. "Al," I said, "do you smell smoke?"

"I'm not sure," he said. "We both smell so smoky, but it does seem like there's a little in the air."

We stood there awhile trying to figure out where it was coming from, and finally Al spotted a blue haze coming off the ridge to the east of us. After watching it for a few minutes we were convinced that we would at least have to investigate, so we worked our way down to the little stream that had given us so much help, stepped across, and climbed up to the ridge above. It was smoke all right. Before us was a jumble of small logs all smoldering away, surrounded by blackened brush. We just stood and stared at it for awhile, both hungry, dirty, and worn out, and now this.

"Al," I said, "let's just sit down a minute and think about what to do. No need to rush into things."

Neither of us said anything for several minutes. We had been planning on a hot meal and then warm sleeping bags, but that was out the window. After thinking it over we decided it would be best for Al to go up to the lookout and call in, then get some food and come back. Meanwhile I would work on the fire and, if we were lucky, possibly have it out before dark.

"Just head straight up this ridge and you'll hit the main trail," I said. "If you're in doubt watch for the phone line, then you're sure you're not on a game trail."

"Okay."

"And don't forget to call in. They must be wondering what happened to us by now."

"I won't forget."

"Now, don't get lost. If you can't find the trail, come back here."

"I'm sure I'll be alright—don't worry." So he shouldered the cross-cut saw—we wouldn't be needing that—and started off up the ridge.

I was concerned, however. He was a new boy and I was responsible for him. It couldn't be more than a half or three-quarters mile to the trail, but who knew what was between here and there. Yet leaving him here alone wasn't a good idea either, so we had to make a choice one way or the other. At any rate, he would be back in a couple hours at most.

There was no time to sit around worrying. The little stream was somewhat closer here than at the first fire, but the slope to it was a good deal steeper, making for a tougher climb. By the sun's position it looked like about four o'clock when I started hauling water and dousing one log after another. It was taking longer than it should have, but I was so worn out that every trip to the stream required a five-minute rest before I could try again. After what I guessed to be two hours, Al had not returned and I began to worry. Could he have possibly gotten lost? I doubted it, but I had been lost the better part of a day the year before and I knew how easily it could happen. Every time I struggled up with water I hoped to see him, but it was getting later and later and still he wasn't back. Darkness descended with still no sign of Al, and I doubted he would try to find me in the dark even if he could. What in the world could have become of him? Not only was I worried, but having not eaten since early morning, I was very, very hungry and tiring fast. There was nothing for it, however, but to haul water until the fire was out and then head for the lookout and hope for the best.

I used the last set of batteries and hauled water with the aid of a flashlight. Finally, at what I estimated to be two o'clock in the morning, I was satisfied that the fire was out. The batteries had lasted only a couple hours, so for the remainder of the time I'd had to work by starlight, and there wasn't much of that. I made one last trip to the stream so I could at least have water when I got to the lookout, and then I shouldered the fire pack and started out.

The going was fairly easy, but in the darkness there were so many things to stumble over that it seemed to take forever. Every time I came to a log across my path, I sat down on it to rest thinking that it might be better just to go to sleep and wait for daylight. That was soon rejected by hunger and worry about Al. When I figured that the trail wasn't too far ahead, I broke off a long stick and held it high over my head in case I passed under the phone line without seeing it, and it's a good thing I did. After what seemed like hours, but was probably less than an hour, the stick struck something above. I gave it another rap—twang, the line at last! Looking up I could barely make out the thin wire. Had it not been for the stick, I'd have walked right past it.

A couple steps and my boot crunched on gravel on the trail. Breaking the stick in half, to use like a blind man uses his cane, I started up toward the lookout less than a mile ahead. It was getting lighter and trees were starting to take shape. The trail was easier to follow. Looking to the east the sky was turning gray and stars were no longer visible near the horizon.

I threw the stick away, and soon the outline of the lookout ahead began to take shape. A palace couldn't have looked more inviting. If Al was there my worries were over. I set the water bag down, slid the pack off my shoulders, and opened the door. The stench of vomit was overpowering. What had happened here?

"Al?"

Silence.

"Al, are you in here?"

A groan.

It was dark as a tomb. Should be matches on the woodbox. I started toward where I remembered it to be, the adrenalin really flowing now. "Ouch!" I forgot about the packing crate. Crawling over it my hand touched an oilcloth—that would be the table. Now to the left a chair, then the woodbox. Fumbling along the top, I knocked something onto the floor. It sounded like a matchbox. I shook it—yes, there were plenty of matches. I pushed it open, upside down, and matches spilled out all over the floor, but some were still caught sideways in the box. I struck one and saw two candles on the table in tin-can holders. Before I could light one the match burned my fingers. I lit another and got both candles going. Al looked ghastly. He was laying on a bunk, partially in a sleeping bag, head hanging off the side.

"Al, are you alright?"

"I guess so."

"What happened to you?"

He propped his head up on one elbow. "I'm sorry. I guess I ate too fast and got sick. I feel better now. I'll see if I can clean up this mess."

While he got to work with a broom, I propped up a shutter opposite the door and opened a window letting a breeze blow through. I checked the oven and as usual the packer had left two loaves of bread and a slab of bacon there so the mice couldn't get at them. After Al finished cleaning up, we dug through the crates until we found all we would need to make a hearty breakfast and then I got a fire going while Al found all the utensils.

While we ate he explained what had happened to him. "I found the trail with no trouble, and when I got to the lookout I was so hungry I ate a cold can of pork and beans. After that I called in. Then I thought I would lie down and rest for a few minutes before starting back. Next thing I knew, I was sick as a dog and couldn't make it to the door quick enough. I was just too sick and tired out to do anything but make it back to the bunk. Next time I woke up was when you came in. I'm sure sorry."

"Don't worry about it. I'd have probably done the same," I said.

As we cleaned up after the meal, fatigue simply got the better of me. It was full daylight now, so somebody should be awake at the Bungalow. I cranked out a short and a long.

"Bungalow," it was George.

"Good morning, George. The fire's out and so am I."

"Well, I ain't surprised. For awhile there we figured you'd got homesick and left."

"No," I said, "it just took a lot of time and all I want is to hit the sack for about a week."

"You do that. Right now I gotta go make breakfast for our lovesick mule packer."

"How come you're cooking? Where's the new cook?"

"Oh, they left a couple days ago."

"Left?" This was awful news. "Where'd they go?"

"Kelly Creek where they was headed for in the first place. They was just here until the supply truck came along to take 'em up river."

"That's too bad."

"How come—don't you like my cookin?"

"Sure I do. It isn't that."

"I know what it is. You're as bad as Bowlander. We ain't got a lick of work out of him since that widow left. He's just mopin' around."

Now, I could hear Bowlander in the background. "Kin you stop tellin' lies to that boy long enough to fix something for me to eat?"

"I better go now, 'fore Bowlander gets violent. Oh, here comes Shorty now. He'll be wantin' to talk to you."

"Well, howdy. Glad to have you back again. You bit off quite a chunk there, taking that second one, too."

"Well, I figured as long as I was there I might just as well put it out. That's what I hired on to do."

"You must be pretty well tuckered out. What time did you get in?"

"My watch stopped a couple days ago so I don't know exactly but it was just getting light. By the way, what time is it?"

"Six o'clock. I'll put you in for fire pay till now. You've earned it."

"Thank you. I appreciate that."

"No thanks necessary. You boys did more than I would ask of anybody. Now I want you to get rested up. Tomorrow I'll be sending a new boy up there. I'd like you to show him around some and then you come down here before going to Bear Butte. That'll be your lookout this year."

"That's fine with me, but just one thing—if I don't call in for the evening test call, please don't call me. The way I feel now, I doubt I'll be awake then."

"Don't worry, nobody's gonna bother you today. Now, if Al is awake, I'd like to talk to him for a minute."

So I put Al on the phone and went outside to put the shutter down to keep out the light—nothing was going to interfere with my sleep. When I came in Al was hanging up the phone.

"I'll be going to Cold Springs today," he said. "I told him what happened. You know, about me getting sick and not going back, so he said I'd had enough rest and could leave anytime."

"When are you leaving?"

"Right after I get you some water from the spring. I used almost all of what you brought me cleaning up the floor."

"You sure you feel up to it?"

"You bet. After that big breakfast, I feel fit as a fiddle."

So we shook hands and he stood in the doorway. "That was some time we had, wasn't it?" he said.

"Sure was."

"I'll be quiet when I come back in. Good night."

He closed the door and was gone. I peeled off my filthy, smoky clothes, crawled into the sleeping bag, and just passed out. When I awoke, there was only darkness where the window in the door should be so I rolled over and slept again. The next thing I knew the phone was ringing. When I crawled out and answered, daylight was showing.

"Clarke."

"Well, good morning, sleeping beauty, ain't it about time you was up and about?"

"George, could it possibly be six o'clock in the morning? I never heard of anybody sleeping that long."

"Well it is and you did—must be some sort of a record."

"I guess I must have been pretty well worn out."

"I reckon you was. Say, do you remember them fellas that took off on that raft aimin' to take it clear to Kamiah?"

"Sure, I remember."

"It's a pity you wasn't here to see 'em come a-hobblin' in barefoot the next morning."

"Barefoot—what happened?"

"The raft hit a rock and come apart about three miles down stream. They lost everything but the clothes they was wearin'."

"You mean the tent and sleeping bags and those expensive guns?"

"Yep, everything. Luckily they didn't lose their lives to boot."

"Well I'll be darned."

"By the way, your little ladyfriend called from Kelly Creek yesterday to see if you was still alive."

This was interesting. "What did you tell her?"

"I said you was busy sleeping your life away and couldn't be disturbed. I done the right thing didn't I?"

"I suppose so."

"Well you think about that while I go fix something for Bowlander. He's starting' to come around again. At least he's got his appetite back."

I did think about it. Should I call her? Probably just make a fool of myself, but then again maybe I should call. When I got back to the Bungalow and showered, I got up the nerve to call, but Shorty was in the office. He would take a dim view of such goings on. I would call from Bear Butte where I would enjoy the privacy that such a call required. But when I got there I kept putting it off until, finally, I lost my courage entirely and I never did make that call.

Ten
Shoestring Trout

Chop, chop, chop.

I peeped out of my sleeping bag. Looking out the window, I could see heavy fog and raindrops dripping off the shutters. The ground below was barely visible.

Jerry was already up and dressed making kindling wood. I would get up when he had a fire going and the test call made. My job was cooking, so that meant a little extra sack time.

I had worked with quite a few different people, but Jerry had to be one of the best—strong as a horse and just as willing and always in a good mood. Not only that, he was a problem solver. If the saw got pinched, Jerry figured out a way to get it loose. If a log got jammed, he simply put his shoulder against it and pushed it out of the way. The only thing that he failed at was cooking, so that fell to me whenever we happened to be together. That would not be much longer since our work here at Bear Butte was close to being finished. One more day and then Jerry would be heading back to his own lookout at Big Horn.

I knew he was anxious to get back there. We had come from Big Horn together expecting only two or three days' work, but it had stretched into over a week now, and we still had the three-mile trail and phone line down to Fourth of July Creek to check out. I was dressing when Jerry made the test call.

"Wade says if it stops raining we can head for Fourth of July Creek," he said after hanging up.

We waited until after breakfast to see how the weather looked. I always believed in a good hearty breakfast. Sourdough pancakes, bacon and eggs, and fried potatoes were the usual bill of fare. Nobody left my table hungry. After cleanup the rain stopped and the fog began to lift, so we made lunches and prepared for our day's work.

First I eased out and took a look down at the tower. In weather like this the grouse had a habit of roosting on the support cables making it a cinch to get an easy dinner. No luck today though—the cables were bare.

Our trip down, however, ended at Fourth of July Creek, which was fairly teeming with trout. I always carried a good supply of trout flies in my hatband and several yards of "catgut" (that's what we called leader material in those days) wound around it. One could always cut a pole easily enough.

"You know, Jerry," I said, "I am willing to bet that if we find anything at all across that phone line or on the trail, it won't be much."

He was quick to agree. A fire had swept through here many years ago and very few trees were still standing, so it made sense that there were few, if any, trees to fall. With that in mind we left the crosscut saw behind and took our chances. As we suspected, the phone line was up and intact all the way down. Only a couple of dead saplings leaned against it and they were easily pushed aside.

Eleven o'clock found us at the creek and eager to try our luck. Jerry went to cut some poles while I rigged up the lines. Taking off my hat I found that the catgut had disappeared, apparently pulled off in the brush somewhere on the way down. Jerry came back with two nice poles, all ready to go.

"I've got some bad news."

"What?"

"The catgut must have come off somewhere and I don't see anything that we could use in place of it."

"Boy, *that* is bad news. Let's eat our lunch and maybe we can think of something."

Finding a fairly dry log we sat down to eat. Because of the weather, I was wearing canvas "tin pants," and as we ate, Jerry began pulling away material around my side pocket.

"What the heck are you doing, trying to pick my pocket?"

"No, I'm just trying to get one of these threads loose."

I looked down and he had succeeded in pulling out four inches of thread from where the trouser and pocket material were sewn together.

"What do you intend to use that for, dental floss?"

"Heck no. If we tie enough of these together, they'll make fairly good leader material."

"You could be right at that. Let's see if it'll fit through a hook eye."

We tried it and with a little spit and persuasion it went through. Next we tested it for strength. It was not very strong, but it would be adequate for small trout. We both started pulling threads in earnest, Jerry on the right pocket and me on the left. There was a triangular piece of the canvas material overlapping on each side and due to the shape, the longer threads were on the outside. The more we pulled out, the shorter the threads became. We kept knotting the threads we pulled out together until we each had a piece about a foot-and-a-half long. I handed mine to Jerry and he joined the two pieces together and held the result up for my inspection.

"What do you think of that?"

"Not much to tell you the truth. These trout better be pretty dumb and pretty small or we'll be having Spam for supper."

"Well, the smallest ones are always the dumbest ones, so let's give it a try."

"I'd like to, but we'll need more than three feet of line and we're about out of thread."

We were down to pieces no more than two inches long now, and tying the knot used up most of that, so we were about at a dead end as far as thread was concerned.

"Let's finish our lunch and think on it," said Jerry.

"Good idea."

I took out one of my leather boot laces and held it up.

"How's this?"

"Hey, that should do it."

We tied the lace to the pole and fastened the thread to the other end and we were ready for business.

"Would you like to try?" asked Jerry, handing me the pole.

"Don't mind if I do."

I stepped to the creek bank and lowered the fly to the water. A good-sized trout shot out and before I could pull the fly away, he'd grabbed it and snapped the line.

"Now wouldn't that frost you," I said. "If I was after a big one, all I'd get is little ones. Who'd ever think an old trout would fall for a rig like this."

Fortunately the thread had broken just above the fly so we didn't lose much of it. There were plenty flies in my hat and I tied on another and handed the pole to Jerry.

"I think the trick is to stay in the shallower water. That way you can see 'em coming and yank it away from the bigger ones."

We moved up the bank to where the water was shallower and Jerry threw out the fly. Nothing happened at first, but then he pulled out an eight-inch trout and carefully flopped it on the grass.

"Nice going. A few more like that and we can head for home."

Each time one of us caught a fish he'd give the pole to the other one. It was indeed an odd way to fish, trying to keep the fly away from the larger ones, but we had little choice in the matter. Twice more we were too slow and as a result lost two more flies—plus a foot of the precious thread. That brought the heavy shoelace too close to the fly and the trout refused to be fooled. So it was back to the pockets again, pulling out more thread, which by now was down to some very short lengths. Eventually we had a three-foot leader but if we lost any there was no way of acquiring more except to cut up my pants.

It was Jerry who again hit upon the solution. When a trout struck instead of setting the hook, he'd let him hook himself then gently ease him in. This resulted in landing only one fish for every ten or twelve strikes, but given the number of fish in the stream there were plenty of takers. After awhile I got the hang of it, and by mid-afternoon we had enough trout for supper. I don't know if anybody ever worked harder for a few fish, but we felt quite smug over our triumph—like a couple of mountain men living off the land.

The three-mile climb back to Bear Butte revealed only one small log across the trail, which we easily pushed aside. We agreed to say nothing about our fishing expedition, much as we would have liked to. We were really supposed to be working all day and fishing was not considered working. So with that in mind, I made the test call.

"Bungalow." It was Wade.

"Bear Butte here."

"Get all your work done?"

"Yup."

"All the way to Fourth of July Creek?"

"Sure did."

"Many logs across?"

"A few."

"Many fish in the creek?"

What was he driving at?

"I suppose."

"Well, didn't you get any?"

"Why do you ask?"

"'Cause you had all day, and if it'd been me, I sure as hell would be having some for supper tonight."

"Is that right?"

"Yes, that's right, and I know you two galoots too well to think you'd pass up a chance like this."

"I guess we're caught red-handed then. Jerry is just rolling 'em in flour right now."

"That's better. Wish I could have been along. Did you get enough for tomorrow too?"

"No. We were darn lucky to get what we did."

I told him about what we'd had to go through just to get enough for supper.

When he got done laughing he said, "Wait'll I tell Shorty this one."

"He won't be mad, will he?"

"Hell, no. He'd done the same thing if he had the chance."

We got a lot of ribbing over our "shoestring trout," but none ever tasted any better.

Bungalow Ranger Station. From left to right are the tool house, bath house, office, commissary, cookhouse, and icehouse.

The fire tower at Seven Mile Lookout. (WY)

These men make it look easy to strap on climbers and a safety belt and go up a tree, but believe me, it's not!

The Kelly Creek Trail looking upriver toward Bungalow Bridge in the distance, 1919.

The Clarke Mountain Lookout photographed at 11 a.m. on July 14, 1924.

Bighorn Lookout, Feb. 1940

Chateau Rock in 1943. I'm on the right and Bill Fry is on the left. (WY

A packer with the Forest Service contract string on the main trail between Bungalow and Kelly Forks.

Pet rock squirrel in the pot at Chateau Lookout. (WY)

Bird's eye view of Bungalow Ranger Station in August, 1928.

Twenty-five years later. From left to right: Laura Yahr, Carol Yahr, Buckshot, Wade, and me. (WY)

Eleven
Sourdough Porcupine

I was sitting on Clarke Mountain Lookout pondering my problem. A pile of dirty clothes lay at my feet, and I was none too clean either. Somehow I had to get those clothes washed and myself as well, and therein lay the problem.

The nearest water was eleven hundred yards away nearly straight down, and I wasn't about to haul up enough of it to do what needed doing. After several days of heavy thinking I had finally come up with what seemed like a reasonable solution. If this thing worked out the way I figured, it would be a major breakthrough in laundry and personal hygiene technology.

I hadn't said a word to anybody about my scheme, just in case it turned sour, but I was fairly confident that things should work out quite successfully. It was evening and the first phase was about to begin. I picked up my big round, galvanized washtub and headed down to the spring, and I took along a five-gallon waterbag to bring some back for my daily needs. No sense in coming back empty handed.

I could make it back without a stop if I took one five-gallon bag, but if I tried to take two, the rest stops were so frequent that most of the water leaked away, so in either case I wound up bringing back about the same amount. Therefore a single bag was altogether a more practical and far less frustrating way to go.

At the spring I found a nice level spot for the washtub where it would catch the early morning sun and then filled it half full of water. By morning it would be at least a few degrees warmer.

Shouldering my water bag, I started the tortuous climb up as the leaking bag dampened first my back and then began running down my legs and into my boots. This happened every time. It was something you simply learned to accept but never really learned to like. Struggling my way upward, I kept running over in my mind what needed to be done in the morning. Not only did I plan on doing the laundry and taking a bath, but I was out of bread, and if things went the way they were supposed to, there would be time to bake a couple of loaves besides. With luck, everything would work out. First of all, the weather had to be perfect.

At last I stumbled through the door and quickly dumped the remaining three gallons in the clean garbage can that I kept water in. The other two gallons were soaked into my pants and boots. With what little daylight remained, I hurried out to gather as many clean, flat rocks as I could find. They were an essential part of the plan. The north side of the slope was nothing but a jumble of rocks of various shapes and sizes, so finding what I needed was not too difficult. It was nearly dark when I had all the rocks inside and pretty well cleaned up.

I went to bed early, setting the alarm for five o'clock. Time was going to be a factor here, and I would have to be ready to go. I had already checked with Shorty and he had given me tentative permission to be away from the lookout in the morning, so everything would have to be completed by noon.

Clarke was known as the "key" lookout for the district. Though one of the lower ones in elevation, it commanded a view of most of the better timber and could see into many places that others could not. Therefore, nobody liked to have the man on Clarke away from his post too long. With luck the weather would hold and I could have the morning to get my cleanup done.

The alarm jangled me awake and I looked out. The sun was already peeping over Junction Mountain. Not a cloud in the sky. Perfect!

Time to get a fire going, get some breakfast, and start those rocks to heating up. I had read somewhere that the Indians used this method to heat their water. Obviously they didn't hang buckets made of birch bark or animal skin over the fire, not unless they wanted to burn a hole in the bucket and put the fire out. So they did the next best thing—they threw some rocks in the fire and when they were hot put them in the bucket of water. Not a bad idea.

No reason I couldn't do the same thing and I had the further advantage of possessing a cast-iron stove, which gave me clean rocks to use—no ashes and soot in my bathwater.

By the six o'clock test call, I'd already had the breakfast dishes done and my stove was covered with rocks and more were pre-heating in the oven, all getting hotter by the minute.

I rang a short and a long.

"Bungalow." It was Shorty.

"Clarke here. You're up pretty early aren't you?"

"Yup, just couldn't sleep."

"Well, no point in wasting a nice day like this. How's chances of getting my washing done this morning?"

"Looks pretty good. Weather should be okay and nothing bad in the forecast, so I guess we can spare you for a few hours. Best you be back by around noon, though."

"That I will. Everything is about ready to go right now, so there should be no problem getting back here by then."

"All right. Be sure to call in soon as you're done."

"You bet. Talk to you later."

Now things could get rolling. I tested the rocks on the stovetop. A drop of water sizzled. Putting on a pair of gloves, I wrapped each rock in my dirty clothes to retain the heat and put them in my pack sack. Then I stoked the fire up and took the rocks from the oven and put them on the stovetop. They should be nice and hot when I came back. I hoisted up the pack, which was really a load, and hurried off to the spring carrying a box of soap flakes in my hand. Halfway down the heat started to penetrate and I had to stop and set the pack down for a minute or risk raising a blister in the middle of my back. Soon I was off again and then I slid to a stop at the spring.

The water in the tub was a bit warmer than the spring, but not much. Fifty pounds of heated rocks ought to do something about that. In they went, followed by the dirty clothes, followed still further by the clothes I had on. I'd brought along a pair of clean shorts and that would have to do until the others were dry. No danger of anyone seeing me so scantily clad, not around these parts anyway. That was one of the fringe benefits of being out in the boondocks.

Testing the water again, I found that the temperature had risen quite nicely. Time to dump the soap flakes in and get going. After much sloshing around and wringing out, the water turned dark brown and the clothes seemed to take on a somewhat lighter hue. Now, it was time to rinse. Over went the tub after I took out the clothes, and I quickly refilled it from the spring. No shortage of rinse water. That completed, I hung the clothes on some handy branches to dry and headed back up the trail. No need to carry the wet clothes now. They'd be considerably lighter after an hour or two.

Back at the lookout again it was time to get at making my bread dough. I jammed more wood in the stove. The fire had cooled down a bit in my absence and I wanted those rocks good and hot for my bath water. Hastily I got my ingredients together, got the right amount of sourdough starter, and, after mixing it all together, I "fed" my leftover starter and began kneading away.

Now I ran into a snag. The dough had to rise in a warm place for an hour or so and my oven was much too hot. The little thermometer in the door registered around four hundred degrees. Well, the sun was shining brightly and the south side of the house seemed like an ideal spot. The lookout had no tower and simply sat on a large rocky mountaintop. The sun had already warmed the rocks there so why not? I had seen very few animals about, only some shy little pikas, which we called "rock rabbits," but they were quite timid and lived in the rocks on the north side and the dough would be safe enough.

I placed the two bread pans on the rocks against the house, wrapped my heated rocks in some old newspaper, loaded them up, and took off.

At the spring once more, I quickly deposited the heated rocks in the tub, which I had refilled before I left, and waited for the water to warm up. Thoroughly pleased with the way things were progressing, I couldn't help but chuckle over how I had accomplished so much without hauling any water up that murderous trail. In one fell swoop I had revolutionized the laundry business on Clarke Mountain. I stuck my toe in the water. Not bad. Certainly not hot, but tolerable. Well, nobody stays in a washtub that size very long anyway. The dimensions of this washtub were such that one's toes had to be upright on one side while your back was tight up against the other. Knees were against your chin. Any washing was done pretty much from a standing position and the sooner I got cleaned up and out of there the better.

Feeling much refreshed but lacking a towel, which in my haste I had forgotten, I jumped around a bit to dry off, got back into my shorts, loaded the clean clothes in the tub, and started back up again.

I soon discovered that a washtub full of wet clothes was not easily moved up a steep, rocky incline. Indeed, it was far more of a chore that I had anticipated. Well, that was only one small drawback. Overall, my scheme had been a whopping success. All that remained now was to get the oven back to four hundred degrees, throw the dough in, and that would be that.

However, as I neared the lookout I could see something in the vicinity of the bread pans. A fairly large gray shape was slowly moving up and down, but for the life of me I was unable to figure out what it might be. As I drew nearer the tempo of movement underwent a dramatic increase. Whatever it was could hear me coming and was getting panicky.

Closer still I finally made out a large porcupine with his front feet embedded in the bread dough, one foot in each pan. How long he had been trying to extricate himself, I couldn't imagine, but he must have been stuck there for some time. I couldn't help but laugh, even though my sourdough bread was ruined, for he looked for all the world like an old man, patiently kneading away at the dough. When I was almost upon him, he became desperate and tipped over one of the pans, which enabled him to free one foot and this gave him enough leverage to free the other one. There were enormous gobs of sourdough clinging to each foot, and some came loose and immediately became attached to his hind feet.

The ground was covered with all manner of sticks, pine needles and cones, and small pebbles—all of which stuck to the mass of goo that he was already dragging along. He resembled a walking brush pile as he slowly waddled off. He had probably doubled his weight in the short time he'd been here.

What dough he left in the now tipped-over pans was beyond salvage, so there would be no bread today. Might as well let the fire go out. But then I thought better of it. Why not make some rice instead? I had all afternoon and who knew when I'd have the time again. Cooking rice was something that took time.

So, after calling in, I hung my clothes over the railing to dry and put some rice on to boil. I went outside for more firewood and my eye caught something off to the southeast. I looked again, scarcely able to believe what I was seeing. A pillar of smoke was rising from a stand of timber several miles away and it stood out so plainly that I couldn't imagine how I'd missed spotting it earlier. Back in, I scrambled up the ladder to the cupola where the map board stood. Clarke was the only lookout that had living quarters below and a ladder up to a small cupola above, which housed the mapboard and phone.

I rang Bungalow before making any attempt at locating the fire. This one needed instant attention.

"Bungalow."

"Shorty, this is Clarke. We've got a serious smoke coming up to the southeast. I haven't got a location on it yet, but I'll have it in a minute."

"Let's have a bearing on it."

I swung the finder around and gave him the bearing, meanwhile studying the terrain to get a location.

"Looks to me like it's about two miles up the Pinecreek Road, probably off to the left, but close to the road."

"Are you sure it's not the motor patrol starting up? They're grading up there somewhere and they throw up quite a smoke when they start up."

"Can't be. There's way too much smoke for that and it's not letting up. In fact, it's increasing every minute."

"Ok. Let's get a hold of Chateau. He should be able to see in there."

I could hear the crank turning.

"Chateau."

"Clarke says he's got a pretty good smoke coming up a couple miles up the Pinecreek Road—can you see in there?"

"Just a minute, let me see here. Holy cow! I'll say there's a smoke. It's really coming up. How did I miss seeing that?"

"Must have just started. Give me your bearing and we'll pin-point it."

John gave him his bearing.

"Just a second while I get this plotted out here. Yup, it comes out right where you put it. Just hold on, here comes George."

I could hear Shorty say, "George, throw a couple fire packs in the pickup and get ready to go. I'll be right with you."

Now he was back to me again.

"Does it look like we'll be able to handle it or will we need more help?"

"I think you'll need all the help you can get on this one. As you know, it's in green timber and it's throwing up a lot more smoke now than when I first called."

John seconded my opinion.

"Ok. George looks like he's ready, so I'll make one more call and we'll be off. Keep your eyes on it."

"Sure will and good luck."

The fact was, I couldn't take my eyes off it. The smoke was boiling out now and rising rapidly, a sign of a lot of heat below. If it ever got into the treetops there'd be hell to pay. Hopefully Shorty and George would get there in time.

Suddenly I heard a hissing sound and remembered my rice. It was boiling over. I'd barely tended to it when the phone rang.

"Clarke."

"How does it look now?" It was Norma, who'd taken over the switchboard. She must be the only person left at the station.

"Not too good. Smoke is getting heavier all the time. Truth is I'm plenty concerned, and I don't mean maybe."

"Oh, I hope everything will be all right," she said. "Shorty really went out of here in a hurry, but he did call the nearest blister rust camp first and they're sending a truckload of help."

"That's good 'cause it looks like they'll be needing 'em. One good thing though, I don't see any flames, just smoke so far."

"Of course, if flames did appear, that would mean a crown fire and Shorty and George might as well turn around and get out of there and start praying for rain. It would take a major effort and many men and machines to get that out."

Norma was probably as concerned as I was. "Call me if there's any change," she said and we hung up.

Now there was nothing I could do but keep an eye on it and watch so my rice didn't boil over again—and keep my fingers crossed.

I looked at my watch. A half hour had passed since I'd first spotted the fire. If they left ten minutes later, that would mean they should be getting there within the next five or ten minutes. Maybe it would take ten more to get to the fire. If no flames appeared, they might be able to save the day. I kept looking at the smoke and then back at my watch trying to make the hands go faster.

Norma called again and all I could report was more smoke, but still no flames. Finally, after what seemed like hours, there was a definite improvement. The smoke changed from white to occasional puffs of gray. They must be there now, throwing dirt over it, cooling it down. I called Norma to report.

"I see some gray smoke now, and unless I'm mistaken they got there in time and are working on it."

"Oh God, I've been so worried. Shorty's wife just called and of course she's worried too. I'll call her right away."

"You do that. I'll keep you posted."

Now there was definitely a change for the better. The smoke was starting to diminish and was not rising as fast—a good sign. The blister rust crew was probably there by now, too. Things were looking up.

When I was sure things were under control, I called Norma with the good news and she relayed the message to Fay, Shorty's wife.

Despite all the excitement, my rice was still cooking away, nearly done now, and my clean clothes were drying nicely. So it looked like everything would turn out okay. My bread dough was the day's only casualty, and I'd gotten a good laugh out of that, so all in all things could have been a lot worse. The smoke continued to lessen and about an hour later George called.

"How's she look from up there now?"

"Almost out. Just a little smoke coming up. How was it?"

"Coulda bin a lot worse if we'd got there later."

"That's what I figured. It must have sprung up awful quick. I know I looked around shortly before and there was nothing. Then all of a sudden there it was puffing up to beat the band."

"Well you sure got Shorty woke up. He was so excited he run off and forgot his cork boots."

"What was he wearing?"

"Nuthin' but carpet slippers."

"Carpet slippers—boy, I bet he did the fandango. That must have been a steep slope covered with slippery pine needles."

"You shoulda seen him. I didn't do no laughin' though, not till them boys got there anyway."

"Luckily he didn't slide right in the fire."

"He stayed on the downhill side or he might of."

"I'll have to comment on that when I talk to him."

"He's gonna call you soon as he gits cleaned up. Don't say nuthin' about me tellin' you."

"Your secrets are safe with me, George."

"That's what I figured. I gotta go. Here he comes now."

About ten minutes later Shorty called.

"Sure am glad you spotted that smoke when you did or we'd have had a real one on our hands."

"That's the way it looked to me. I was mighty glad to see it let up when it did. That's when I knew you and George were there."

"I guess we made 'er in the nick of time. She was about ready to take off. The blister rust boys are mopping it up now."

"Looked to me like it was on a pretty steep slope. Was it?"

"Sure was slippery, too."

"Good thing you had your corks on."

A long silence. "You been talkin' to George?"

"What, who me?"

Then we both burst out laughing. Shorty knew he was going to be a long time living that one down.

I was so amused, I clean forgot to brag about my laundry breakthrough or my sourdough porcupine. Well, I'd save that for another day.

Twelve
Bears in the Building

Old John and I had been working on the trail from the river up to Bear Butte for several days. John was a really interesting character. He had been in the German navy and after coming over here had made his living capturing live cougars to sell to various zoos. He generally was living the life of a backwoodsman, trapping and living off the land.

To John a day's work meant exactly that—work all day. On the job at eight a.m., exactly an hour at noon, and start back not a minute before five p.m. I always looked forward to the noon hour since he would tell about some of his harrowing experiences capturing cougars. I'm sure they were true because John didn't have an imaginative bone in his body. His little finger had been bitten off by one of the big cats.

We were living in what was called the "cook car," a four-wheeled trailer containing everything we needed for a fairly comfortable existence. Our little house on wheels was parked by the river, so I was able to supplement our food supply with an occasional meal of trout.

In order to get to our trail across the river we would pull ourselves over in a cable car. There were two seats in the car facing each other just wide enough for two people. There was enough sag in the cable so that the car would coast out to the middle and from there on we would have to pull like the dickens on the rope running through the car to make it to the other side. Once that was accomplished, one person would jump out and hang onto the car while the other handed out whatever equipment we had and then got out himself. Only then could the car be released to coast back out to midstream again.

On returning from work one evening, we were astonished to find our car out in the middle and occupied by two ladies chatting away, oblivious to everything. No doubt, they had coasted that far and lacked the strength to go farther either way. This was apparently of little concern to them, so absorbed in their conversation were they that they failed to take any notice to us.

I called, but the roar of the river was too loud for them to hear, so I gave a couple jerks on the rope. This got their attention, and through hand signals they indicated that they wanted to come over to our side. When I pulled them closer, I could see they were middle-aged, matronly ladies, both wearing huge straw hats. One had on bib overalls.

"Howdy, ladies," I said as I gave them a hand out of the car. "What in the world brings you here?"

"Oh, we're camped over yonder," said the one in overalls pointing to a tent on the other side that I hadn't noticed.

"Our husbands come over this mornin' to go fishin' in Fourth of July Creek and we was fixin' to join 'em, but couldn't quite make it across."

"So that's it," I said. "Did you know where the creek is?"

"You bet, we bin here b'fore, but we all come over together then so we didn't know how hard a pull it was."

"Okay. Well don't get lost."

"Oh, don't you worry now. We know where we're goin'."

With that they started off and John came up to grab the car. He was a confirmed bachelor and was very bashful around women. He had stood way off to one side all the while. I got in and he started handing me the equipment, then, straightening up and staring across he said, "I vonder vot he vants?"

Turning around, I could see Shorty getting out of a pickup truck.

"Must be something up, or he wouldn't be here," I replied.

Shorty went straight to the platform on the far side and grabbed the rope to help pull us across. This was typical of him. He was the boss, but he never stood around with his hands in his pockets when he could be of some help. Shorty held the car for us as we got out and unloaded.

"What's up?" I asked.

"Got a special job for you. Hope you can handle it."

"I'll try anything once—you know that. What is it?"

"Well, Wade called in from Chateau this afternoon. He got there around ten o'clock this morning and walked right in on two bears that were busy tearing the place up. The way it sounds he had a pretty close call."

"I bet he did. Where's he now?"

"On his way to Bar Point. Took him most of the day to catch the mules. He had nine in the string and they all scattered to hell and gone when the one bear came running down past 'em."

"What about the other one?"

"I guess he shot it up pretty good. Said he hit it six times before it went out the window and then he shot a full clip into it as it went over the rock. He doesn't think that one will survive, but you can bet your boots the other one will be back."

Wade always carried a Colt Woodsman .22 pistol, not exactly an ideal weapon for bear, but under such conditions I suppose you use whatever you happen to have. While we drove back to the Bungalow, Shorty began to brief me on what to expect.

"I've got a little Winchester 30-30 you can use, but there's only one shell for it at the station. Wade says there's a full box at Chateau, though, so as long as you don't run into any bears on the way up, you should be okay."

"How bad did they tear up the lookout?"

"Wade says it's a real mess. They got in through one of the windows, broke the whole section out, and I guess all the food has been broken into, so you can imagine what the place looks like."

"What about the window?"

"Wade nailed a manty over it." (A manty was a term packers used for the tarpaulin they wrapped over their packs.)

"I hope it's still in place when I get there."

"Chances are it will be, but you never know. Most likely he'll wait awhile before coming back, but again you never know. Bears are hard to predict. One thing is for sure, though, he knows there's food there and he'll be back for it before long."

"How long do you think?"

"No telling, but more than likely it'll be pretty soon."

"How long should I stay up there?"

"Till you get him. Unless I miss my guess it'll only be a day or two."

When we pulled into the yard Shorty said, "George is holding supper for you. I'll see you after breakfast tomorrow morning."

I took my pack into the bunkhouse and headed down to see what George had on the menu. He saw me coming and ran out to give his old steel triangle a few turns around with the striker, making enough noise to wake the dead.

"What's for supper?"

"You're late. All that's left is cold oatmeal."

"Is that so?"

"Yup, Bowlander's et up about everything else."

"If the oatmeal is cold, how come there's smoke coming out of the chimney?"

"Thought you'd like it cold or I'd a put it on the stove."

"Maybe I'll just go in and look around. There might be something else that's edible."

"Suit yourself. There's some stuff I was gonna throw out anyway. Probably spoilt, but for you that don't matter."

Naturally the table was loaded with all sorts of mouth-watering goodies.

"This is what you were gonna throw out?"

"Yup."

"Maybe I'll just have that cold oatmeal."

I was hungry as a bear and dying to dive into all this delicious food, but the game had to be played.

"I'll go get it."

George disappeared into the kitchen and began rummaging around.

"What's the matter, can't you find it?"

"Hold yer horses. It's around here someplace."

"Well, hurry up. I'm hungry."

At last George reappeared with an empty bowl.

"What's that?"

"This here's what it was in. Mice musta got at it. You'll just hafta take a chance with them leftovers."

"Well, I suppose it's that or starve. Just remember, if I get ptomaine poisoning, it'll be on your conscience, if you have one that is."

"Oh, I've got one all right—jest don't believe in overworkin' it, that's all."

One thing I had learned about George, if he didn't like you he simply ignored you completely. On the other hand, if he did like you he would tease you unmercifully, but always with a grin and a twinkle in his eye that let you know it was all in fun. With me he seemed in perpetual good humor, a favorable sign.

Now he sat across from me, turning serious for a change.

"I hear you're going bear huntin'."

"I guess so. That's what Shorty says anyway."

"How many bears you shot?"

"None."

"That's what I figured. Well, I shot a few and before you go out and do something dumb, there's a couple words of advice you better listen to."

"Shoot."

"For one thing, if he don't come around before you hit the hay, you'd best sleep with one eye open, 'cause they do like to move around after dark. First thing you know, he'll be in bed with you and I can think of lots of things I'd rather bed down with than a stinky bear."

"You and me both."

"Another thing. If you do hit him pretty good, don't go galvantin' after him. Just leave him be. Nuthin' I hate worsen' packin' out a dumb kid's got himself busted up by a bear."

"I'll be careful, George, you know that."

"No, I don't know that. People get excited and they don't always use the few brains they got."

"Don't worry. I'll be okay."

"I s'pose you will, but if I wasn't so important around here, I'd go along and make sure you was okay."

"You know they couldn't get along without you here, George, so I'll just have to go without you. Come on, let's clean off the table. I'll dry dishes for you."

"Darn right you will. You et enough for ten people. Now you can work off some of your bill."

When the dishes were done I retired to the bunkhouse and started packing what I would need to take along to Chateau. I'd hardly started when George came in.

"Wade's on the phone. He wants to talk to you."

In the office George handed me the phone.

"Hi, Wade, hear you had a little excitement today."

"That I did. Enough to last me for a while anyway."

"What happened exactly?"

"Well, I had a box of perishables under my arm as I walked in the door and I was looking over my shoulder at a smoke near Tamarack. Soon as I got inside, the wind blew the door shut behind me and there they were right in front of me. Both of 'em started growling right away. Well, I dropped that box on the floor—Bam!—and that backed 'em both up a foot or two and gave me a second to get my gun out."

"The sow was closest so I shot for her eye and all she did was shake her head, so I shot for it again and she got up on her hind legs and came for me, popping her jaws. I emptied the rest of the clip right in her belly. That put her down on the floor rolling around."

"Now, the boar came for me on his hind legs and I thought sure he was gonna slap me, but the other one got up on the bunk and went out the window and he followed."

"By now, I had the clip out and was loading it up as fast as I could, and by the time I got out the door the sow was sort of stumbling down over the side of the rock. I shot a full clip into her and she lost her footing and rolled the rest of the way down. Last I saw, she was still on her feet, but by now she should be done for."

"The boar went down the stairs and scattered all the stock, and I spent the rest of the morning and half the afternoon rounding 'em up."

"Whew. Glad you're still here to tell about it. How much of a mess did they make?"

"I can tell you this much, you'll be all day cleaning it up and then some. I left enough food for a few days, 'cause everything that had been there before was broken into and ruined. They didn't miss anything that I could see."

"What if he gets into the stuff you left for me?"

"He won't. It's in the oven."

"Oh, good. I'll have to remember that before I start a fire."

"Best you do or you'll be mighty hungry. Maybe you'll be cooking up some bear meat when I get back there."

"When will that be?"

"I'm going on to Cold Springs tomorrow and with a little luck should be back to Chateau late the next day. I'll be hungry as hell, so see to it you have something fit to eat ready for me."

"I always do, Wade, you know that."

"I guess you do at that. Just wanted to make sure. One more thing—I want you to be careful. That is one big bear and they are nothing to fool with. Don't take any chances, you got that?"

"You bet. George just got done lecturing me and I expect I'll get another one from Shorty in the morning, so I should be pretty well prepared."

"That's good. Just be sure it's all sinkin' in."

"It is Wade. I'll have supper ready for you day after tomorrow."

"Well, let's hear all about it," said George when I hung up.

After I finished Wade's account of what had taken place, Bowlander wandered in and I had to do it all over again. Then he and George started recounting all their bear experiences covering the last forty years until I finally called a halt.

"Boys, if I'm going up there tomorrow, I've gotta get some sleep."

So off to the bunkhouse I went, but getting to sleep was easier said than done. What with all the excitement, advice, and anticipation, most of the night was spent tossing and turning. Toward morning I must have drifted off, because the next thing I knew George was banging away on the cookhouse triangle and the sun was up. Struggling into my clothes, I hurried down to the washhouse and then on to breakfast. Bowlander and George were already eating.

"Better grab some grub, 'fore Bowlander gits it all," hollered George.

"You just take your good-natured time," said Bowlander. "If we run out, he can just go make some more—ain't that right?"

"Absolutely," I agreed.

"No it ain't," cried George. "Once I set down to eat, my cookin' time is done. Besides, the stove's only got enough heat left in it fer dishwater and that's that."

Of course there was enough food for the three of us and then some and we all knew it, but George and Bowlander had to have their fun. After breakfast I headed up to the office. Shorty was waiting.

"Well, good mornin'. Get a good night's sleep?"

"Sure," I lied, "ready to go."

"That's fine. Now here's my rifle," he said handing me a Winchester carbine. Reaching in his pocket he pulled out one shell.

"Sorry I don't have more, but Wade says there's a full box at Chateau, so that won't be a problem."

Next he showed me how to load the rifle and gave a few instructions.

"It's a bit light for elk and maybe not just what you'd want for bear, but it shoots right where you aim and at the moment it's all we've got."

"It'll be just fine," I said.

"Well, then, you might as well take off. You'll have plenty of cleaning up to do when you arrive."

"Okay. I'll call in when I get there."

"Good. And one other thing I'd like you to know, you're the only one of the boys I'd let go on a deal like this. I've seen you handle your own rifle (a .22), and I know you have some experience so that's why I'm letting you do this, but be extra careful, will you?"

"I sure will be, and I appreciate your trusting me."

"No problem there. Now get going." He gave me a slap on the back and I grabbed my pack at the bunkhouse and was off. When I passed the cookhouse, George was waiting.

"Hold on a bit, I've got something for you."

"Not more advice, I hope."

"No, but there ain't no harm in good advice, long as you foller it."

"I will George. Now what have you got for me?"

"Never you mind, just something to tide you over in case all the grub bin et up by them bears."

He was jamming a bag in the top of my pack, pulling me off balance.

"Careful there, you'll tip me over."

"If that's all it takes you better stay where you're at."

"Not a chance. When you're done back there I'd better get going or I'll never get there in daylight."

"Don't be so all-fired impatient. I gotta git this thing buckled up right or you'll lose half your stuff. Now hold still."

There was nothing for it but to stand there and let him yank away. Finally he was done.

"There, now, you can go off and not leave a trail of food and clothes behind you."

"You're sure? May I go now?"

"Yup. Git outa here, an don't shoot yerself in the foot."

"I will if I want to," I called back as I hurried off.

It was high time to get a move on. Chateau was four and a half miles away and I wanted to get the place in some semblance of order before dark. As I crossed the bridge I looked back and George was still standing there. I waved to him and he gave me a little wave back and then turned back toward the cookhouse.

I climbed over the gate at the old CCC Camp where the livestock were kept. Wade had most of them, but there were several horses and mules still there. One of the mules decided to follow me, but at the upper gate he had to stand and watch me go on without him.

The day was ideal—sun shining, birds singing, then a doe bounded off startling me and I decided it was time to load up the one shell I had. I didn't want to be caught flatfooted if the bear should appear. By the time I reached the foot of Chateau rock, I hadn't encountered anything more threatening than a hen grouse that held me up long enough for her brood of chicks to disappear into the brush.

There was a cleft in the lower part of the rock to climb up and then a stairway that went the rest of the way to the top—a climb of probably three hundred feet. Now was the time for extra caution. Nothing stirred when I neared the top, rifle at the ready.

The little house looked peaceful enough, and to my relief the manty over the torn-out window appeared undisturbed. Nevertheless, I took a careful look in before I opened the door. There was nothing, only the most terrible mess I had ever seen. Punctured cans were strewn about everywhere and the floor was crusted over with heaven only knew what. A fifty-pound flour sack was torn open along with several sugar sacks and their contents were spilled out over the entire mess. Egg shells were stuck tight to the gooey crust on the floor together with dried beans, rice, a butter and honey pail, and several pounds of coffee. The stovepipe had been knocked down and its contents added to the monumental mess. Not even the mapboard had been spared. Claws had slashed across it snapping the wire.

"Well, first things first," I thought as I set my pack on the bunk, which appeared to be undamaged. At least they hadn't slept in it. Getting the stovepipe up again seemed a logical start and then a fire to heat water. But first the oven had to be emptied.

Good old Wade. He had left me two loaves of bread, some condensed milk, a small canned ham, some eggs, potatoes, bacon, and enough canned goods to last awhile. Then I remembered what George had put in my pack.

The bag contained some sandwiches, fruit, cookies, and a sourdough starter. That ought to tide me over for one day, and with luck maybe I could salvage enough flour and sugar for sourdough pancakes in the morning. At least I wouldn't starve.

Best of all, there was a full box of shells on the table. I fed six into the rifle right away. Now, Mr. Bear could shine around anytime he chose. I'd be ready—loaded for bear.

Once the fire was started I began filling the garbage can with punctured cans. It was then I noticed something strange. There had been eighty individual cans of fruit on hand when the bears broke in. Of these thirty were Libby's pears in white cans, twenty Del Monte's peaches in green cans, and thirty Dromedary grapefruit in yellow cans. The bears had apparently put the cans between their teeth and punctured them and licked up the liquid as it ran out. Unable to get at the fruit inside, they'd simply grabbed another and done the same thing. The odd part was every can of peaches and pears had been bitten into and only two cans of grapefruit, though they were all mixed together on the floor.

Now, I don't think bears are able to read and people tell me that they are color blind and surely they can't smell what is in a sealed can, but somehow they figured out what was in those cans. One thing for sure, they didn't care much for grapefruit. With the garbage can full, I grabbed a couple five-gallon water bags that didn't seem to have been damaged and set off for the garbage pit and then the spring.

I debated whether or not to take the rifle and finally decided against it. Going down I would have the full garbage can plus the empty water bags and coming back I would have eighty pounds of water plus a garbage can—more than enough to carry. If I did see the bear, chances are I would be too overburdened to shoot anyway.

The garbage pit was around on the side of the rock, perhaps fifty or sixty yards to the right after you hit the bottom. Nearby stood the outhouse that Jack had built the year before. He was always after everybody, including Juanita, the office girl, to come up and tryout "the house that Jack built." So far as I know, nobody ever did.

There were timbers across the garbage pit into which old crating had been nailed and then dirt thrown over that. In the center was a large cover which could be lifted off to keep the flies and animals out. After dumping the garbage, I filled the water bags at the spring about a quarter of a mile away and started back.

The climb up the rock was a real chore and I was thankful for having left the rifle behind.

The fire was going nicely, so I filled every container with water and started them heating while I broke out the lunch that George had so thoughtfully made for me.

After lunch it was time to take another run to the garbage pit and spring, and when I returned I filled the garbage can with the last of the cans and poured all the hot water out on the floor. Hopefully this would soften up the encrustation a bit.

There were a few cans of butter packed in salt water that were too large for the bears to get their teeth into. They were pretty well battered but still intact, so I would have butter. Needless to say, the syrup had gone the way of the rest of the food, so it would be butter mixed with some salvaged sugar on the pancakes tomorrow. Oh well, I had eaten worse.

I had more water heating now, and with the last of the garbage going out, one more trip to the spring would be enough. Besides, I was getting pretty well bushed. Returning once more, I dumped the rest while the water did its work.

When I felt rested up enough to tackle the mess, I took off my boots and pants and went in and got started. After some experimenting it was apparent that I would have to scrape the stuff loose with a butcher knife and then sop up the water with a rag. Not a very speedy way of doing things, but it was working.

The garbage can was soon filled with the filthy water so I set it outside the door and used a smaller bucket instead. When it was full, rather than carry it down to the pit, I simply sailed it over the rock. If it attracted flies, well, that was too bad. I'd had enough of struggling up and down that rock for one day. The miserable job seemed to take forever, but at last it was done. I was willing to bet the floor was the cleanest it had ever been.

My knees and feet were a different matter, however. From kneeling in that goo for hours, I was a real mess from the knees down. Fortunately, I'd left some water heating on the stove and with that I was able to get cleaned up fairly well.

Now, I was really tuckered out, so I leaned the rifle against the house and sat outside, waiting for the floor to dry. A cow elk and her calf appeared down below, peacefully browsing on some brush. Suddenly the cow raised her head and started testing the wind, apparently trying to identify some smell. She returned uneasily to her browsing, then, jerking her head up once again, caught a whiff of something that sent her and the calf bolting out of there at top speed. There was no way she could have winded me. I could only conclude that the bear must be somewhere upwind of her, but try as I might I could see nothing.

The phone startled me out of my concentration. A glance at my watch showed it to be five minutes after test call time.

"Chateau."

"Are you still alive up there?"

"Yes, George, I'm alive—just been so busy I forgot the time."

"Seen any bears?"

"Nope, not yet, but I did see one hell of a mess that they left behind."

"You done anything about cleanin' it up yet?"

"Of course I have. I was just outside waiting for the floor to dry."

"You got it all cleaned up then?"

"Just about."

"Wade called—said he'd be over your way tomorrow if he don't run into any more trouble."

"Good. I'll have supper ready when he gets in."

"What you gonna feed him, bear steak?"

"Maybe. That depends."

"Well if I was you, I wouldn't try servin' none to Wade. I don't expect he'd be any too fond of it."

"Probably not, and by the way, thanks for the food. I'm too tired out to make a big supper, so I'll just finish off the stuff you sent along."

"You do that and remember what I said about sleepin' with one eye open."

"I'll try, but that's a pretty tall order. See you later."

The floor needed a little more drying out, so I took the remaining food that George had sent and settled down out on the catwalk with the rifle handy. I kept an eye out for any movement down below, but nothing stirred. When it was too dark to see, I went in and lit a candle. The Coleman lantern had been wrecked so a flashlight was my only other source of light. There were two bunks on the side where the manty was hung, one right under it and the other to the left under a window that was still intact. After deliberating awhile, I opted for the one under the window. That way I could at least see out. I took off my clothes, blew out the candle, and crawled into my sleeping bag, leaving the flashlight and rifle close alongside.

Sleeping with one eye open simply wasn't going to work. Furthermore, it was too dark to see anything with two eyes, let alone one. So if Mr. Bear wanted to come, let him come. I was too tired out to care.

Sometime later, though, I woke with a start. Did I hear something or was it my imagination? No, there it was again. The wind? Could be. I was wide awake now listening. Again, this time unmistakably, a board on the catwalk creaked. Something had put weight on it right outside the window. Straining my eyes I could see only darkness. Again the faint sound of something on the catwalk.

I groped for the rifle and laid it across my body pointing at the window. "Could he hear my heart beating?" I wondered. I knew I could. The hammer made a slight click when I eased it back, sounding quite loud in the silence. Whatever was out there heard it too and the creaking moved toward the front of the house.

As silently as possible, I slid out of the sleeping bag and, with the rifle in one hand and flashlight in the other, tiptoed slowly to the door. Moving the flashlight under my arm, I yanked the door open and grabbed the light and swung it around just as a dark shape hurtled down the stairs.

Bringing the rifle up I hesitated and decided not to shoot. No chance for a killing shot, and I'd hate to report in to say that I'd let a wounded bear get away. Better to wait.

Well, that's that, I thought, he's scared off now and won't be back. I carefully let the hammer down on the rifle and put it back within easy reach, along with the light, just in case, and got back into the sleeping bag.

I lay awake for sometime, my heartbeat still going pretty good from the excitement. Eventually, though, sleep took over, but not for long. Again, I jerked awake to the sound of running water. Where could that be coming from? Puzzled, I came fully awake.

The garbage can, of course. I had left it outside the door full of dirty water. Something had tipped it over and the water was splashing on the rock. Again I slipped quietly out of the sleeping bag and stuck the rifle under my right arm and the flashlight in the same hand. No clicking hammer this time. I could do that quickly enough when I brought the gun to my shoulder. Reaching the door, I yanked it open, turned on the light, and saw absolutely nothing—just the garbage can lying on its side, a little stream of water still dribbling out. I could only conclude that bears must have very good ears or I was making more noise than I thought.

Well, what now? Might as well go back to bed. If he keeps coming back, sooner or later he'll make a mistake. Maybe. Arranging my artillery I crawled in again. This was getting to be one long night. When my heart finally settled down I dropped off right away and slept soundly.

Dawn was just breaking when I awoke. I was facing east looking into a rose-colored sky. Might as well go have a look around, I thought, so I crawled out and went to the door and stepped outside. Swallows were already doing their aerial acrobatics around the sides of the rock, feeding on the first early morning insects.

The tower over at Bar Point, where I'd spent most of the previous summer, stood out plainly against the brightening sky. It promised to be a perfect day. Looking around for any movement I could see none, so I stepped farther out on the rock. Everything looked normal at first, but then I noticed that the cover was not on the garbage pit.

Had I forgotten to put it back? No, I could distinctly remember looking down and seeing it in place last evening. Looking more closely, I could see something moving, and then one corner of the top over the whole pit started to raise up and out poked a huge black head. Somehow he had gotten inside and was in the process of moving the whole thing off, timbers and all. He hadn't seen me, or at least he gave no sign of it, so I went quickly back in the house for the rifle. I slipped on my pants and a pair of moccasins and went back out.

Perhaps he heard me or caught the motion when I appeared, for he spotted me instantly. Figuring on an easy shot, I was caught unprepared when he burst out. My first shot was pure luck. A puff of dust appeared on his back and I knew he'd been hit, but he slowed not at all and went galloping to my right. The next shot hit a rock right ahead of him.

"Damn, led him too much."

It did, however, turn him around and he took off to my left, quartering away. Three more shots, as fast as I could work the lever, kicked up dust ahead, behind, and under him. I'd have to do better or he'd escape. The last shot did turn him enough so that he was going straight away from me. Carefully now, I shot again and was rewarded with another puff of dust from his back farther forward than the first one. Either confused or badly hurt, he stopped and turned broadside to me. The distance was now two hundred yards or more, so I held high on his shoulder and fired. Nothing—he simply disappeared. Working the lever, I waited for him to show himself. Nothing stirred except the swallows, clouds of which had poured out of their nests on the rock no doubt disturbed by the shooting.

After what seemed like several minutes, but was probably only seconds, there came a wail, sounding almost human.

"W-O-O-O-O-O-O-O-O-O-O-O-O-O-O"

It must have lasted at least a minute, maybe more. Assuming that this meant the end of Mr. Bear, I promptly forgot all the advice I'd been given and went bounding down the stairs like a wild man. Reaching the bottom, I ran around to the garbage pit and began to wonder just where he might be. Everything looked the same, not at all the way it had from above. A few drops of blood and several black hairs showed where he had been first hit, but he had gone back and forth after that, so I struck off in what seemed like the right direction hoping to find some signs. No tracks were visible on the hard ground.

Moving cautiously ahead, I came upon what appeared to be a pockmark where one of the bullets had hit. Must be getting close, I thought. Ahead was a small mound where a tree had probably been uprooted many years ago. Once up there I should be able to see better. Still exercising all the caution I could muster and waiting for my heart to stop pounding, I stopped to see how many shells were left, just to be on the safe side. Sliding the lever ahead I looked in—empty. George was right, people get excited, and they don't always use the few brains they've got. At the moment it seemed mine were few indeed, and I certainly wasn't using them.

Well, what to do? I stood for a minute undecided. Should I go back and reload? Probably. Yet everything was so quiet. A bird came and sat in a tree on top of the mound. Surely a bird wouldn't do that with a bear nearby, or would it? After thinking it over, I decided to go to the mound and look things over, no farther. If I couldn't see any sign of him, I'd go back and reload.

When I approached the mound and peeped over, something big and black appeared on the other side. There he lay, stone dead, a big blue fly already walking on one of his eyes. Carefully, I poked him with the rifle barrel. No reaction. I took a deep breath, the first one in sometime. My heart was still going like a triphammer, so I sat down on a nearby log to settle down a bit. This was probably the most exciting moment in all my seventeen years.

Looking at the animal more closely, he seemed to be the largest black bear I'd ever seen. Even lying there on his side, he looked huge. I noticed a tree about as thick as my wrist that had been bitten off, probably as he was dying, giving an indication of the power of those jaws. After a few minutes, I began to settle down and think about what to do next.

"I must call Shorty," I thought but it was four-thirty in the morning. He wouldn't appreciate a call right now, so I'd just have to wait until test call at six o'clock. I could make some breakfast, but somehow food had no appeal. I was still too excited.

Well, I'd walk back to the lookout—that might calm me down a little. But what would I do when I got there? Once back in the house, still with no appetite, I decided the best thing would be to write a letter to my girlfriend. That would kill some time. Then another letter to my mother—I'd been meaning to do that anyway. Now there'd really be something to write about. I was fairly bursting to tell someone of my heroics, but for now, a couple of letters would have to suffice.

I looked at the clock. Quarter after five and the letters were all done. Still too early to call. I'd only make a fool of myself. Well, there was still plenty time to run down and take a couple of pictures. I rummaged through my pack looking for the camera. It had to be here somewhere.

Then it dawned on me. In my haste to get going I had forgotten to take it along. What a dilemma. Here was the chance of a lifetime to show my triumph and no camera. How could I have failed to remember that? I would just have to think of something.

Time seemed to stand still, but finally it was six o'clock. I rang.

"Bungalow." It was Clyde, the dispatcher.

"Good morning, Chateau here."

Being as nonchalant as possible I said, "I got him, Clyde."

"Got what?"

"The bear. I shot that bear earlier this morning."

"Oh, that's good."

Frankly, I had expected more of a reaction than that. He was entirely too matter-of-fact.

"What should I do with it?"

"I don't know."

"Well, where's Shorty?"

"He left for a blister rust camp half an hour ago."

"Oh, well, maybe you ought to get hold of him and find out what he wants me to do."

"I s'pose I could."

"Well, will you do that?"

"Yeah. It'll be awhile, though. He won't even get there for at least another hour."

"Okay. I'll just have to wait then."

"I guess so. I'll have him call you soon as he gets there."

"Okay. I'll stick around."

I hung up feeling a bit let down. What was the matter with Clyde? He acted like people went around shooting bears every day of the week. He never even asked how it happened. Shorty would call soon and he would be more impressed.

Might as well start a fire and get some breakfast. I wasn't hungry, but maybe I would be later. I had set up half my sourdough starter for pancakes the evening before and "fed" the rest of it, so I added the remaining ingredients and soon had pancakes in the pan. Miraculously the bears had somehow overlooked a jar of jam that was set way back on a shelf, so that took the place of the syrup they hadn't overlooked. Just as I put my hands in the dishwater the phone rang.

"Chateau."

"Well, good mornin' Mr. Bearslayer. Are you still all in one piece?"

"Yes, I am George—fit as a fiddle."

"You didn't shoot yerself in the foot?"

"No, I did not."

"Well, I am truly surprised. I was plumb worried about you, you know."

"I don't know why. I can take pretty good care of myself."

"Well, maybe you can and maybe you can't. Let's just say I'm damn glad it's over and you're okay."

"Was there ever any doubt?"

"In my mind there was. You're just a kid whether you know it or not, and kids ain't always too careful."

"Well (I was especially careful not to tell him about the empty gun), I was plenty careful, if you want to know the truth, but I was a bit concerned when he came around during the night."

"I bet you was. Did he try crawlin' in with you?"

"No, I never let him get that close. I'll tell you all about it when I get in. Okay?"

"Sure thing. I'll be awaitin'."

After dishes were done, I busied myself straightening up the place and finally Shorty called.

"I hear you got him."

"Yup, around four-thirty this morning."

"Where was he?"

"He started out from the garbage pit, but was probably two hundred yards out or more when I got the last good shot into him."

"That's a load off my mind."

"What do you want me to do with it?"

"Bury it."

"Okay."

"Wade should be in there late this afternoon and he'll go on to Cave Point in the morning. If the place is all cleaned up, then you can head back to the Bungalow right after breakfast tomorrow."

"Okay. I'll come down as soon as I get cleaned up."

Now for the task of burying the bear. This was really the last thing I wanted to do. What I really wanted was to show it off to somebody, but nobody was around. Wade wouldn't be here until evening and besides he had already seen the darn thing, mighty close up at that. And no camera. I was still kicking myself about that. Well, no need to cry over spilt milk. Might as well make the best of it and get on with the job, much as I hated to do it.

Grabbing a shovel and axe at the shed down below, I made my way back to the bear and began digging. The ground was quite loose, but tree roots were laced all through it making it difficult. I'd get a shovelful or two and then have to chop more roots. Eventually though, I had a hole that looked large enough. Not any too deep, but out here in the boondocks, who would know the difference? Still smarting over the lack of a camera, I got an idea. Why not cut off a paw and skin it out? At least I could show Wade proof of the kill. Otherwise somebody might think I made the whole thing up. Yes, some people might—you never know.

A couple whacks with the axe and the job was done. Now I felt better. At least there was some proof. Now to get that bugger in the hole. This proved easier said then done. Rolling him over simply couldn't be accomplished. He was just too heavy. Using the small tree he had bitten off as a pry pole didn't work either. It just bent and finally snapped. I remembered seeing a crowbar in the shed. When I returned with it, the flies were really swarming around. I guess burying was the only answer. After much grunting and prying the thing finally rolled over and slid into the hole.

I took one last look at my prize and covered it over. Dropping off the tools at the shed, I made my way back up to the lookout. I left the paw outside, already having second thoughts about skinning it out. Flies were crawling around on it and there would be no hope whatsoever of preserving it. I would show it to Wade and then get rid of it.

Time had flown by. It was well past noon and time for a bite to eat. Later, I would have to haul water and firewood, being nearly out of both. So the afternoon passed.

It was a pleasant evening, and I sat out on the catwalk overlooking the trail to the east. Just before sunset I spotted Wade and his packstring approaching, so I put on coffee and started cooking supper. He'd be plenty hungry, that's for sure. Only two mules were still carrying packs, and it wouldn't take too long to unload. None of it was meant for Chateau, I was sure, so he'd need no help from me. Supper was just about ready when Wade came in.

"What the hell is that thing out on the catwalk."

"What does it look like?"

"Looks like you got him all right."

"That I did, early this morning. Didn't you know?"

"No. I called in early and haven't talked to anybody since."

"Well, I just saved a souvenir so you'd know I wasn't telling any tall tales. You've seen it—now I can give it a heave-ho off the rock."

"You do that, but first let's have some food. I could eat the south end of a northbound skunk I'm so hungry."

"Funny you should say that, cause that's just what we're having."

"Well, don't just stand there, dish it up."

Wade hadn't been fooling either, he ate like he'd been starved for a week. After the dishes were done, we sat and talked awhile, swapping bear stories. Wade pointed out exactly where the bears had been when he walked in on them.

"I was as calm then as I am now," he said.

Sleep came early. Both of us were completely worn out. No bears would bother us this night. I woke several time to hear Wade peacefully snoring and a distant horse bell down below.

In the morning we parted after I helped him catch the stock and load up. I looked forward to getting back to the Bungalow, where everybody would be anxious to hear all about my adventure.

I wasn't disappointed either. They all turned out when I strode in trying to look nonchalant and probably not doing well at it.

After I finished telling all about it, even Bowlander had to admit, "Son, you done all right. I couldn't a done no better myself."

That meant a lot to me.

Thirteen
A Close Call

There are probably not a lot of people around anymore who have spent much time on the business end of a six-foot crosscut saw, more appropriately called a "misery whip" by those of us who pulled them. I have spent hundreds of hours toiling away on these wretched things with all kinds of people on the other end. Some folks have a natural talent when it comes to sawing and others never seem to acquire any knack for it at all.

To saw with Clyde, our dispatcher, was pure pleasure. Everybody said so. No matter how poor a sawyer you were, when you sawed with Clyde, the saw just seemed to sing through the logs with scarcely any effort at all. Then there were others—George for one who, despite probably thousands of hours spent sawing away, never got the hang of it. Several factors entered into perfecting your technique.

First of all you had to pull the saw straight, not bend it around behind you, as some were prone to do. Then you let your partner pull it back—*you* didn't help by pushing. This only resulted in bending the saw and getting dirty looks or comments from across the log.

Another thing you avoided was pushing down on the saw, thinking that this would make it cut faster. Of course, it did nothing of the sort. It only made both of you tire faster.

For as simple as it appeared to be, working one of these "misery whips" could be tricky business and woe be unto the unlucky person who got a saw "rider," "pusher," or "bender" on the other end.

So it was that toward the end of my second fire season, when the fire danger was minimal and the lookouts were coming down, that Shorty decided it was time to open up the trail to Elizabeth Mountain. This hadn't been done for several years, and since there was quite a bit of valuable timber up there, the trail needed to be cleared of fallen trees should fire strike and people and pack animals had to get there in a hurry. Four of us headed for Kelly Forks to do the job—Shorty, George, Tom, and myself.

Kelly Forks was a snug little log cabin nestled alongside the Clearwater about eighteen miles upriver from the Bungalow. We arrived there about midafternoon, in time to get the place shipshape and for George and me to get a fire going and supper started. We didn't waste any time because, situated as Kelly Forks was right beside the river, we had high hopes of getting some fishing in that evening. After supper, Shorty got his fly rod out and motioned for Tom to come along.

"Long as those guys like to cook so much, let's see if we can get something for 'em to put in the pan for breakfast."

"Who said we like to cook?" grumbled George, as they fled out the door.

"Looks like we're stuck with each other," I said.

"That and the dirty dishes to boot. Don't know what I ever done to deserve this."

"Could be worse," I said. "Wait'll tomorrow. I bet we'll be sawing partners."

"Cripes, I hope not—if you ain't the worst kid to have on the other end of a saw that I ever seen."

"Oh, stop your moaning. You're just as bad or worse and you know it."

George and I had sawed together several times and were about as incompatible as two people could be. Otherwise we got along just fine, but put six feet of crosscut saw between us and everything simply fell apart. Hopefully, Shorty would separate us tomorrow.

By the time we had the dishes cleaned up there wasn't much time left for fishing, but we hurried out anyway and got a couple whitefish apiece. Shorty came in with some more, so we'd have plenty for breakfast.

The Clearwater River had a good population of trout, but it also has a lot of these mountain whitefish, which in my opinion were fully as tasty as the trout. If you could find hellgrammites (aquatic larva of a dobson fly) under the rocks along the shore, they were a real dynamite bait for these fish. You could catch as many whitefish as you could find hellgrammites—it was that simple. The problem, of course, was finding hellgrammites, which were not all that plentiful. I can recall at the falls, just upstream from the Bungalow, where the water must have been thirty feet deep, you could see hundreds if not thousands of whitefish silhouetted over a large white rock that lay on the bottom. Getting a line down to them was nearly impossible because of the current, but drop a hellgrammite down anywhere near them, and *bang*! you had yourself a whitefish—and they were delicious.

At daybreak George was already shaking me awake.

"Come on. Git up and make a fire. I got other things to do."

"Okay, okay. I'll be with you in a minute."

George didn't know it, but I had laid a fire the night before. All I had to do was touch a match to the kindling and it was lit.

Mountain mornings, especially near the river, are inclined to be pretty cool, so I grabbed my clothes and stood by the stove to slip into them. Shorty and Tom came out and did likewise. Soon the fish were frying with the whole works—bacon, eggs, potatoes, pancakes, and coffee. George was one fine cook, even if he wasn't worth a darn at sawing. After breakfast, Shorty and Tom went out to load the tools in the pickup while we cleaned up the dishes.

It began to look like Shorty had already selected Tom as his sawing partner. I doubted if he had ever sawed with Tom, but he had with George and me and was probably figuring that Tom couldn't be any worse.

When we arrived at the trail Shorty said, "Come on Tom, we'll take the first log and let them go on ahead to the next one." This is the way we were to proceed, leapfrogging our way ahead.

After we left them at the first log, George waited until we were out of earshot. "Well, I said my prayers last night, but it didn't do a damn bit of good."

"I know what you mean. I did the same."

We hadn't gone a hundred yards and there was our first project, a tree fallen right across the trail. Sometimes you can get by with only one cut, if one end or the other of the tree is of a manageable size. Then you can move the lighter portion out of the way. If there was a glimmer of hope, George and I were inclined to try it. Anything to avoid making a second cut.

In this case, though, there was nothing for it but to make two cuts and then roll the offending log to the side. We were off to a bad start.

George was on me right away.

"Quit ridin' the saw."

"I'm not. You're bending it around behind you, that's the trouble."

"Like hell I am."

"Well, you're pushing on it then."

"No, I ain't."

To prove my point, when it was time to pull I didn't and George pushed and bent the saw.

"See, I told you—you're pushing."

"If you wasn't so damn weak, I wouldn't hafta."

Shorty and Tom had come up on us and were hearing all the bickering, much to Shorty's amusement.

"Boy, are you two at it already? This is only the first log."

"It ain't funny," said George. "Anytime you feel like changing partners, just lemme know. I'll be happy to oblige."

"No thanks. The way it sounds I better keep the one I got," and off they went.

Well, after rubbing away on that miserable log for the better part of an hour, we finally rolled the middle piece over the side, gathered up our tools, and went on up the trail. We passed two freshly cut logs before we caught up with the others. They were working on a third one.

"Let's take five," said Shorty, and we all sat down to rest.

Tom passed the water bag around and we all took a drink.

It looked like Shorty knew what he was doing when he chose Tom for a partner. Tom was a big, husky kid from Ohio who had come to us in midseason. He had proved to be a good, willing worker who caught on quickly and he was a welcome addition to the crew. He had spent a few days with me on Bear Butte and I had been sorry to see him go.

Shorty began needling George. "Looks like you fellas had a little problem back there."

George shook his head. "I guess we got a dull saw."

"That's too bad. I'll get you a different one tomorrow."

"Throw in a peavey too. I think we'll be needin' one." A peavey was a long pole with a hook on one end used by loggers to roll logs.

Shorty was grinning, enjoying himself at George's expense. I caught him giving Tom a wink. The rest of the day went fairly well until midafternoon when we came upon a large dead tree across the trail. No hope of making just one cut on this one. It was simply too big. Well, we bickered our way through the two cuts, but our cut-out piece was firmly wedged in and no amount of pushing and straining would budge it. We would have to cut some pry poles. With the two of us grunting and straining, we finally managed to pry the piece out only to have the upper portion of the log slide down and block the trail again.

George wiped his brow with an old red bandanna. "Just look up there. There's a good forty feet left just waitin' to slide down soon's we git another hunk cut off."

"You're right, but let's try something else first."

"What you got in mind?"

"If we can pry the end up a little, just enough to get it started sliding, I think the whole thing'll take off."

The slope was pretty steep and if we raised the end up just enough to clear the edge of the trail, gravity would do the rest.

"What do you think, George?"

"Worth a try."

So we put a couple rocks beside the log and got the pry poles underneath and started pulling down. After much bouncing, the log inched its way to the edge of the trail and without warning suddenly took off like a huge torpedo, cutting down everything in its path. After a great deal of smashing and crashing there came a loud "bonk" when it slammed into a boulder and stopped. It must have been pretty funny because we laughed so hard we had to sit down. Shorty and Tom came running up.

"What the heck was that?"

"Oh nuthin' much," said George, wiping his eyes. "We was just movin' logs is all."

"Sounded like a herd of elephants," said Shorty. "What really happened?"

So we told him how clever we had been, thereby avoiding half a dozen saw cuts.

Shorty grinned and the turned sober.

"That worked pretty good, I'll admit, but don't go getting careless and wind up under one of those logs. I'm not too anxious to pack anybody out of here on a stretcher."

We were quick to assure him that we were just naturally the cautious types, but he did have a good point. A log like that headed in the wrong direction was no laughing matter. Fortunately that one had gone straight ahead, but it could just as easily have hit something and swung to the side, clipping one of us. Yes, we would have to be careful. Shorty was right.

The rest of the day passed without incident and then we headed back down the trail. All in all we had made good progress, clearing about a mile and a half of trail.

After supper, Tom and Shorty were out the door and down to the river again, leaving George and me with a dishpan full of dirty dishes.

"Somehow this ain't workin' out the way I planned," George complained.

"You're right," I said. "Maybe they'll take over the cooking tomorrow."

"You ever eat any of Shorty's cookin'?"

"No, not really."

"Well, you ain't goin' to, either, long as I'm here."

"Is it that bad?"

"Bad ain't the word for it."

"So I guess we're stuck."

"Bet your boots we are. No sense crabbin' about it, just hurry up, though, so's we kin' go fishin'."

Before long we were at the river and just before dark came in with a few fish. Shortly after, Shorty and Tom came in—Tom with a guilty grin on his face and Shorty laughing so hard he was almost doubled over.

"What's goin' on?" asked George. "You two find a whiskey bottle somewheres?"

They both shook their heads. Finally Shorty settled down enough to make sense.

"I was fishing about fifty feet from shore and Tom didn't have a pole so he was turning over rocks looking for hellgrammites."

"What's so funny about that?" asked George.

Shorty had to stop for a minute, then continue.

"I looked over at Tom and right behind him was a young bear. Must have been coming down to get a drink."

"Quietly as I could, so as not to spook the bear, I said, "Tom what is behind you?"

That started Shorty into another laughing fit and it took awhile before he could talk again. Tom stood there looking red as a beet.

"Next thing I know, Tom is going by me like a streak clear out to midstream, and the bear is going twice as fast back to where he came from."

Of course, we all got a good laugh at poor Tom's expense, but he took it pretty well. What else could he do? He knew he was in for plenty of ribbing over that one.

While we sat around talking until bedtime, Shorty would break out laughing every once in awhile, no doubt over the bear incident. Poor Tom said very little that evening, suffering his embarrassment in silence.

The next morning, after breakfast, Tom busied himself by getting water and splitting firewood, which was beginning to be in short supply. I suppose he was avoiding the rest of us in order not to be the butt of any more bear jokes.

When we left, George made sure that a peavey was included with the other tools. That would be quite an advantage in rolling those stubborn logs that we tried to avoid sawing. Of course, that meant carrying not only our usual equipment, which consisted of an axe, saw, a pack containing our lunch, a wedge, and a four-pound maul, but also now a big, awkward peavey. Quite a load. Not only that, but we were now a mile and a half up the trail and we'd have to lug all that heavy equipment up there before even getting to work. But if that was the price we had to pay to avoid sawing, it might prove to be well worth it.

The first log looked fairly easy, so George quickly volunteered us for that one. We disposed of it with little trouble, thanks to our trusty peavey, which turned out to be worth the trouble of lugging along.

When we caught up with Shorty and Tom they were struggling with a huge log that they had cut off and were having very little success trying to maneuver it off to the side.

"Hold on boys," yelled George. "We'll have 'er off in a jiffy," as he sunk the peavey hook in and started lifting. I grabbed hold of the pry pole with Tom, and between the four of us we got the job done in short order.

"Now that's what I call teamwork," said Shorty.

"Right," George answered with a laugh. "If you fellers do the sawin' we'll do the movin'."

Shorty shook his head. "I don't know about that. We just might come out on the short end. Tell you what, though, we'll try to stay ahead, so you're always behind us with that peavey of yours. That way, if we get a real tough one, we'll just leave it for you to roll out. How's that sound?"

George looked at me. "That seem like a good deal to you?"

"Anything to get out of sawing with you George. Anything at all."

So that would be our plan of attack from now on. We stopped at the first log and the others went on.

"What do you think George?" I asked, looking it over. "One cut or two?"

The tree had fallen across the trail at an angle with the top on the upper side. It apparently had been dead for sometime, the upper portion being a mass of short stubs where the ends of the branches had fallen off.

George was surveying the situation.

"Let's cut 'er on the lower side and maybe with the peavey and a pry pole we kin' git it to rollin' off."

"Okay, that looks like the best bet."

So we proceeded with our usual bickering and cussing until we had the cut made. Next, I cut a nice long pry pole, and while George held the bottom end with the peavey, I pried the top around until we had the whole long piece lying in the trail. Now all we had to do was roll it over the side.

"Wait a minute," said George. "Gotta catch my breath."

"Good idea." We were both puffing pretty hard.

A couple minutes went by.

"You ready?" asked George.

"Yup."

"Just lemme git a bite with the peavey and then we'll both heave together."

"Okay. Wait'll I get my pry pole under."

Once I got my pole under, I nodded to George, and we both gave it all we had.

The log started to roll, ever so slowly, nearing the edge of the trail. The slope was very steep, so once it started to go, there'd be no stopping it. Right at the edge, I needed a new "bite" for the pry pole, but I was unable to get it under—so I threw the pole aside and grabbed a couple of the short stubs that protruded from the trunk, and, from a kneeling position, leaned forward and kept the log rolling slowly. Now things began to happen real fast. George's end went over the side first and my end began to raise up and gain momentum. When I let go one of the stubs came around and inserted itself right into the canvas cuff of my right glove. There was no way to free myself. I was going over with the log and couldn't do a thing about it. Already another stub was caught in the front of my shirt, sealing my fate. I tried to pull back but my feet were off the ground. Then suddenly, something had a hold of my ankles and was hanging on for dear life. My dear life, as it turned out. I felt like I was being pulled apart. The there was a ripping sound as the canvas cuff of my glove tore away and buttons went flying off my shirt and suddenly I was free. The log went crashing off downhill without me.

"Thanks, George," I croaked when I got my breath back. I looked around at him. He was pale as a ghost.

"Cripes, kid, that was a close one."

"I know. If you hadn't held on, I'd have been a goner."

"All's I kin' say is we was mighty lucky. By the way, yer bleedin'."

"Where?" I felt nothing—probably in shock.

"Yer wrist and yer chin. What's left of yer shirt's got blood on it, too. Here, lemme take a look."

George looked me over.

"Yer skint up some, but it 'pears like you come out of it in one piece."

"Thanks to you. How did you ever get to me that quick?"

"I looked over to make sure you was clear when she started to go and that's just when that stub caught in yer glove. I didn't waste no time gittin' there once I seen that."

"I never saw you coming. I figured I'd had it."

"You come close enough to suit me. By the way, I wouldn't say too much to Shorty about this."

"Are you kidding? I'm not gonna say a word, not after that little talk he gave us about being careful. No siree."

"Well, when he gits one look at you, he'll be askin' what happened."

"Is it that noticeable?"

"Pretty hard to miss and Shorty don't miss much. Here lemme wipe you off 'fore we take off. Yer chin looks about the worst. The stub that snagged yer shirt musta caught you there when it went over."

"Funny, but nothing hurts except my chest."

"I expect you got poked pretty good there, but yer shirt'll cover that—what's left of it anyway."

So we started off and caught up with Shorty and Tom about a quarter mile up. Shorty heard us coming and turned around.

"Gracious!" (This was his favorite expression—I never heard him cuss.) "What in the world happened to you?"

"Oh, a branch caught me when we pushed that log off. It's nothing much."

"That may be, but you look like you tangled with a wildcat and came out second best. Let's get this log taken care of and then have lunch."

He never said anymore about it, but I knew he was thinking his share. We were getting into more open country now, so there were fewer fallen trees to contend with, and by midafternoon we were a good four miles up and it was time to start back. On the switchback below where I'd almost cashed in, there sat the treacherous log that had caused it all, right smack in the middle of the trail where it had rolled to a stop.

"This the one that got you?" asked Shorty.

"Sure is. I guess it wants another crack at me."

It didn't take the four of us long to roll it off, and when we were done, Tom handed me a bit of cloth that he'd pulled off the stub he'd been pushing on.

"This yours?"

"Must be. You can have it for a souvenir if you want."

"Gee, thanks."

When we got back to Kelly Forks, Wade was just pulling in. There were a couple campgrounds nearby that he and Shorty intended checking after supper. I tried to get past him and get on a different shirt, but he caught me anyway.

"Whoa, there, young fella. What you been doing, rassling a bear or somethin'?"

"No, I just had a little argument with George."

"Is that so, George. You did this to my boy here?"

"Damn right. It don't pay to git smart-alecky around me, and I'd bear that in mind was I you."

Wade pretended to be frightened.

"Anything you say George. Want me to make a fire?"

"Hell yes, and don't waste no time about it neither."

Shorty joined in.

"Can I be of any help, George?"

"Course you kin. Go git some water and fill up the dishpan. We need firewood too."

It was all in fun, of course. Everybody was flying around except George, who sat down and calmly pulled off his boots. His turn would come soon enough when the cooking started. At suppertime poor Tom got another round of razzing when Wade heard of his previous evening's adventure. When we'd finished eating, Shorty got me aside.

"Feel like doing a little hunting this evening?"

"I guess so. What did you have in mind?"

"Well, you know we keep livestock in the pasture here quite often."

"Yes, I know."

There was a pasture of perhaps ten acres alongside the cabin between the road and the river fenced in with barbed wire. "Wade and I talked it over. If that bear that scared Tom last night makes a habit of coming through here, he's liable to spook the stock and we could wind up with some of 'em tangled up in barbed wire. Best we get rid of him before that happens."

"I left my revolver back at the Bungalow."

"Doesn't matter. Wade brought his Colt along. You can use that."

"Okay, if that's what you want. I'll take care of it."

"Good. Let's go see Wade."

He handed me the pistol.

"Shoot for right behind the ears. That'll put him down, sure."

"Okay."

Shorty put a hand on my shoulder. "Climb up on that rock ledge at the far end of the pasture. That's right were he came under last night, and chances are he'll be using the same path again."

"Okay."

I started off not overly enthused with the prospect of shooting a small harmless bear who had done nothing at all to deserve being shot. But then, I'd hate to see any of our horses or mules tangled up in a barbed-wire fence, either, so I would do whatever needed doing. The view from the rock ledge was beautiful with the river down below and the mountainsides up above. Swallows were skimming down over the water getting their fill of a hatch of insects. Trout and whitefish dimpled the surface as they fed. Right below me a huge beaver hauled himself out of the water and began gnawing on a sapling on the bank. A family of otters came by playing follow the leader, diving and surfacing in the undulating current. Everything seemed so at peace that I hoped no bear would come and force me to spoil it all. My life had been spared earlier by George's quick action and it seemed wrong to take the life of some poor creature on such a day.

My wish was granted for no bear appeared. Perhaps Tom had frightened him enough that he chose a less congested spot for his daily drink.

I hoped so, for I heard no more of him.

Fourteen
A Model-A Mishap

I hadn't seen the Bungalow in three years and, Lordy, how I missed it. I had been discharged from the Navy in September and had to wait for spring before going back to Idaho. Fortunately, there was a job opening at a commercial fishery that I was able to land to tide me over the winter.

Cars were incredibly hard to come by at that time since production had stopped for about four years during the war. Luckily, I was able to find a 1940 Chevrolet that was in reasonably good shape at an affordable price. As soon as spring started melting the snow, I headed West, covering 2,300 miles in three days.

My heart was doing a real tap dance when I rounded the last curve and pulled in front of the flagpole—home at last. There was a joyful reunion with Wade and his wife Buckshot (I never did know her real name), and it was oh so good to be back in the mountains once again. After all the hugging and handshaking settled down, I said, "I can't wait to see Shorty, too."

At this Wade looked a bit downcast. "Shorty's not here anymore. He was transferred to Priest River."

This was not good news. When I left he had assured me that if I chose to come back he would see to it that I would get a full-time job instead of working just during the fire season. Maybe I should head for Priest River.

I explained this to Wade, but he wouldn't hear of it. Neither would Buckshot.

"We've waited all this time to have you back, and now you're already talking about going away again," she replied.

"Well," I said, "this is going to be a tough decision."

"I know," said Wade, "but Ken, the new ranger, seems to be a nice fellow and the alternate's not a bad sort either."

"The alternate," I said, "I thought you were the alternate."

"No," he said. "I'm now the dispatcher. Stanley has more years than I have so he got the job and I got backed down to dispatcher. These things happen once in a while."

I didn't like the sound of this, either, but before I had time to digest it Wade said, "Come on, I'll take you over and you can meet both of them and then make up your mind on what you want to do."

He took me over, and Ken, the ranger, expressed his pleasure at having me back and said if I wanted to stay on after the fire season he would see what he could do. Stanley, on the other hand, was not unfriendly but not exactly cordial either.

"That's just his way," Wade said later as we walked back. "You'll get used to it. He's just not the friendly type."

In the end I decided to stay and Wade helped me unpack my things and put my car in the garage up at the old abandoned CCC Camp across the river, where he and Buckshot were now living in the former commandant's house. I spent the rest of the evening with them. After all, they had been like a father and mother to me, and we had an awful lot to catch up on.

Later, when I walked back to the ranger station in the dark, it seemed so good to be back that I cast aside my uneasiness over not having gone on to Priest River.

Several days later I was walking past the office when Ken poked his head out and said, "Could I see you for a minute?"

"Sure."

"I understand that you have a car."

"That's right."

"Could I ask a favor of you?"

"Ask away."

"You see," he said, "when I was in the Army, I married a girl over in Scotland, and she just got over here now. As a matter of fact, she'll be arriving at Lewiston on the train at one o'clock Saturday afternoon."

"You want to borrow my car?"

"Well, yes, but I really don't like to drive someone else's car over roads like these. I'd feel a lot better if you drove, and I'd pay for the gas, of course."

"I don't see why not," I said. "I was planning to go in soon anyway to pick up a fishing license and a few other things. That will work out just fine."

We agreed that with Lewiston being a three-hour drive, plus a couple of short stops on the way, we'd have to leave no later than 9:30 Saturday morning. Meanwhile, Bob, one of the other boys, asked to go along, and I said fine.

After breakfast Saturday morning, Bob and I got all showered up and ready to go, and I walked to the CCC Camp to get the car.

Well, 9:30 rolled around and no Ken. We stood around waiting beside the car for another fifteen minutes and then Bob said, "Looks like somebody isn't in any hurry to fetch his new bride."

"Could be," I said. "Let's drive over to his house and pick him up." Off we went and pulled into his yard. There was no sign of Ken. I was just getting out of the car when Ken appeared at the door, coffee cup in hand.

"Be with you in a minute," he said and went back into the house.

Bob looked at me and shook his head. Another ten minutes went by before Ken finally came out and got in the car.

"Running a little late," he said, "but I gotta stop at the office for a minute."

So back to the office we went. Ken went in and after ten more minutes went by, Bob said, "If that train is on time, there is going to be one unhappy lady getting off."

We were finally off with absolutely no hope of arriving on time—not unless the train was late, of course, but in those days trains were famous for being on time.

To give you some idea of what the road from Bungalow to Pierce was like, it is fair to say that it was strictly not for the faint of heart. It covered twenty-eight miles of hairpin turns, steep, unguarded drop-offs of up to a thousand or more feet, rocks, mud holes, and you name it. To make it in an hour was virtually impossible. An hour and a quarter was possible but bordering on suicidal. If one wanted to see the sun come up again, an hour and a half was more like it.

Most of the hairpin turns were completely blind and you had absolutely no idea if there was a car coming at you until it came into view at a distance of approximately ten feet—too late to do anything but smash head on or go over the side, the road being only wide enough to accommodate one car. To reduce the risk of colliding or worse, people would lay on the horn when they approached these curves, hoping that the oncoming driver would hear it and take some sort of evasive action. I never did this and it wasn't long before Ken took note of it.

"Aren't you going to blow your horn?" he said.

"Nope."

"How come?"

"I don't think it's a good idea."

Ken was starting to get under my skin, not just because of his lack of consideration toward his new wife, but also because of his general officious attitude. It didn't take long before he started again.

"I just can't understand why you don't blow your horn!"

"Look, Ken," I said, "if I'm blowing my horn and the guy coming my way is blowing his, neither one of us can hear the other one. If it's quiet in the car, I can at least hear what's coming at me." That held him for awhile but not for long.

"I'd still feel better if you'd blow the horn," he said.

"Well, if you're that uneasy about it, I'll turn around and we'll forget the whole thing." That got his attention.

"Oh, no, no need to do that. I see your point—maybe it is a good idea. I never thought of it that way."

Bob, sitting beside me, was trying not to laugh, but I could see it wasn't easy. He wasn't overly fond of Ken and was really enjoying himself. From that point on there was very little conversation coming from the rear seat, though Bob and I chattered away up front. After filling up in Pierce and getting our licenses, we headed on to Orofino and

Lewiston. Shortly before we got to Orofino, Ken spoke up again.

"I'll have to stop in at the Forest Service Office for a few minutes, so if you'll just park in front, I'll run right in."

"Wouldn't it be better to stop on the way back?" I said. "We're going to be pretty late as it is."

"No," he said, "I'd rather do it now. That way we can drive straight through on the way back."

"Okay," I said. "It's your wife that's going to be sitting there, not mine."

So I parked in front and Ken took his time getting out and then had to come back for something he forgot. Finally he disappeared into the building. Bob and I settled down to wait. It was already past noon and we were both hungry. A restaurant was just down the street.

"I wonder if we could chance running down there for a bite," said Bob.

"I was thinking the same thing," I said, "but you know who'd get the blame for being late if he comes back and we're not here."

"You're right," said Bob. "We'll wait."

So we waited. Half an hour went by. An hour went passed. At quarter of two Ken finally came out.

"Took a little longer than I figured," he said.

"It must have," Bob agreed. "Incidently, in case you don't know what time it is, your wife has been waiting about three-quarters of an hour already."

"I know," he said. "She'll have to wait a little longer, I guess."

Bob just shook his head. I pushed as fast as I dared and finally pulled into the Lewiston depot. It looked deserted. Ken got out and held the door open as if he wanted Bob to join him. No doubt he wanted help with the luggage.

"I'll just wait here, if you don't mind," said Bob. "You can explain why we're so late, and don't blame us."

So Ken went in by himself.

"I hope he gets his stupid head bit off," said Bob.

"If he does, he's sure got it coming," I answered.

But wouldn't you know, here he comes out of the depot with a sweet lady who is all smiles and she's carrying the suitcases. I could scarcely believe my eyes. She wasn't the slightest bit upset that nobody was there to greet her, let alone having to wait for an hour and a half in a strange country before somebody finally showed up. I could only wonder what Ken had offered in the way of an explanation. It must have been a good one. Well, we got her luggage stowed away in the trunk and she and Ken got in the backseat and we were off for the Bungalow.

As we got underway, Bob asked Mary if she was hungry.

Before she could answer, Ken, now in a hurry, said, "Maybe we better get there as soon as possible. George is putting on a big spread tonight and we'd best get there on time."

"Yes," Bob said, "we wouldn't want to keep anybody waiting, would we?"

As we followed the Clearwater River past Spalding and on to Orofino, Mary kept expressing her amazement at the beauty of the country and we filled her in a bit on Chief Joseph and the Nez Perce who lived there. We crossed the bridge at Greer and started up the eight-mile grade climbing higher and higher, and Mary kept telling me in her Scottish brogue to "please be keerful and dunt go over-r-r-r-r the side."

Bob's comment was, "You ain't seen nuthin' yet."

We stopped for gas in Pierce and than started up the twenty-eight-mile obstacle course to the Bungalow. After several miles we began to notice beer cans every mile or so along the road.

"I didn't see those cans when we came out," said Bob.

I hadn't either, but we soon discovered where they were coming from. First there was just a faint dust haze in the air which slowly increased until at last we could see two vehicles ahead. One was a Model-A Ford, which was followed by a small Ford stake truck. We hardly had the truck in view before a beer can came sailing out the passenger-side window, followed by another from the driver's side a mile farther. This continued unchanged, mile after mile. First one side, than the other.

"The way I figure it," Bob said, "if they keep this up, a case ought to last just about to Bungalow."

"That's about what I was thinking," I said. "But there's no way they'll even get that far without a pit stop. As a matter of fact, I don't see how they got this far. I know I couldn't."

"I see what you mean," said Bob. "They have had six or seven cans apiece, and, unless they're spilling most of it, which I doubt, there's a limit to how much a human body can hold."

I was hoping that when the inevitable stop came, they would have the good sense to pull off where the road was wide enough for me to go on around and thereby spare Mary the embarrassment of such an event. Her first impression of America, even though she smiled through it, couldn't have been too good, and what was going on in the Ford ahead could only make it worse. Well, we knew they would have to stop sooner or later, and stop they did—but so suddenly that all I could do was stand on the brakes and hope for the best. It all happened fast. One moment we were going along just as nice as you please and then, with no warning and for no apparent reason, the Model-A was skidding out of control sideways in the road, gravel and stones flying up in a cloud of dust, headed for the edge of a two-hundred-foot drop. When everything stopped, the Model-A was perched on the very edge, front bumper out beyond it, front wheels at a crazy angle, a fraction of an inch from going over. The truck had stopped about five or ten feet short of the car and we were about the same distance behind the truck.

"Whew!" exclaimed Bob. "That was a close one. Another inch and they'd have been goners."

Ken and Mary had been kind of dozing in the back seat, but they were wide awake now.

"What happened?" asked Ken.

"I'm not sure," I said, "but by the looks of those front wheels, I can venture a pretty good guess."

By this time two middle-age women had climbed out of the car, obviously quite shaken by their experience. Then out of the truck came two burly looking men, lumberjacks I supposed looking at their boots and stagged pants held up by suspenders. I assumed they were the husbands of the two women. Well, they got out of that truck and strode just as casually as you please between it and the car and stood there facing away from each other.

"Let's get out and see what's going on," said Ken.

From where he sat what was going on was not as obvious as it was to Bob and me.

"Just hold your horses," said Bob. "We'll get out in a minute."

By now there were two puddles forming in front of the truck. Ken was not one to be easily put off, however.

"Why aren't we getting out?" he asked. "Those people may need help."

Bob was getting a bit annoyed.

"Ken, will you just wait. What they're doing right now doesn't require any help at all. Just be patient.

Apparently Ken understood, or at least he seemed to, because all he said was, "Oh." Mary chimed in with, "Oh dear."

We finally got out when the man who had been the passenger in the truck crawled under the Model-A while the driver stood talking to the still ashen-faced women.

"Howdy," said Ken, "looks like you've got a little trouble here."

"Tie rod come loose," came from under the car. "I'll have 'er fixed and be out of your way in a jiffy."

"Why don't we get this thing back from the edge?" I said. "No telling how solid that bank is."

"Not a bad idea," said the man under the car as he heaved himself out.

So we all got hold of the car and managed to move it back onto less precarious ground. Now the driver began rummaging under the truck seat. "Should be some wire and a pliers around here somewhere," he replied.

"What do you need that for?" asked Ken.

"Well, to put the tie rod back on, naturally. Ain't nobody goin' no place with it off, is there?" he replied, obviously annoyed at such a foolish question.

"Wait a minute," said Ken, "you're not going to just wire that on are you?"

"Well, Mister Ranger, unless you got the right size bolt in the pocket of them fancy pants of yours, I aim to do just that."

Ken was wearing his ranger's uniform and from this guy's attitude, rangers were not among his favorite people. Mary seemed to sense that things were taking a wrong turn, even if Ken did not.

She moved beside me and asked very quietly, "What does a tie rod do?"

"That's what connects the steering gear to the wheels. If it comes off, the wheels turn anywhere they choose," I answered.

"Is that why the car went the way it did?" she asked.

"Right you are."

"And they're just going to wire it on?"

"So they say."

"Oh, Lord!"

"Maybe Ken can talk 'em out of it, but I have my doubts about that."

Ken, of course, was nowhere near ready to give up.

"Look," he said, "we've got a whole bin full of nuts and bolts at the ranger station and a blacksmith that can make anything. Why don't we just push the car out of the way enough so we can get by and you can get what you need and come back and fix it right?"

"Well now, Mister Ranger, just where do you figger on finding a place wide enough where you kin git around this car?"

He had a point there. As far as I could see in either direction there was hardly room enough for one car, let alone two. That had Ken stumped momentarily, but not for long.

"Why not wire it on and then just go where we can get by, park it there, then you can go get whatever you need and come back and fix it?"

This sounded reasonable to me, but this guy was having none of it.

"Look," he said "if you wasn't standin' here a-jawin' at me I coulda had this thing fixed ten minutes ago. Now stand aside. If you gotta do something, get aholt of them front wheels and do what I tell you."

That left Ken speechless, for once, and surprisingly he did as he was told, probably avoiding a busted nose in the bargain. The gent under the car was not unaccustomed to violence, if I was any judge. So everybody—that is, except the driver of the truck, who was just finishing his second can of beer and was nonchalantly reaching in the cab for a third—pitched in.

"More to the left," came a voice from under the car.

One of the women had climbed back in the car and was trying to help by moving the steering wheel and was not doing too well.

"Not so much," came the voice again, "back up a little."

Nobody knew who he was talking to, so we'd move the wheels at the same time the steering wheel was turning the other way. Our boy was rapidly losing patience. Meanwhile, his partner was calmly opening another beer.

Finally, after a great deal of cussing, everything accidently lined up and the voice said, "Hold 'er right there till I get this here wire on."

At last he pulled himself out from under the car and glared at his partner.

"Get me a beer if there's any left."

Apparently there was, because in less than two seconds he had a beer in his hand already opened.

Ken still thought he had a chance, "Look," he said, "when you go by the ranger station, stop for a minute and we'll get you a bolt."

"Won't have time," he said. "We're in a hurry."

This guy was in a surly mood and it wasn't going to take much. Ken being Ken persisted.

"Well, I don't see how you can let a car run around like that. Just stop at the station and I'll get you a bolt myself. It'll only take a second."

That did it. Before Ken could back away, the front of his shirt was grasped by a huge fist and he was yanked up chin to chin with one tough hombre who was mean and drunk to boot.

"Look, Mister Ranger," he shouted, "there's only the women in that car."

To which both ladies nodded in agreement. Women's lib was still light years away in these parts.

Mary's reaction was somewhat different. Her hand flew to her mouth and she gasped, "Oh, dear me."

One could only speculate on what her thoughts might be regarding her first real day in America. A lesser person would have probably been on the first boat headed back to Scotland. She recovered quickly, however, and ran to Ken, who had now been released and was trying to smooth out his shirt front with his hand. A couple of buttons were going to need some attention too. That settled things down and everyone got back in their respective vehicles and our little caravan began to roll once again.

As we crossed Shanghai Divide, Ken, who had been unusually silent, suddenly regained his voice.

"I bet they'll think it over and stop for that bolt."

"How much you want to bet?" asked Bob.

"I didn't meant I wanted to bet," said Ken, "but I think the women will have sense enough to stop."

"I think they don't and they won't," said Bob. "They're more scared of their menfolks than they are of going over the side."

This was undoubtedly true. Meanwhile the beer cans resumed flying out of the truck at the same rate or even faster, if that was possible. Where was all that beer stored in that small cab I wondered? Under the seat? Hardly. That was taken up with tools and a roll of wire. On the seat? Not much room there. Those two bruisers took up nearly the whole seat themselves. Had to be on the floor, the only place left, but that wasn't any too spacious either. Well, no matter, it was in there someplace, that's for sure. When we headed into the home stretch, Ken got his hopes up once again.

"Looks like they're slowing down," he said.

It didn't look like it to me and then they sailed on through, leaving only a cloud of dust and a couple of empties in their wake.

"Thought sure they'd stop," said Ken. "If they sober up they'll probably stop on their way out."

If they ever did stop, Ken kept it pretty quiet, because that was the last we ever heard of the Model-A.

Good old George, however, salvaged something from an otherwise horrendous day for Mary. He had an absolutely sumptuous meal prepared on that old cast-iron range of his and everybody turned out to welcome Mary to the Bungalow. At long last, she got a touch of western hospitality.

Everybody was introduced in turn, and when it came her turn to say a few words, all she said in her Scottish brogue was, “Thank you all so very much for coming to meet me. Now let’s eat. I’m famished.”

George leaned over and whispered in my ear, “She’s famished.”

No doubt she was.

Fifteen
A Three-Fire Night

"Bungalow."

"Bear Butte test call."

"Good morning," said Norma, "are Bighorn and Junction on?"

"Bighorn here," said Bob.

"Junction too," added Gene.

"Okay, boys, hang onto your hats, I'm going to give you the weather report. Looks like we may be in for a pretty exciting day." It was six o'-clock in the morning and Charlie and I had just rolled out. I looked at the sky—a few puffy clouds, nothing serious.

"Everybody ready?"

"Okay."

"Here goes. Partly cloudy to cloudy a.m., with increasing cloudiness p.m. Severe thunderstorms can be expected by mid-afternoon, accompanied by high winds and possible hail at higher elevations. Fire danger is extremely high; numerous lightning-ignited fires are likely. Maximum precautions are to be taken. Any questions?"

"Yeah, when does the next bus leave town?" That was Bob the comedian.

"No busses today," Norma replied. "I'm sure Wade will want to talk to you when he comes in, so just sit tight for awhile."

"What was that all about?" asked Charlie.

"Looks like we'll be getting some business this afternoon."

"Oh!"

"The heavy thunderstorm kind. Should be real interesting."

Charlie had only been here about two weeks and hadn't gone through fire school, nor had he experienced one of our severe thunderstorms yet. He was in for a real treat, if the forecast was accurate. We would soon find out if it was. About half way through breakfast Wade called.

"Are all the boys on?"

Everybody was.

"Okay. Now you've heard the forecast and you know what that means. First of all, I want you to get plenty of water and firewood on hand this morning. If we get a storm, you won't have any time later. Check your fire packs. Make sure everything is in good order. Get a good hot meal in you this noon. You may not get another for a while. Make sure the light over your map board is working and fix anything else that might need attention. Do it now. I'll call you later and we'll get all our clocks synchronized. That's it."

"Well, Charlie," I said, "if what they predict comes to pass, you are about to experience your first real thunder-boomer."

"I've been through lots of thunderstorms before," he replied, "why should this be any different?"

"Do you see those copper cables attached to the stove, map board, and bed springs?"

"I was going to ask you about that. How come?"

"They were put there for a darn good reason. Every one of those cables is connected to a larger one that runs down to the spring, so we're well grounded. Being the highest point around, we'll attract any number of strikes. Be forewarned—it's scary, but we'll be safe enough."

"You mean the lightning actually hits this place?"

"Bet your life it does—again and again. Let's finish breakfast now and then get started with the water and firewood."

While Charlie cleaned up after breakfast, I filled the woodbox and then we took turns hauling water. Meanwhile the clouds kept building, looking more and more ominous. I made a big meal at noon and Charlie ran down to refill the woodbox after the dishes were cleaned up, just before we heard the first rumbles of distant thunder off to the southwest. I gave the firepacks a check and a moment later the phone rang.

"Bear Butte."

It was Wade. "Are all you boys on?"

"I'm on at Junction."

"Bighorn is on."

"Good. Do you have your clocks handy?"

Everybody acknowledged.

"Okay. Set them at 1:31—everybody got that?"

"Right, okay."

"Okay. Now boys, this storm is going to be a bad one from all reports. This will be the last call. Don't use your phones again until it's over unless it's an emergency. I've got to go now. Talk to you later."

As I moved the clock ahead, Charlie questioned why that was important.

"Well," I explained, "as soon as we start taking lightning strikes, I'll record the time and bearing. You just get a sight on each one and let me do the rest."

"But why?"

"I'm getting to that. Let's say we get a big strike behind Buckingham Ridge. Everybody can see the strike go down, but nobody is in a position to see where it hits. If it should flare up, we've all got a fix on it at the same time and Wade can plot on the map exactly where the fire is. Of course, if we start getting ten or fifteen strikes a minute, we'll just forget it. Nobody could make any sense of it anyway. And by the way, be sure you don't use the phone during the storm. There'll be so much static on the line that you won't be able to hear anything, and you don't want to run the risk of getting an earful of lightning."

In the distance we could see black clouds stretching all the way across the horizon, the first lightning strikes starting to appear. Thunder was continuous and getting louder. Not a leaf stirred. Charlie swung the finder at a distant strike.

"Not yet. Still too far off. When they look like they're in our district, then we'll start."

All we could do now was watch this monster edge closer.

"I see what you meant," said Charlie. "I've seen storms before but not like this."

"It's not here yet."

"I know, but I can see already what it's going to be like."

"It'll be a huffer, no doubt about it."

Ding, went the phone.

Charlie looked at me, "What was that?"

"Lightning hitting the line. I think we can start taking strikes now. Let's see. It's 2:13, let's go."

"You want me to sight on all of them?"

"No, just those that look like they're in our district. When they hit close, don't bother. We can see those good enough."

The lightning strikes were really coming now. They were not up to us yet, but they were streaking down one after another. Charlie swung the finder back and forth while I tried to keep up with marking down times and bearings. When we got to fifteen strikes a minute I called a halt.

"It's no use. There's too many."

The wind was picking up, and a few raindrops dotted the windows. Thunder was a constant roar though the main storm was still a few miles away. Minutes later, the storm hit us with full force. Lightning blazed down in all directions and the tower began to lurch back and forth in the furious wind. Standing upright became difficult. It was black as night, except for the almost constant lightning flashes. Charlie was shouting something at me, but it was lost in the roar of thunder and the screaming wind. Finally, he grabbed my shoulder and turned me around, pointing at one of the shutters.

A support had fallen down and the shutter was now bouncing violently up and down in the wind. Within seconds the screws tore out of the other support and there was a ripping sound as the hinges gave way. Then the shutter disappeared over the roof only to reappear on the other side sailing lazily down toward the spring. Suddenly there was a loud *Bang*! and the floor shook.

"What was that?" Charlie hollered in my ear. He was pale as a ghost. I probably didn't look much better. We both ran to the north side where the sound seemed to have come from. With relief I saw that the heavy trap door over the stairs had fallen down. It was held up by a hook and eye and the hook must have jiggled loose. Rain was coming down in torrents now, with the wind driving it through every possible crack. The south bunk was getting soaked, so Charlie grabbed the sleeping bag and threw it on the other bunk while I followed with the mattress. As we did so there was a blinding flash and pieces of bark and wood rattled off the windows. A chunk of wood the size of a boat oar went cartwheeling past not ten feet from the building.

A dead snag at the edge of the yard had just taken a strike and was blazing furiously, in spite of the rain. The phone bell was going ding, ding, ding almost constantly now as lightning hit the line again and again. We'd be lucky not to have a broken line when this was over. I could smell and taste copper. I knew what was coming and instinctively I ducked. CRASH! Little balls of glowing fire rolled around on the stove top, then vanished.

"You see why everything is grounded?" I shouted over the din.

Charlie nodded, managing a weak smile.

The fire in the dead snag seemed to be subsiding, the rain apparently being too much for it. At last the wind began to ease and the storm drifted off to the northeast. Thunder still rolled, but it was not over us anymore—thank goodness.

It was time to start looking around for fires. There had to be plenty after all this, and there were.

"I'll check south and east, you look north and west," I said.

Visibility wasn't too good, but I could see smoke on Cook Mountain to the south then another and another maybe a mile apart. Smoke was coming up near Davis Creek lower down.

"What do you see, Charlie?"

"I haven't looked west yet, but there's two for sure right across there on Buckingham and what's that over there on Green Mountain?"

"Yup, that's another. Now look over where I'm pointing at Flat Mountain. Does that look like smoke to you?"

"Sure does. In fact, it looks like more than one."

"That's what I was thinking. We'll know more when it gets dark. Then you can really see the flames. Just hope we don't get fogged in or we'll be completely blind."

"Let's see if the phone works," I cranked out a short and long.

"Bungalow," Wade's voice came through.

"Hey, it's working. This is Bear Butte."

"I was just going to ring you. I can't get through to anybody on the north side of the river."

"Oh, boy, that's not good."

"You bet your boots it's not. How do things look up there?"

"So far we can spot maybe a dozen smokes, but I'm sure there are more."

"Are Bighorn and Junction on?"

"Bighorn here."

"I'm on at Junction, too."

"Well, that's welcome news. What can you see?"

"Lots of smokes," said Gene at Junction. "I've got a bearing recorded on each one but haven't had time to work out an accurate location yet."

"About the same here at Bighorn. I see those over at Cook and Buckingham and a couple over on Clarke. By the way, is Clarke's phone working?"

"Yes, it is," said Wade. "I just talked to him a few minutes ago, but Cave, Chateau, and Cold Spring are out."

The situation was critical, because none of us could see much on that side of the river. Clarke could see a little on the west end and Junction could see some on the east, but Bear Butte and Bighorn were completely blocked off by Buckingham Ridge and Pot Mountain.

"Okay boys. We'll just sit tight for now. Stanley and Bowlander are going up to Chateau to see if that's where the line is broken. I'm going to call Canyon. They've got a man on Wallow Mountain, and if that line is okay, he can see into a lot of that country that we don't know about. So work out the location on those smokes and I'll get back to you as soon as I can."

Charlie and I set to work trying to figure out exactly where each fire was located. The final description would be something like the SE ¼ of the NW ¼ of sec. 26 T39 R8E, or pretty close to that. Sometimes we were able to pin it down very well, but not always. A lot depended on the terrain. Occasionally there was just plain human error, mine included. Nobody was very pleased to be off on a wild goose chase, sent to put out a fire that was nowhere near where it was reported to be. I could recall one time when I was on Bar Point and Jack was on Chateau and Mike was at Cave Point. We were having our Sunday afternoon social conversation when I noticed a huge pillar of smoke going up from Elk Mountain. All three of us could see it plainly, but we were in complete disagreement about its location. Of course, we called in immediately and Clyde, the dispatcher at the time, said, "Stop arguing and just give me your bearing on it and let me work it out."

We did this and hung on while he started drawing his lines across the map. Where the lines intersected would be the source of the smoke. We were still arguing about who was correct when Clyde cut in again.

"It's off the map. I gotta get a bigger one."

"What!" Nobody could believe it.

"That's right, the lines ran off the end of the map over an inch apart. I'll get back to you."

He was back on in a minute. "Well, we can forget that one. I just got a call. The sawmill at Weippe is burning down."

From where I was that was nearly fifty miles away and I was willing to swear that it was not more than ten. So mistakes were easily made, even though we tried to avoid them. After looking the country over very carefully, we were able to spot fourteen smokes and, along with Junction and Bighorn, we counted twenty-seven in all.

Most of them could be seen by at least two of us so we could get an accurate fix on those. The others had to be done strictly by matching known points, contour lines, and any reference point we could come up with to pinpoint them as well as we could. Once that was accomplished, I made a quick supper while Charlie kept scanning the country for any smokes we might have missed. Meantime we talked to Wade several times. The lines on the north side remained out, but Wallow Mountain could still communicate and was able to report two fires on that side of the river in our district. Of course, nobody was going to do anything about them without orders. Getting the phone line operating was clearly a top priority.

Wallow Mountain was in the canyon district, but if worst came to worst, the ranger over there would send his man to help us out. When it grew dark we could still see seven or eight red pinpoints. The rest were either dying out or were hidden from our view with the smoke showing only in the daylight. Stars were shining when I went to take a walk outside, but everything was still soaked from the heavy downpour. About ten o'clock the phone rang.

"Bear Butte."

"Are you still up?" It was Wade.

"What a question. You know darn well we're up."

"How are those fires doing on Cook Mountain?"

"Just a minute. I'll turn off the lantern so I can see. Okay. The two that are close together are flaming up real good, but I can barely see the other one off to the left. It's still there though."

"How about the one down near Davis Creek?"

"Can't see that at all, but that's down in a canyon anyway, so it would be too low to spot now."

"All right now. You've checked your fire packs, I take it?"

"Yup, ready to go."

"Are you in the mood to take a hike?"

"Whenever you say."

"How about right now?"

"Suits me. You mean both of us or just me?"

"You'll have to handle this alone. I'll need Charlie up there to keep an eye on things. We need all the eyes we can get right now."

"I understand. Soon as I get my boots on I'll be on my way."

"Thanks and good luck to you."

"You're going alone?" asked Charlie.

"I guess so."

"I don't envy you one bit."

"Can't say I'm in love with the idea, but one must do what one must do. Besides, I've done this before a time or two."

"I know, but it seems awful cold and dark and wet out there."

"That it is, but I can warm up in front of a nice fire soon. Think of it that way."

"Anything I can do for you?"

"Yeah. While I'm getting my boots on, take about half of those K rations out of that one fire pack. I'm sure I won't be gone for three days. No point in dragging those things around if I don't have to."

"That's all?"

"Rob some extra batteries out of the other pack. I'll probably need 'em."

"That's it."

"Yup, I'm ready. Just help me on with the pack and we'll get the headlamp on so I can see where I'm going and I'll be on my way."

"You gonna take a saw?"

"Don't think I'll need one."

"Okay. Well take care of yourself."

"I will. With luck I could be back sometime tomorrow."

So I was out the door and underway. Stars were still shining and the wind had dropped, but everything was soaking wet. It wasn't long, in spite of my canvas "tin pants," before my legs were soaked through from the wet brush along the trail slapping against them. Other than that the going was easy. The trail was very plain in the little circle of light that bounced ahead showing the way. Two of the fires were still visible, but that would soon end when the trail led downward to Camp George Creek. It would probably be several more miles before they reappeared. Jerry and I had been over the trail early in June and had found it ran largely through quite open country and was easily traveled.

That day had been a cold, miserable, rainy day and we were both soaked to the skin. We had the job of opening up the trail but found nothing at all blocking it. Most of the dead trees along it had fallen over years ago. That put us way ahead of schedule and normally we would have turned around and gone back, but we were both so cold we decided to go on to the Cook Mountain cabin and see if we could warm up a bit.

Our district, and with it our responsibility, ended about a half mile short of the cabin. Since it was early in the season, there was still snow on the ground, and as we pressed on toward the cabin it kept getting deeper and deeper.

"How much farther is it?" asked Jerry.

"Can't be very far," I answered, pulling myself through the heavy snow. It was almost hip deep now.

We struggled on and at last the small cabin appeared through the timber, a welcome sight. Neither of us had been there before, so it was a new adventure. The cabin was deserted, of course, and nobody had been in it since fall. By luck we found a loose board over one window and with a little persuasion got the other boards off easily enough. Two loose nails held the window in place, and once they were removed the window came out and we were inside. It was dark except for the small window we had crawled through, but a lantern was on the table and Jerry soon had that going.

"Hey, this is all right," said Jerry.

"Soon as I get a fire going it'll be a whole lot nicer," I answered.

The woodbox was full and it didn't take long before we had our feet toasting in the oven and our jackets drying over a chair. The pack with our lunch was still outside and Jerry volunteered to go out for it.

"While you're out there, fill this with clean snow," I said handing him a saucepan.

"What for?"

"So we can make this for dessert." I had spotted a bag of butterscotch pudding mix on the shelf, which I held up for his inspection.

"Not bad. Not bad at all. What do they call this, foraging?"

"No, I think it's more like living off the land."

We spent another hour over a leisurely lunch, complete with dessert, cleaned everything up, and with great reluctance went back out into the cold, hard world. We carefully put the window back in and the boards back on and headed for home, much cheered by our pleasant interlude.

I had to chuckle over that incident as I started upward. If things went well, I might just get there again. Maybe even in time for breakfast if things went exceptionally well. Now I could see the fires again fairly close. Soon I'd have to leave the trail and strike off cross-country. Best to change batteries first. My headlamp was getting dim. That accomplished,

I swung off the trail and started toward the first fire, about a half mile away. The other one was closer to the trail but higher up. The third was not in sight. Sometimes finding a fire can be troublesome, but not this time. Both were lit up nicely. I approached the first and it turned out to be only a burning stub. I came to a small stream not fifty feet from the fire.

"How lucky can you get?" I asked myself. Putting this thing out was a cinch. All that was needed then was to dig a shallow trench around the perimeter and that would be one down and two to go. So far so good.

Fire number two proved to be a replica of the first one minus the handy stream. But before tackling that one, it was time for a break. I found a handy log to sit on and by the warmth of the fire I opened a box of rations and took my time disposing of them. By now it was around four a.m. and the first hint of dawn was beginning to show over the ridge to the east.

With renewed vigor, I set to chopping out the live coals and cooling down the fire with shovelfuls of dirt. The soil here was soft and loose, ideal for my purposes. By the time the trenching was completed, full daylight had arrived and I headed back to the trail to see if I could find fire number three.

After finding the trail, I hadn't gone a hundred yards before striking the fresh tracks of a lone mule. No horse tracks, no human footprints, just one mule.

"Now what the heck would he be doin' out here all by his lonesome?" I asked myself.

The tracks continued for about a quarter of a mile and then took off to the west. Puzzled by this, I decided to have a brief look for the fire and then go on to Cook Mountain cabin, now only a mile away. There would be somebody there and he surely could give me a good idea of exactly where the fire was located and he might have some information on that mule. The only mules in the area wore the U.S. brand of the Forest Service, so somebody had to be missing one.

I knew the fire was fairly close to the trail, but there was no sign of it and I went straight on to the cabin. Smoke was coming out of the chimney and I could smell bacon frying when I walked up to the door.

I was greeted by a red-headed boy.

"Well, howdy there. Bet you're up here a-lookin' in after them fahrs."

What a southern accent this guy had.

"You bet. Two are now history, but the third one is going to be a little harder to find."

"That won't be no problem. I got 'er down perfect. In a bit I'll take y'all up in the tower and show you right whar it's at."

"That'd be great. I guess by you're accent that you're not from around here."

"Heck no. I'm from a little ole town in Looziana, say, and I bet y'all ain't had nuthin' t'eat this mornin'." He stuck out his hand, "Name's Claude."

"I'm Warren. I did have some K rations earlier, but that bacon sure smells good. Is that cajun-style bacon?"

"No siree, it ain't. The USFS don't supply us with much in the way of spices and such, but I'll just slice some off here and do the best I can with it. You pretty hungry?"

"Yeah, I guess so."

"That's what I like to hear. How many eggs, three or four?"

"Maybe a couple."

"Is that all? I'll put on three. Can't be havin' you goin' hungry."

"Okay. While you're doing that, I'd better call in and let 'em know how things are going. I'm going to report on that mule, too."

"What mule is that?"

"I struck the track of a lone mule about a mile down."

"Well, won't George Pitcher be happy to hear that. He's been huntin' that mule for better'n a week." George Pitcher was the Pierce district head mule packer.

So I rang up the Pierce ranger station and told him about the mule. Herb, the ranger, was pleased to hear the news.

"George Pitcher is down at the Wietas now. I'll get a hold of him right away if I can. You say the tracks are fresh?"

"Last night or early this morning—since the rain anyway."

"Good. He'll be up today or tomorrow at the latest."

"Okay. Now could you ring the Bungalow for me?"

"Sure thing."

"Bungalow." It was our George.

"Good morning, George."

"Good morning. You ain't back already?"

"No. I'm up at Cook."

"What're you doin' there? You're suppose to be puttin' fires out."

"I was, but I got hungry. My chef is preparing breakfast now."

"Is that so? What's he got, a restaurant up there?"

"Sort of. He specializes in Cajun food."

"*What* kind?"

"Cajun."

"Has he got the food in a cage or is he in one?"

"No, no. That's a style of cooking. They do it down south. He's from Louisiana."

"Does it taste any better comin' out of a cage?"

"There is no cage, George. The word is C-A-J-U-N. It's a style of cooking—spicy."

"I know all that. Hell, I prob'ly forgot more about cajun cooking than you'll ever know."

"I'm sure if you ever did know anything about it you forgot it."

We were all laughing now. "Its a good thing nobody's listening in or they'd put us both in a cage," I said.

"Ain't that the truth. You go have your fancy breakfast now and I'll give Wade the news when he gets in."

"Okay. I should be calling in later this afternoon when I get back. I gotta go now—breakfast is being served."

I didn't realize how hungry I was until I started eating. Claude was a good cook and I had no trouble downing the extra egg. When the dishes were done we went up in the tower. The little enclosure at the top was barely big enough for the two of us.

"Y'all see that big rock sticking up yonder?" asked Claude, "Here, I'll put the finder on it."

I looked through the finder. "Yup, I see it."

"Well, the fahr wasn't no more'n a couple hundred feet this side, right on the ridgetop. No way you can miss it."

He was right. After saying goodbye and thanking him for his hospitality, I had to look a little, but what was left of the fire was exactly where he said it was. Finishing it off took no more than an hour, but digging the trench around it in the rocky soil took much longer. When everything was completed, I took my time with a box of K rations and then started the long haul back to Bear Butte. As I passed Davis Creek, I took a good look down the shallow canyon where we had seen smoke but could see nothing. At last Bear Butte came in view and soon Charlie appeared. He gave me a wave and started down the stairs. We met about a quarter-mile out.

"Here, let me take that," he said and he helped me get rid of the fire pack.

I felt like I was walking on air without the heavy burden.

"You get 'em all out?" he asked.

"Yup, no problems."

"Glad to hear it 'cause I've got sort of a problem here."

"Oh, what kind of a problem?"

"Well, I'd kind of figured you'd be back this afternoon, so I got out the cookbook and thought I'd make somethin' for supper."

"What are we having?"

"Spanish rice."

"That's nice."

"Well, it would be, but I never made rice before."

"O-O-O-H, don't tell me—let me guess. You've got every container in the place full of rice, right?"

"Right, and it's still expanding. I had no idea that stuff blew up like that."

"Neither did I the first time I made rice. Everybody makes the same mistake."

"That's good. I was afraid I was the only one."

"Not by a long shot."

There were kettles of rice completely covering the stove top and several were about to run over. Charlie looked worried, but I just had to laugh. "Looks like we'll be having rice for awhile."

"Yeah, I guess so."

"Well, Charlie, if you don't mind, I'm going to call in and then stretch out for a bit. You can call me when supper is on—okay?"

When I called in, Wade answered. "Bungalow."

"I'm home again, those three fires on Cook Mountain are now history."

"Glad to hear it. You must be a little pooped out."

"That I am. Charlie has taken over the cooking, so I'm going to relax. By the way, is the line fixed on the north side of the river?"

"Yes it is. Stanley and Bowlander went up last night and found a break this side of Chateau. Carl went out from Cave this morning on one fire and Marv went out from Cold Springs. They should be back in sometime tonight. Altogether we had twenty-seven fires. By tomorrow we should have 'em all mopped up."

"What about those two on Buckingham? I see they're still smoking."

"I know. That's pretty rugged country. If they don't go out, we'll have to get some jumpers in there. Right now there's none available. Everybody's out."

"Okay. We'll keep watching 'em."

I took a short snooze before Charlie woke me with the news that the Spanish rice was ready.

"I hope you're hungry," he said.

"I am, but not that hungry." Every available container was filled, and we had at least a week's supply. We managed to empty one kettle, but half a dozen remained full to the top. I helped Charlie clean up the dishes, but then I simply ran out of gas.

"I'll see you in the morning," I said as I crawled into my sleeping bag. The next thing I heard was Charlie making the morning test call. Feeling quite refreshed after a good night's sleep, I got the fire going and started preparing breakfast. I thought it would be a real relaxing day. The smoke was still visible on Buckingham, so we'd have to keep an eye on that, but otherwise things were pretty well under control. Halfway through breakfast the phone rang. It was Wade.

"Good morning. How are you feeling?"

"Not bad."

"That's good. How'd you like to take another little hike?"

"Where to?"

"Same place as yesterday. Ken wants you to patrol those three fires."

"Wade, those fires are out—dead, cold, kaput."

"Now you know that and I know that, but Ken is one hard guy to convince about anything, as you well know, and unfortunately he's the boss."

"Maybe I'd better talk to him."

"I'm afraid you can't. He left the orders and then took off for one of the blister-rust control camps."

"Oh, that's just great."

"That's what I thought. He makes the snowballs and I gotta throw 'em."

"I guess that's it then."

" 'Fraid so, but one thing I want you to remember—you'll be on fire pay, so take your good-natured time."

"You just bet I will."

"What's going on?" asked Charlie when I hung up.

"Ken wants those fires patrolled, so I gotta go back up there and see if I can find 'em again."

"Oh man, that's expecting too darn much if you ask me."

"That's not what's bothering me. It's that he didn't take my word for it that they were completely out. Shorty always trusted me. This guy doesn't."

"I see what you mean. Are you gonna lug a fire pack all the way up there again?"

"Heck no. I'm not even packing a lunch. I'll drop in on my friend Claude at noon. He'll feed me, I'm sure."

Charlie insisted on doing the dishes alone, so right after breakfast I was off. It promised to be a really beautiful day—birds were singing, the sun was shining, not a cloud in the sky, and I was traveling light. What more could one ask for? Finding those dead fires might not be too easy, but I had all day so there would be no need to hurry. My tracks were still quite plain in the soft earth when I came to the spot where I had left the trail, so it was a simple matter to follow them straight to the first fire. Everything was cold, as I knew it would be. After taking a short rest and looking over the countryside, I started off in search of my next objective. That proved a little more difficult, but after a bit of circling around, I spotted an empty K-ration box and there was what was left of fire number 2, cold as could be. It was still early enough, so I took another short rest and as I sat there ever so faintly came the sound of sheep. Somebody had told me that there was a herd of sheep headed this way and this was what I was hearing. Part of the National Forest here was government range and there was enough open grassland to feed quite a few sheep.

It was time to head for Cook Mountain. If I moved right along, I should make it in time for lunch easily. Once on the trail I noticed horse tracks and they left at the same spot where the mule tracks did, so I knew George Pitcher was tracking down his escapee. Claude was glad to see me again. "Kinda figured you'd be back. Y'all ain't in no hurry are you?"

"Not really."

"That's good. In a minute ah'll make a fahr and fry up some ham and potatoes. That sound good to you?"

"Sure does."

"By the way, George Pitcher went through here earlier. Ya'all git to see him?"

"No, but I saw his tracks."

"Good. If he don't ketch his mule too quick, he'll likely stay here tonight. I could use some company. Gits a bit lonesome around here."

"I know what you mean."

After we ate, we chatted awhile, but finally I had to say goodbye or I'd never make it back for supper.

"Y'all take care now," Claude called after me and waved.

The last fire was as dead as the other two, and after giving it a brief check, I struck off down the trail. There was a small patch of timber on the way and just after entering it, I heard the creak of saddle leather and around the bend came George Pitcher with his long lost mule in tow.

"Well, howdy there son. Ain't seen you in awhile," he said as he grabbed my hand.

"I see you found your mule."

"Sure did. Say, I bet you're the one found his tracks."

"That's right."

"Well, I'm much obliged. I reckoned ole Silas here'd bin et by a cougar by now."

"Where'd you find him?"

"Down at the sheep camp. Raymond says he heard the dog a-barkin' away early yestidday mornin'—figures it must be a bear or something after his sheep. Loaded his rifle and run outta the tent and here come ole Silas, trottin' in like he owned the place."

"Maybe he was lonesome."

"Lonesome for his feedbag, more likely."

Silas was standing there with both eyes shut, dozing away. He looked like he'd had a rough week.

"Say, son, how'd you like a chunk of mutton?"

"I'm not really too crazy about mutton. Where'd you get it?"

"A lightnin' strike killed five of Raymond's ewes, so he butchered one and gave me a piece. I wanted to refuse, but he's Basque, you know, and their feelings are hurt if you turn down a gift."

"He's a what?"

"A Basque—you know. They come from somewhere in Spain and most all of 'ems sheepherders."

"I didn't know that."

"Ain't you met Raymond yet?"

"No. I just heard the sheep for the first time this morning."

"He'll be up to see you. He don't miss a chance to talk to somebody. Them sheep ain't a lot of company, I guess. Say, how'd you like some sourdough biscuits?"

"Are they from Raymond too?"

"That they are."

"To tell you the truth George, I make my own."

"That's good, cause I prob'ly wouldn't have give 'em to you anyway. You know that sheep camp ain't the cleanest place in the world and when I pictured ole Raymond a kneadin' away at that sourdough, I just plain lost my appetite for them biscuits of his."

"Think Silas might care for a few?"

"Say, now there's an idea, but don't you ever tell Raymond what become of his biscuits."

George got off his horse and got a dozen or so biscuits out of the saddlebag.

"C'mon Silas, time to wake up. I got a special treat for you."

Roused from his reverie, Silas took a sniff and then gobbled down one biscuit after another. When there were no more, he closed his eyes and dozed off again.

"Now there is one tired mule," said George. "Wonder where he's been all this time?"

"If only he could talk," I answered, "he might have quite a tale to tell."

"That's a fact," said George as he mounted up. "Now if I can get Silas started, it's time I was on my way."

"Me too. If I want some supper, I better get a move on."

"Adios and thanks again for helpin' me track down this wild critter," said George and he put his heels to the horse.

It was high time I was on my way too. The sun was headed downward and I still had five miles to go. Again in the distance I could hear sheep, a bit plainer now. They must be headed toward Bear Butte.

No doubt I would soon get to meet Raymond. Most of the way was level going so the miles flew by and before long the Bear Butte tower appeared. No sooner did I spot the tower, than Charlie, who must have been watching for me, came bounding down the stairs and hurried down the trail to meet me.

"We got another problem," he said with a worried look.

"You didn't make more rice?"

"No, nothing like that. You remember that smoke we saw down near Davis Creek?"

"Yeah. That went out didn't it?"

"Well, it did, but about one o'clock today it started smoking again."

"Did you report it?"

"Right away. Wade said we'd wait 'till you got back and see what you thought."

"Oh, okay."

"Yeah, but that's not the problem."

"What is?"

"Well, Wade wanted to wait, see, but about an hour ago Ken called and said there were jumpers available now and we might as well use 'em, so there's a plane on its way."

"In that case, I get to sleep tonight, right?"

"I guess so, but that's not what's got me worried."

"What has?"

"Well, when he called, the plane was already on its way and right before that the smoke stopped."

"Did you tell him?"

"No, I figured what's the use. The plane's already gone and maybe the smoke could start up again."

"That's true. We'll just have to wait and see."

We didn't have long to wait. We'd hardly climbed the stairs before an old Ford Tri-motor appeared headed straight for Davis Creek. The plane circled the area again and again, apparently seeing no more smoke than we could. Then he banked and headed straight for the tower. We both stood out on the catwalk and waved as he thundered past at treetop level, not two hundred feet away. A man stood in the open doorway and waved back and on the second pass, he threw out a long yellow streamer with a weight attached. It landed in some brush and I hurried down to retrieve it. The streamer was easy enough to find, but whatever was attached to it had evidently come off and fallen to the ground, lord only knew where.

Back up on the tower, I held out my hand with the streamer as the plane continued to circle. We both waved to the man standing in the doorway and I gestured frantically trying to get across to him that his message, whatever it was, was lost.

Apparently he understood, for the plane banked away and headed for Buckingham Ridge where two smokes were still visible. The plane circled several times and then a parachute blossomed beneath it, coming down near the uppermost smoke. Again the plane came around and a second chute opened, coming to rest near the first one. Another pass produced a third, and then after several more passes, apparently to check things over, the pilot turned and headed back toward Missoula.

"Show's over," I said, "time to call in."

"Are you going to make the call?" asked Charlie.

"If you want me to."

"I wish you would. They might be mad at me."

"Why should they be?"

"Well, you know about the smoke going out and all that."

"Hey, you saw smoke, didn't you?"

"Yes."

"And you reported it, didn't you?"

"Yes."

"That's exactly what you're suppose to do. There's no way you could predict that it would stop, is there?"

"I guess not."

"Okay. I'll make the call and nobody is going to fault you in any way."

So I explained to Wade what had taken place and he was pleased to hear about the fires on Buckingham being taken care of and hopefully we'd heard the last of the one on Davis Creek. As things turned out, we had.

"Well, that's that," I said. "You got anymore of the Spanish rice around?"

"Only six kettles full," answered Charlie.

"Okay. Go get a couple while I light a fire. I'm hungry as a bear."

Charlie left the next morning for the Bungalow and I was sorry to see him go, though he did leave me with a good supply of Spanish rice. Several days later on my way to the spring I spied a brown canvas pouch on the ground. On it were printed the words, RETURN TO PARACHUTE LOFT...MISSOULA, MONTANA.

I opened the flap and read the message inside.

IF YOU STILL SEE THE SMOKE, WAVE YOUR ARMS.

IF YOU DON'T SEE IT, DON'T WAVE.

Well, we hadn't done what he wanted, but apparently he understood anyway.

All's well, that ends well, I guess.

Sixteen
George's Revenge

As I drove around the last bend and over the bridge, there was George waiting on the office steps.

"How was your trip?" he said as I opened the door.

"Hardly a trip. All I did was go into town."

"Well, I know, but that road ain't meant for kids like you."

"As you see, I am here and never met a car either way."

"No wonder you made it. Did you git my Copenhagen?"

"I surely did."

"I bin' out of it for more'n a week now, and that's long enough. Where's it at?"

"In the trunk, George, just keep your shirt on. You can have it just as soon as I find the key." He was standing right in my way in front of the trunk handle.

"How can I open the trunk with you standing over it?"

"Don't be such a grouch. You don't know what it's like to do without as long as I have."

"It must be pretty awful."

"It is. Now where is it? I don't see it."

"Right here, George," I said handing him a bag containing six cans of his precious snuff. Instantly, his pocketknife came out and he slit the seal and popped a pinch under his lower lip.

"Ah-h-h, that's better. Now I kin' be myself again. What else did you bring me?"

"Nothing. Oh here, you can have this newspaper to read, but don't throw it away. I haven't looked at it yet." The paper had been over a case of Lucky Lager, which immediately caught George's eye.

"Thought you just said you didn't bring nuthin' more for me."

"That's what I said."

"Who is this for then?"

"Me, of course."

"Now what would you want with all that beer? You know it's not good for you."

"Then it's not good for you either, George."

"Now, that's a matter of opinion. Last time I seen a doctor he said I was to have three, four cans a day for my health."

"Is that so—have you been following his orders?"

"No I ain't, cause there's been a shortage, but now I see I kin' start up again."

"Well, as long as it's strictly for your health, maybe I'll share some of it with you."

"Now you're making sense. I always said you was a generous kind of person."

"Cut the flattery, George. Just figure out how to get the stuff cooled. It's been in this hot trunk for a couple hours."

"That won't be no problem. You stay right here to guard it and I'll be right back with a gunnysack."

He disappeared into the building known as the tool cache, and came out with a burlap bag and some twine.

"There now. You just stick a half dozen of them cans in here and meet me down by the incinerator. I got a couple of fishin' poles there and maybe we can git enough fer supper. Wouldn't that be nice?"

"Sure would. I'll be down soon as I finish unloading and change clothes."

The incinerator was a small concrete oven where we burned our garbage located near where the Orogrande Creek emptied into the North Fork of the Clearwater, right behind the station.

I had to hand it to George. He had the beer all weighted down out in the river and two nice trout already gutted on the bank.

"Grab that other pole and git busy. We'll need a dozen more of these with Bowlander at the table."

As we fished and waited for the beer to cool we got to talking about how things had changed since Shorty had been transferred.

"You know, George, when Shorty was here we wouldn't have dreamed of having beer around, let alone drinking it."

"Yer right. He never said we couldn't, but he didn't have to. You just knew he wouldn't stand for it."

George hit it right on the head. Shorty seldom reprimanded anyone—he just didn't have to. Everyone knew what he expected of them without being told. He was that kind of person and the best man I ever worked for—a mighty tough act to follow. As we talked a few more trout fell for our bait, but still not enough for supper. There were some fishermen upstream from us near the bridge and they didn't seem to doing too well either.

Suddenly George said, "Now what in hell does he want?"

A black pickup pulling a horse trailer was stopping on the road above.

I recognized the truck. "That's just Mike, the game warden. I suppose he's going to check out those fishermen."

"You don't have to tell me who it is. I know that pest when I see him."

"Why is he a pest?"

"He just is, that's all."

Come to think of it, I had noticed that George got in a testy mood every time Mike stopped in and ate with us. Actually, I thought Mike was a pretty nice guy and besides he was known to have a good-looking teenage daughter living with him and his wife up at the old Cold Springs CCC camp. One of the buildings there was kept up for living quarters for Forest Service people, and I was always nice to Mike on the off chance that I might be sent there someday. George kept staring over his shoulder and muttering.

"Now look what he's doin' pesterin' them fishermen. Why don't he leave 'em alone?"

"That's his job, George. He's just doing what he gets paid for."

"Well, that's a hell of a way to make a livin' if you ask me."

"I s'pose it is, but somebody's gotta do it."

"That may be, but he's nuthin' but a pain in the neck far as I'm concerned."

Things quieted down for awhile, but George kept glaring up river at Mike, who was still busy with the fishermen.

"You got a fishin' license?" George asked.

"Of course. I wouldn't be standing here looking at the game warden if I didn't, would I?"

"Didn't think you would. Now I'm going to git shut of that pest once and fer all."

"What do you figure on doing?"

"Soon as he looks over this way, you and me are gonna throw down our poles and make a run fer the bunkhouse."

"Why should we do that?"

"Don't ask any dumb questions. Just do as I say."

"Okay, George, it's your deal."

We kept on fishing and I took the time to wet some ferns to cover the fish we'd caught. It began to look like we might not be back for awhile. Eventually Mike finished with the other fishermen and started up the bank toward his truck. Halfway up he turned and looked our way. Spotting us, he gave one of those waves that means, "Stay there I want to talk to you."

Dropping our poles we made a run for it. For all of George's years, which were if not seventy pretty close to it, he could darn near outrun me. I had to go all out to keep up. We burst through the back door of the bunkhouse, George in the lead. As we passed an old table with some of last year's magazines on it, he grabbed a couple, shoved one in my hand, and commanded me to lay down on my bunk and start reading. He plunked himself down on the next bunk, opened his magazine, and said, "Let me do the talkin'."

"George, I will not only let you do all the talking, I insist on it. After all, who was it got us into this in the first place?"

I was determined to take a position of neutrality in the upcoming battle. I was not about to be drawn into his vendetta with Mike.

Mike was a big, well-built man, looking every inch a game warden in his uniform with a badge pinned to his shirt pocket and a thirty-eight special resting on his right hip when he walked in.

"Howdy boys."

"Howdy."

"How's fishin'?"

"We ain't fishin'."

"I can see that, but you were."

"Well, we ain't now."

"Just thought I'd drop in and check your licenses."

"You need a license to read a magazine now?" George said. He hadn't looked up from his magazine yet.

"No, you don't have to have a license for that."

"What for then, to lay on a bunk?"

"No, I'm talking about your fishing license. You have one don't you?"

"I don't need one."

"What makes you think that?"

"'cause I work for the U. S. of A. Government people don't need no license."

"That's where you're wrong. Everybody has to have a license."

In George's opinion anyone who didn't work for the U. S. of A. was at best unpatriotic or at worst some kind of subversive. Mike working for the state probably fell somewhere in-between.

"I'm over sixty-five. I don't need one then, do I?"

"Like I said, George, everybody except kids under sixteen needs a license."

"Hell, I'm old enough to be your father and in all my years your the first dammed warden ever seen fit to ask for my license."

No mention was made of baiting him by throwing down our poles and running.

"George, I'm just doing my job."

"Well, go do it some place else then."

Mike was starting to sweat and looking extremely uneasy.

"I will just as soon as I check your license."

"What if I ain't got one?"

"I guess I'd have to give you a citation then. I wouldn't like to, but I'd have to."

"What does that mean?"

"You'd have to pay a fine."

"How much?"

"I don't know. Whatever the judge decides."

"What if I couldn't pay, would they lock me up?"

"I doubt that, but it would be up to the judge."

"Why don't you just git in that truck of yours and pretend you never came in here?"

"I can't do that, George. Now do you have a license or don't you?"

"Course I got one."

Relief flooded Mike's face. "Could I see it please?"

"Not till I'm finished with this article."

I glanced over. He hadn't turned a page yet and was staring fixedly at a Camel cigarette ad.

"Son, do you have a license?"

"Sure."

"Could I please see it?"

I handed it to him and George shot me a murderous look for caving in so easily. After examining my license, he handed it back, and George finally finished with his cigarette ad, rolled on his side, and pulled a worn-out old wallet from his back pocket.

"Well, I suppose if you gotta see mine, I'll hafta look around for it."

Mike began to relax a little, but George wasn't through with him. The wallet contained old sales slips, photographs, expired driver's licenses, and all manner of needless papers. At last, quite pleased with himself, he selected a folded piece of paper and handed it to Mike.

"Is this what your lookin' for?"

Mike looked it over and said, "It would be if it was two years ago. I'd like to see the one for this year."

"Lemme see that." He snatched it away from Mike. "Should be another in here someplace. Maybe I lost it."

"If you did, there'll be a record of it."

Mike's self-control was being severely tested, but somehow he was still hanging on. George continued patiently looking over his papers, then, coming across a photograph, he passed it to Mike.

"That's my son Joe when he was in the Navy servin' his country."

"Nice looking boy." The implication wasn't lost on Mike.

"Damn right he is. They didn't have to draft him neither—just went right ahead and joined up."

I had no idea whether Mike had been in the service or not and doubted if George did either, but he was going to get his dig in just in case. The wallet's contents were now strewn all over the bunk and Mike stepped closer to help in the search. George, however, would have none of it.

"Get outa my light. How kin I see anything with you hunkered over me?"

"Sorry. I thought I could help."

"Don't need no help. Just stand back so I kin see."

Mike backed off again while George continued examining one document after another. I could see one that looked somewhat newer than the rest and was going to point it out but then thought better of it. George probably knew exactly which one was his current license, but he intended to make Mike sweat until every scrap of paper had been carefully scrutinized. At last there remained only one and that, naturally, was his current license. With a sneer he handed it to Mike.

"Here, look at it all you like."

Taking his time, Mike looked it over and gave it back to George.

"Looks like everything is in order."

"'Course it is. Told you I had one in the first place. Now I s'pose you're aimin' to stay fer supper."

Mike looked at his watch. "Well, it is getting pretty close to that time and I sort of figured...."

George cut him off, "What's the matter, don't your wife know how to cook?"

"Sure she does. She's a good cook, but not quite as good as you."

Flattery was not going to work on George.

"Maybe you ain't givin' her enough practice."

"Oh, I wouldn't say that. It's just that it's easier for her if I eat here sometimes."

"Is that so? Well, did you know that every time you stick them big ugly feet of yours under my table, I hafta make out a stack of forms a foot high?"

"No, I didn't know that. Why?"

"'cause you don't work for the U. S. of A., that's why."

At last there was the reason for George's hostility. I had seen him muttering to himself over some forms, but didn't know that Mike was the cause of it all. There was an old stub of a pencil hung by a string and a couple of small stacks of forms on the windowsill of the kitchen, and George would mark down everyone who ate each meal. No doubt there was one form for Forest Service personnel and another for others. Apparently the one for others caused him a great deal of trouble.

Mike was all apologies. "I'm sorry, George. I didn't realize you had to go to all that trouble."

"Well, I do."

It was plain that nothing short of Mike's departure was going to satisfy George. Mike being the perceptive type took the hint.

"Guess I'll be running along then. So long boys."

"Don't slam the door," George hollered after him.

"Was that nice?" I asked when he had gone. "After all, he did apologize."

"Well, he should after all he's put me through. Let's fergit about him and go have some beer. It oughta be plenty cool by now."

So back we went and he was right, the beer was plenty cool. We each opened a can and picked up our poles and resumed fishing when there was a crunch of gravel behind us.

"Hide the beer," George whispered, "here comes Bowlander."

"He won't say anything."

"I know that, but he'll likely drink it all up on us."

It was too late. "So that's where you two bin a-hidin'. What's that you got in your hand?" he said.

"A fishpole, what's it look like?"

"I mean the other one, inside yer shirt."

"Never mind. It ain't none of your business."

"Bowlander," I said, "we were just having a friendly can of beer, would you care to join us?"

"Don't give him none. He'll git wilder than hell."

Bowlander put a big hand on George's head and ruffled up his hair. "I will if you don't gimme one."

"Oh, give him one then. If he gets outa hand I'll just lay him one aside the head with a rock."

So Bowlander got his beer and fished as we talked until Bowlander brought up an unpleasant subject.

"I seen Mike come out of the bunkhouse awhile ago with his tail between his legs. You know anything about that George?"

"Yes I do. I run him off."

"What'd you do that for? I like Mike."

"'cause he was gittin' to be too much of a pest."

"Never pestered me none."

"No, well you never had to make out all them forms every time he sits down at the table."

"Is that what's got you so worked up?"

"Ain't that enough?"

"No it ain't. Why don't you call him up and say yer sorry and I'll make out them forms fer you."

"You got trouble enough figurin' out how to spell yer own name, let alone makin' out them complicated forms."

"Well, if you don't call him, I will. When there's three of us at a table, he's the only one I can talk to that makes any sense. Don't know why you hadda go runnin' him off like that."

George shoved his fishpole in Bowlander's face and said, "Here go ketch yer own supper, I got work to do," and he stormed off.

It wasn't long before the cookhouse chimney started smoking.

Bowlander looked at me and winked. "Say, he is a mite ticked off ain't he."

"This is nothing. You should have seen him go after poor Mike."

The fish quit biting, but the triangle rang out supper call on time and, of course, George had a meal fit for a king laid out for us. Lee, the blacksmith, joined us for supper and took note of George's bad humor.

"What's the matter, you got a stone in your shoe or something?"

Bowlander spilled his own version of the whole thing, much to Lee's amusement. By the end of the meal George had returned to his old jovial self and Bowlander even volunteered to dry dishes, so things were back to normal again.

That was the last of Mike's taking meals at George's table, though. He would wave as he drove through, but his stops were strictly business.

Seventeen
The Lead Shaver

I was sitting in the bunkhouse writing a letter when George came in.

"Whatcha doin'?"

"Writing a letter."

"Who to?"

"My mother."

"That's nice."

"Glad you approve."

"Where's that gun of yours?"

"In my seabag right on top. What's the matter, Bowlander picking on you again?"

"No, but I don't need no gun to take care of that big galoot. Don't tell him I said that."

"What do you want it for then?"

"There's a rabbit in my garden."

"Chase him out."

"I would, but he'll be in there again soon as my back is turned. There's only one answer, so lemme have that gun 'fore he's got all the lettuce et up."

"Okay. Just help yourself. It's right there on top."

"Where's the shells?"

"Should be half a box right there somewhere."

"All I need is one."

"Better fill it up. I've seen you shoot."

"Don't get sassy. One's all I'm gonna need and that's all I'm takin'."

"Anything you say, just don't shoot any holes in the cookhouse."

"Don't you worry none. I'll be back in a jiffy."

Out he went and a minute later a shot rang out. He was back in shortly.

"Did you get him?"

"Heard me shoot didn't you?"

"Answer my question."

"Course I got him."

"Now, I s'pose we'll be having rabbit on the menu tonight?"

"No siree. I heaved him in the crick and that's what I shoulda done with that wore-out gun of yours."

"George, that gun has provided me with many, many chicken dinners and it is probably one of the finest weapons you've ever had your hands on. What's more, I paid twelve bucks for it five years ago, so you know it's an expensive gun."

"Somebody seen you comin', if you ask me."

"What makes you say that?"

"Cause it's shavin' lead, that's what."

"It's doing what?"

"Shavin' lead. Come out here in the light and lemme show you."

"Oh, all right, if I must."

The revolver we were arguing about was definitely not of the best quality. Instead of having a solid frame like the more expensive ones, where the cylinder swings out to the side, this one hinged ahead of the trigger guard and the barrel and cylinder swung down, like on a double barrel shotgun.

"Lookit here," George said, pointing to some blue residue on the left side of the barrel. "See that, that's lead."

"Hmmm. I saw that before, but thought it was powder."

"No, it ain't. The cylinder don't line up right with the barrel and lead is gittin' shaved off every time you shoot."

"Why would that be?"

"Like I told you, it's wore out. Look here—that little doohickey that turns the cylinder is rounded off so much it don't turn it far enough."

I could see what he meant and after trying it out, it was plain that George was right, but I had a simple solution.

"Look George, all I have to do is pull the hammer back and then turn the cylinder till it stops, then it'll be lined up right."

"I just knew you was gonna say that and it'll work as long as you don't forget, but all you gotta do is forget just once and you can likely as not git your fool head blowed off."

"In that case, I'd better not forget."

"Best thing you can do is forget to take it along tomorrow and leave it here where it ain't gonna blow up on you."

"Well, you just shot it and it didn't blow up."

"That don't mean it won't the next time. If I was you I'd leave it right where it's at till you git it fixed or better yet throw the damn thing away."

"Well, let me think about it."

"You better think about it. Nothin' I hate worse than seein' a kid missin' half his face."

With that he went out. Naturally I opted for taking the gun along up to Junction, where I was headed the next morning. I did resolve, however, to be extra careful and to use it as little as possible.

Next morning Wade took me as far as the horse bridge and I hiked up the seven miles to Junction. After I got there, just to be on the safe side, I put a shell in the gun, turned the cylinder until it stopped, and stepped behind the tree. I stuck my arm around the other side and fired. It worked perfectly. Well, that was the answer. As long as I gave the cylinder that little extra turn everything would line up and there would be no problem.

Several days went by and I was kept busy working on the phone line, cutting away anything that might be a possible ground. One evening I came in and was peeling potatoes and trying to decide what can of meat to open for supper, when I glanced out the window and spied a fat grouse strutting past, about thirty feet away. That solved the meat problem, as long as my aim was good.

Grabbing my revolver, which was fully loaded, I eased out the door as quietly as possible, pulled back the hammer, and knelt down so I could steady my arm on the railing.

Taking careful aim I squeezed the trigger. There was a tremendous explosion. I was blown back against the building hitting my head on the window casing. In my haste, I had completely forgotten to turn the cylinder.

In a daze, I looked down at the revolver through a red mist. Amazingly I was still clutching the thing, which had come open, barrel hanging down, the now empty cylinder exposed. I could see out of my right eye, but when I closed it I could see nothing out of the left one. Still in a daze, I stumbled through the door, my ears ringing so loudly I couldn't hear my boots striking the floor. My face felt like it had been peppered with buckshot.

There was a small mirror on the washstand and I staggered over to it to assess the damage. The left side of my face was covered with blood, apparently coming from around the eye. Trying to stay calm, but still partly dazed, I dippered some water into the wash basin and washed away enough blood to look things over. The vision in my left eye cleared up immediately, but more blood soon covered it again. Washing it again, I took a closer look and there was something shining. Plucking at it with my fingernails, I pulled out a hunk of brass shell casing.

I sat down and held a wet washcloth over my eye for a while, and had a serious talk with myself. Through my foolishness, I had come within a whisker of losing my eye.

Still badly shaken, I looked at my revolver. The cylinder, of course, was empty. Had the concussion set off all the shells, I wondered? By the force of the explosion that is what must have happened, for I never found so much as a fragment of any of them around, though I looked the area over carefully later.

Faintly, over the ringing in my ears, I could hear the phone. I looked at the clock. Bighorn must be making test call. I picked it up and could barely make out George's voice.

"Bungalow."

"Bighorn test call."

"Junction here too."

"Good, are you all done eatin'?"

"All done, just getting cleaned up now," said Jerry.

"I'm not started yet."

"How come?"

"Got in a little late and had to go for water," I lied.

"Say, will you stop hollerin', if you yell any louder we won't need no phone."

"Oh, sorry. You weren't coming through too good and I thought maybe I wasn't either," I lied again, more quietly this time.

The ringing in my ears was so loud I hadn't realized I was yelling.

"That's better. Thought you might bust my eardrums there for a minute. Now go make yourself some supper."

That was a close one. If George had suspected what I'd done he'd have surely questioned me about it, and if he ever found out I'd never hear the end of it.

Eventually the bleeding stopped and I fixed myself something to eat, but somehow my appetite just wasn't up to par. Under the circumstances, that was understandable. Fortunately, the powder and fragments that hit my face hadn't penetrated to any degree and after a few days I looked pretty much the way I had before my foolish accident.

The ringing in my ears, however, took several weeks to subside, but eventually that too went away and my hearing returned to normal. But it was a lesson painfully learned. One that, but for a fraction of an inch, could have ended in a disaster for me. The lead shaver was still, unbelievably, intact, but it went into immediate retirement and I never fired it again.

Eighteen
Stanley and the Stove

My stove was shot, and there was no getting around it. I could still make bacon, eggs, and pancakes on it, but the firebox was burned out and the flames went right into the oven. Baking anything was out of the question, and I was clean out of bread—not a crumb left. So, at evening test call when George answered, I said, "George, my stove is burned out. I can't bake a thing with it. What am I gonna do?"

"Well, you've been falling over that new one that Bowlander brought up this spring every time you set foot in the woodshed—why don't you use it?"

"Is that what's in that crate?" I said, "I thought it was canned goods."

"Maybe if you wasn't so blind you'd a had that thing goin' a week ago."

I took off down the stairs to take a look and sure enough, after hammering one side off of the crate, there was a brand new stove. I tried lifting one end. With all my strength I could barely get it off the ground.

The front side of the stove was exposed and I opened the oven door and found all sorts of parts wrapped in paper—the lids, the legs, the grates, the poker, the ash box—all heavy stuff.

After taking them out it was somewhat lighter, but it would take some doing to get it up four flights of stairs—seventy-two steps in all.

I called back.

"George, I found it, but how am I supposed to get that thing up the tower? Even with all the parts out, it still weighs about a ton."

"As you oughter know," he said, "cast-iron stoves ain't famous for being lightweight, but from what I seen, you got some sort of a brain and you ain't too weak, so you should be able to figger out a way. If not, Stanley is coming up your way next week and maybe he'll give you a hand." That's just fine, I thought, Stanley, the alternate ranger, was about sixty years old and didn't appear to be in very good health.

This was going to take some planning. I was determined to get that stove up the stairs, but right now I was getting up at 5:30 a.m., making breakfast and a lunch, doing a test call, washing dishes and cleaning up, working all day brushing out a trail, and then back by 5 p.m., preparing the evening meal, doing a test call, and washing dishes again plus getting water and firewood. The day was pretty well used up and so was I.

After several days of pleasant weather it finally clouded up and rained. No work on the trail this day, so today would be the day the stove ascended the stairs.

After breakfast, with the lookout all tidied up, I went down to the woodshed. I had come up with a plan that seemed to be the only possible solution and now was the time to try it out.

The crate was still extremely heavy—probably 300 pounds—but I could lift one end enough to turn it over. A couple of flops end-over-end and it was out the door headed across the yard toward the stairs.

The rain really got down to business and I was soaked through, but there was no turning back. I gave a heave, turned the crate over, and gained a couple stairs. I couldn't let go of the thing or it would slide right back down, so it had to be held from the bottom all the time. I would put my shoulder against it and hold on until I got enough strength back to flop it over again. Slowly I got to the first landing, a fourth of the way up, in time to get the weather call at eleven o'clock. Then I lit a fire in the old stove to dry out a bit before the next ascent.

By noon, half the mountain had been climbed and I was at the second landing, exhausted but in the groove, gaining confidence with every flip-flop. After a bowl of hot soup I went back to work, being extra cautious now since the steps were wet and slippery and so was the crate. A slip could send that cast-iron monster crashing down pinning me or, worse, crashing through the rail and taking me along. I had put on my cork boots as an extra precaution again slipping.

Another hour and I gained the third landing. One more to go. Barring any mishap, supper would be cooked on the new stove. I was elated.

Back again after a rest and dry off, the flip-flopping went on. Only forty-five minutes and I was at the top—absolutely triumphant.

Once through the door the stove slid easily on the floor, but the old stove still had to be disconnected and dragged out. Now, though, it was hotter than blazes since there was still a fire in it. There would be plenty of time for it to cool off while I hauled up all the parts for the new one. Then I'd still have to uncrate and assemble the new stove, and that would take awhile.

The easiest way to get the legs on it was to block the stove up on some pieces of firewood and then slip the legs on and pull out the wood after they were fastened. Then I took the lids off to lighten up the old stove and smoke poured out. To heck with it. I disconnected the stovepipe, set it on a couple pieces of crating, and pushed it out the door. It could sit out there and smoke all it wanted.

Now it was just a matter of getting the lids on and the stovepipe connected and I'd be in business. Everything fit and she was ready to light up. As soon as the fire got going good the stove started to smoke. I'd forgotten it was covered with grease that would have to burn off.

The place turned blue with terrible, acrid-smelling smoke. I opened the windows but not much went out. By now I was coughing and had to go outside where the rain continued to come down. By luck, the old stove was sitting under a shutter that afforded some shelter, and by putting the lids back on I had a nice warm seat. A little smoke still was coming out, but not enough to bother. Inside it was still blue and I'd run in occasionally to throw some more wood on the fire to hasten the burning-off process.

After an hour the smoke started to taper off and a half hour later I could re-enter and close the windows. They would need some serious washing after all the greasy smoke, but that would be another day; right now I was going to dry off, warm up, and relax and enjoy my new treasure.

At test call time, George was at the switchboard again. Trying to sound as nonchalant as possible I said, "Would you please find out what I should do with the old stove?"

"So that's what you been up to. I figgered if you fell over it once too often you'd get it out of your way."

"What should I do with it?" I said.

"Where's it at?"

"Out on the catwalk."

"Just leave it be. Stanley's coming up and he can tell you where to get shut of it."

"Aren't you going to ask how I got the new one up here?"

"No I ain't, 'cause I already know."

"How?"

"Same as everyone does—by going end over end. Bowlander even figgered that out twenty years ago." I could hear Bowlander chuckle in the background.

Somewhat deflated I said, "Guess I'll bake some bread on my new stove."

"Good idea," said George. "Maybe I'll come up there and help you eat it up—then again maybe I won't 'cause it probably won't be any good anyway."

"It'll be good, don't you worry," I said and hung up.

Apparently I was more impressed with my feat than George was, so I wrote a letter to my mother telling her all about it. Mothers are always impressed by their son's deeds.

After a three-day baking binge, Stanley showed up late one afternoon. He was coming from Junction and had stopped at Fourth of July Creek and caught a salt bag full of trout, a rare treat.

While he tended to his horse and a mule, I read the mail he had brought me and started to make supper.

He had walked down the trail to close the horse bars after turning the horse loose. Then he had tied the mule to the tower leg.

When he came up I asked, "How come you tied up that mule? Won't he stay around?"

"That's why I got here so late," he said. "I spent half the morning running him down, and I'm gonna make sure he doesn't get away again."

We had just started to dig into our supper when the tower gave a sudden lurch that felt like an earthquake. We both ran out the door and looked down. There was a large buck deer practicing up for the coming mating season by using Stanley's mule for a sparing partner. In trying to defend himself, the poor mule about pulled the whole tower over.

The buck would back away and then advance with head down in a threatening manner and give the mule a poke with his horns, which were still in velvet. Then he would jump out of the way when the mule turned and kicked. It was clearly a mismatch—the deer was way too agile for a tied-up mule.

"I'll put a stop to this," I said and ran in for a couple pieces of firewood, handing one to Stanley. I fired first, missing the target by ten feet. Stanley's aim wasn't too good either. He succeeded only in hitting the mule in the back, and the lurch that followed threw both of us against the rail. I ran in for more wood, but the deer became apprehensive and went to grazing in the yard.

"You got any shells?" asked Stanley. He had apparently noticed my revolver lying on the bunk.

"Not a one," I said. "Why?"

"I sure would like to get that deer," he replied.

"You mean to scare him away?" I said. Shooting him seemed a bit extreme to me. He hadn't really caused that much trouble.

"No," he said, "to eat. I could quarter him up and pack out the meat tomorrow. By evening the wife could have the whole thing canned. There must be a hundred mason jars in that house we're living in."

This came as a surprise to me. Rangers and alternates are also game wardens of a sort, and deer season wasn't due to open for at least a month, but if he wanted to get that deer, I wasn't averse to being a party to the crime.

We went back in and finished our now cold supper. Later, Stanley walked out on the catwalk to have a look around and came dashing right back in. "Come here quick," he said. I ran out and looked down where he pointed. The buck was directly under us, pawing at a hole in the ground about the size of a washtub caused by animals searching for salt. We were really supposed to pour all our dishwater in the garbage can and dispose of it in the pit but everybody simply threw it off the tower. There was some salt in the dishwater, and that wound up in the soil and attracted the deer.

"Man," Stanley said, "he must go over 200 pounds—you sure you don't have any shells?"

"I'm sure," I said. "I turned the place upside down last week when a bunch of grouse were roosting on the guy wires. There's a full box at Bungalow that I forgot to bring up but that won't do us any good."

"Does that buck come around often?" he asked.

"Everyday," I said. "In fact, there's usually another one about the same size, but he's a little more wary. Then there's a little doe that hangs around most of the time. I can almost touch her she's so tame."

After watching the deer for awhile Stanley said, "If we only had something heavy to drop on him, I bet I could get that deer yet."

"Look behind you," I said. There sat the old stove. Dropped from forty-five feet it could crush an elephant, let alone a deer.

We instantly set to work removing anything removable—lids, legs, etc. Then, with a mighty heave, we balanced it on the top rail.

"This ought to do the trick," said Stanley. We waited for the deer to get directly under the stove. When everything looked just right Stanley nodded and we pushed it off.

A falling object of this magnitude that has as many holes in it as this one happened to have tends to generate quite a bit of noise as it drops, and deer, being possessed of an extremely acute sense of hearing, are prone to leave an area of danger in great haste. Our friend had already reached a safe distance and turned around to watch when the stove hit.

At the moment of impact it virtually disintegrated. Shrapnel flew in all directions and a volcano of ash spouted out in a cloud that slowly settled, completely whitening an area thirty feet in diameter. Even the tower rocked, but, as Stanley explained later, "That was just the mule having a nervous breakdown."

The deer had now retreated a hundred feet or so from the place where the attempt on his life had taken place and he eyed it suspiciously, as well he might. Slowly, though, he circled downwind, testing the air for signs of danger. He stepped closer, carefully sniffing each piece of scrap iron, gradually making his way back to the salt hole, his craving for salt overcoming his better judgment.

Stanley had a better plan. Seeing we still had a formidable arsenal of cast-iron parts, why not drop the grates first? They would make lots of noise and lull the deer into a false sense of security, and then we would follow up with the silent, but deadly, lids for the coup de grace, a plan that surely could not fail.

We each took a grate, and when conditions were just right, Stanley dropped his straight down toward the now very suspicious deer while I heaved mine out toward his anticipated route of escape.

Mine landed not ten feet from Stanley's and the deer was a good fifty feet away when they hit. Well, we hadn't really intended to do any damage with the grates anyway. They were just part of the softening-up process. When the silent lids came down, that would be another matter.

Again the deer repeated his cautious return to the salt hole, taking ten minutes or so to determine that everything was safe. This time we were armed to the teeth—a lid in each hand and the four legs balanced on the rail ready for instant launch. Even the spider, the piece that the lids fit into, was going to go. It was now or never. At Stanley's nod, all four lids were released, followed by the legs and spider.

Had either of us been schooled in aerodynamics we would have known that a round stove lid passing through the air becomes a sort of overweight Frisbee that tends to plane off in one direction or another. The legs and spider, on the other hand, fell true but created enough wind noise to warn our intended victim in plenty of time for him to escape once again.

Well, our ammunition supply was exhausted and the area below looked like a battlefield, so we had to give up. Only firewood remained and if we wanted a hot breakfast we'd better not throw all that away. Besides, it was getting dark and the dishpan was on the stove full of dirty dishes, sitting in what was now cold, greasy water.

During the night the tower would lurch occasionally. No doubt the deer was getting bored and was amusing himself by worrying the poor mule. As we drifted off to sleep Stanley, ever hopeful, had mumbled, "if that mule's rear hoofs ever connect, I may have me some venison yet." But at dawn there was only one bleary-eyed mule down below and no deer to be seen anywhere.

After breakfast, as he was preparing to leave, Stanley said, "I'll see if I can get up here again in a couple weeks and I'll bring your shells along."

When he did return, not only with my ammunition but with a weapon of his own, the deer wisely stayed away only to reappear after he had left. Whoever referred to them as "dumb animals" had never run into this critter. I never did find out if that deer survived the hunting season or not, but I like to think he did and that his offspring are just as smart as he was and are still roaming those beautiful mountains.

Nineteen
Farewell to Bungalow

Things at Bear Butte were not going well. The cable car down at the river had broken down and as a result I'd had neither mail nor perishables for three weeks. Even the sheepherder, Raymond, had stopped visiting me. Maybe that was just as well, he'd not been all that much company anyway.

Raymond was tending a flock of six hundred sheep on the side of Cook Mountain and he'd been a regular visitor until the cable car broke down. His first visit had been on a Wednesday six weeks ago. I'd just returned from my weekly trip to meet the supply truck at the cable car to pick up my pack of perishables and mail. By luck I'd just cut into a big juicy cantaloupe when he came up the stairs accompanied by his collie dog. He introduced himself, and to be hospitable I offered him half of my cantaloupe. He accepted, of course, and had shown up every Wednesday thereafter until the cable car broke down and no more cantaloupe were forthcoming. So much for loyal friendships.

To make matters worse, my right thumb was pounding away, painful as all get out. That had been my own fault and I was kicking myself for being such a fool. The cause of it all was Pete, my friendly rock squirrel. There were two of them, Pete and Repeat, and of the pair Pete was the tamer one.

Every morning I kept two pancakes for my little friends, and when I'd finished breakfast all I had to do was open the door and whistle and up the stairs they'd come for their breakfast. They never ate them on the spot, but dragged them backward down all seventy-two steps. Where they took them I never knew, but they soon returned for their morning raisins. Pete in particular had a fondness for raisins, and this is how I figured I would get to pet him.

My plan was to hold the raisin between my right thumb and forefinger in the usual manner and when he was really enjoying the treat I'd start raising my hand. I'd often done this and every time he'd put his little paws on my finger and stand up on his hind legs. Now came the tricky part. I would slip my thumb gently over one of those little paws, and hold him fast with my other hand. It worked to perfection. I held him gently but firmly in my left hand with only his head sticking out. At first he struggled, but as I talked to him he gradually calmed down and I figured it was petting time. I got in one stroke and then there was a searing, white-hot pain in my right thumb where his sharp teeth were embedded. I tried to shake him off, but he hung on with the tenacity of a bulldog. It wasn't until I set him firmly on the floor that he released his grip and sat there chattering angrily at my treachery.

Fortunately a river of blood flowed from my wounded thumb, for who knew what manner of bacteria had gone in along with those wicked teeth? No infection developed but my thumb was a source of pain and worry for a week or more. Pete, as far as I was concerned, could stay forever unpetted.

My other animal friend, the little doe I called Bambi, was a great comfort to me. She came every day for the salt I poured on a stump beside the bottom landing. I would talk to her as she licked at the salt and she would stare at me with her gentle brown eyes. We became, over the summer, quite good friends and though I'm sure she trusted me to do her no harm, she would only allow me to come within inches of her. Touching her was off limits.

Our relationship got a boost one evening. I was sitting on the catwalk watching the sunset when I caught a flicker of motion down near the spring that turned out to be Bambi. She would go dashing off out of my sight behind some brush and then reappear only to go running pell-mell back again to the same spot. I watched for a few minutes then decided to go see what all the fuss was about. It took only a short time to get to the spot where she was wild eyed and repeating her antics. Looking over to where she ran, I saw a large black bear busily eating huckleberries and paying no attention to her whatsoever.

I shouted at the bear, but he continued to nibble away. I debated going back for my revolver, but thought better of it. I picked up a rock instead and fired it at Mr. Bear, whereupon he let out a "woof" and took off for parts unknown.

Bambi then ran to where the bear had departed and emerged proudly with a little fawn in tow. She followed me back to the lookout with her fawn and they spent the night under the tower. Apparently she viewed me as her protector. In the morning they were gone and though she still came everyday thereafter, she never brought her little one with her.

It had been cold and raining for over a week now, and to keep warm I'd used up a lot of my firewood. This was a real problem at Bear Butte since most of the usable dead trees had been cut down over the years. This meant going farther and farther away in search of wood. I'd been hauling it in an old dilapidated wheelbarrow that somebody had made years ago. The wheel was just a cut-off piece from a round log with wire wrapped around to keep it from splitting apart. It worked better than carrying the wood in my arms, but not much. I was getting wet everyday on my wood gathering, and with a fire going all the time, I could barely keep ahead of the stove's great appetite.

Then a call came from Wade.

"How'r you fixed for firewood?"

"Pretty good."

"You have a two-week supply?"

"Yeah, maybe three."

"Good. How long will it take you to get closed up and down to the river?"

"Maybe two or three hours. Why?"

"With all this rain, the fire danger is way down and we're pulling some of the lookouts in. Fire season's about over anyway."

"Did somebody fix the cable car?"

"No. You'll have to cross at the ford."

"Wade, that river's gotta be high after all this rain."

"I know, but that's where Ken insisted on picking you up."

"Let me talk to him. It would be just as easy for me to come down over Bugle Point and he could pick me up at the mouth of Johnny Creek."

"That's what I told him to do, but he's the boss and he left an hour ago to check the campgrounds up river."

"I don't know about that ford, Wade. Even when the water was low I never tried it. It looks awful treacherous to me."

"I know it is, and if I had any transportation here, I'd pick you up at Johnny Creek and he could sit and wait for you at the ford till hell froze over for all I care."

I'd never heard Wade talk like this before. He and Ken must not be getting along too well.

"Are all the trucks gone?"

"Yeah. Ken and Stanley each took one and the big one's got a dead battery. I'd use my own car to get you, but the brakes are all apart."

"Well, that's it then. I'll be coming across at the ford."

"I don't like to see you trying that, but I'm afraid you'll have to. Listen, stay always on the upstream side. There's a fairly shallow bar going across, and if you get off on the downstream side you're gonna be in deep, fast water, so watch out."

"I'll try, but I'm not real happy with this."

"Neither am I and Ken knows it."

"Okay. Soon as I get organized I'll be off."

"Good luck to you and be careful. Be sure to stay on the upstream side."

"I will."

This was not good news at all. If Wade was concerned, I had every reason to be. Furthermore, I was really angry with Ken. All he would have had to do is drive two miles out of his way to pick me up and avoid a risky crossing. Even if I got across okay, I'd still be soaking wet, and with the weather what it was, it was going to be most unpleasant. With his reputation for being late, who knows how long I'd be out there waiting? After cleaning up the lookout, I gathered my things and slipped into my pack and went into a cold, drizzling rain.

My little deer was patiently waiting for her daily salt ration and I was sorry to disappoint her, but it was too late. The salt was already put away. She followed me to the edge of the yard and then turned back. I stopped and took one last look at Bear Butte, where I'd spent so many pleasant days, wondering if I'd ever see it again. Standing in the rain did my somber mood no good, so I turned and started down the trail.

Arriving at the ford I looked the situation over, and what I saw was not reassuring. The water was higher than I had ever seen it before, though still crystal clear. The take-out spot was at a forty-five-degree angle upstream, which meant bucking a swift current. Coming from the other side would have been far easier. As a precaution I put my wallet and watch in the pack. With luck they might stay dry.

"Well, no guts no glory," I said to myself and stepped in.

I knew that these clear mountain waters were very deceptive so it came as no surprise that what had appeared to be knee-deep water was actually hip deep and after a few more steps rapidly became waist deep. The current was tugging at my legs and rocks began to roll beneath my boots, but I struggled slowly ahead, trying hard to stay on the upstream side of the rock bar.

When the water began lapping at the bottom of my pack, I knew I was in trouble and could go no farther. Going back wasn't going to work either. I'd surely be taken downstream and the only place to get out was where I'd entered. Below that was a long stretch of sheer rock cliff. I was at the point of no return with no way to go ahead. I stood for awhile to catch my breath, leaning into the current and pondering my next move. Maybe I was already on the downstream side of the bar. It was hard to tell. Perhaps, if I forced my way upstream, the water would be shallower.

Leaning farther upstream, I lifted one foot and then the other one was swept right out from under me. All I saw was green water, but I popped quickly to the surface, my canvas pack acting like a life preserver. My hat was just out of reach, floating away, but I made a lunge for it and got it. There was nothing for it now but to let the current take me and try to make some progress toward the far shore. Occasionally my boots would strike bottom, enabling me to push a few more feet, but most of the progress came from using my hat like a paddle. The current was so swift that the cable car soon passed by overhead, suspended out over midriver, the broken rope dangling down. How I wished I could have crossed in it.

Eventually I worked my way closer to the far shore and the water became shallow enough to get a foothold now and then. About a quarter mile downstream, I finally pulled myself up onto a bunch of boulders on the shoreline and I stayed there gasping for breath until I started shivering with cold. Then I scrambled up to the road twenty feet above. Teeth chattering and feet squishing, I walked slowly back to the cable car platform where Ken was supposed to pick me up.

Taking off my pack, I dug out a light jacket, which was soaked, but it did afford some protection from the cold rain that was still coming down with a vengeance. Miserable, cold, and wet, I left the pack and started off down the road in a futile attempt to warm myself. As I walked my anger toward Ken increased with every step.

The time to make a very important decision was close at hand and today's happenings pushed it to the forefront. I had come out here in the spring expecting to be offered a full-time job, but with Shorty having been transferred, it was a whole new ball game. Ken had promised to see what he could do, but every time I brought up the subject he'd been evasive. Well, today was the last straw.

After an hour of walking back and forth, the green pickup finally came around the bend and pulled up. Ken rolled the window down.

"You better get in here. You look like a drowned rat."

"Come out here first. I want to show you something."

"Can't I see it from here?"

"No, you can't. I want you to take a good look."

"Well, alright, if it's that important. Now what is it?"

Pointing across at where I'd entered the river I said, "You see where the ford starts on the other side?"

"Yes."

"And you see where it comes out over here?"

"Yes, I see it. What are you getting at?"

"What I'm getting at is you damn near got me drowned trying to get across here."

"Are you kidding? It couldn't have been that bad."

"Oh, no? Go ahead and try it. I'll wait right here."

"Well, I'm not going to get all wet, but I'm sure I could do it easily enough."

"Go ahead then. Prove it."

"I'm just not going to. That's all. Let's get in the truck. You're wet enough already."

Reluctantly I got in and we drove on for awhile in silence. After I'd cooled down somewhat, I asked the question that was uppermost in my mind.

"Just what have you done about getting me a permanent job?"

"Well, to tell you the truth, I've been pretty busy and just haven't gotten around to it."

"Just when do you figure on getting around to it?"

"Actually, it's pretty late in the year for something like that, what with budget and all."

"In other words, you haven't done anything about it and don't intend to."

"Well, I wouldn't put it that way exactly."

"That's exactly the way I'm putting it."

"I could keep you on for another month, maybe even two."

"That's not good enough."

"Under the circumstances, I don't know what else I can do."

"I do."

"What's that?"

"You can make out my time. I'm through."

"You can't mean that."

"I mean exactly that."

"Look, I know you're cold and wet and maybe angry, but let's not do anything right now. Think about it over tonight and by morning you'll change your mind."

"Don't count on it."

Only the swishing of the windshield wipers broke the silence the rest of the way. George was waiting when we pulled in.

"Geez kid, am I glad to see you. Looks like you got yourself a good ducking."

"That I did."

"Listen, you git on up to the washhouse and take a shower 'fore you ketch pneumonia. I got a good fire goin' and the waters hot."

"Thanks a million, George. Just let me go get some dry clothes first."

"No you don't. I'll bring 'em. I know where they're at. You jest hurry up and git outa them wet clothes."

By the time my stiff, cold fingers fumbled the buttons on my shirt loose, George was there with dry clothes and a towel.

"I was plenty worried about you, tryin' to cross at that ford. How was it?"

"Not good."

"What I figured, but you made it."

"Yeah, about a quarter mile downstream."

"Oh, I see. You know, me and Wade done our best to talk him out of it, but he just don't listen to nobody."

"You're telling me. That's why I told him to make out my time."

"I was afraid you might. That is one crying shame. You know he ain't really a bad sort, but he's just too damn stubborn for his own good."

"I know only too well."

"Him and Wade had one hell of a row over this, and if I hadn't stepped in, I guess Wade would of whipped him right then and there."

"Was it that bad? I could tell Wade was mad, but I didn't know it had gone that far."

"Unless I miss my guess, Wade ain't gonna put up with much more."

"You mean he'd quit after all these years?"

"That's what I'm thinkin'."

"Oh, man, that's awful. I'll go talk to him after a while."

"You do that, but I'll bet his mind's made up. Now hurry up and git in that shower 'fore the water gits cold. I'll have supper on when you finish up."

This was terrible news. I knew that Wade had been with the Forest Service over twenty years and to leave now would not be good. I would have a talk with him. Maybe it wasn't as serious as George made it out to be. Feeling much better after a hot shower, I went down to the cookhouse and George greeted me with more news.

"Soon's yer done eatin', you're to call Bob at Chateau."

"Oh, did he say what he wanted?"

"That he did."

"Well?"

"It looks like you'll be havin' some company on yer way home."

"You mean he's quitting?"

"What he said, but you'd best talk it over with him."

"I sure will."

"There's more. I'll let Bob tell you."

I hurried through supper, which was eaten in grim silence. I had known for sometime that this day had to come, but now that it was here, I felt completely drained—not just from the unnecessary cold swim, but from the awful feeling of loss. I had loved this job and these people so much, and now it was all coming apart. What I'd planned as my lifelong career was finished. I'd have to go back home and find a job, but there could never be another like the one I was leaving, of that I was certain.

In a somber mood, I called Chateau and Bob got right to the point.

"I heard you're leaving."

"That's right."

"How'd you like some passengers on you way home. We'd pay all expenses."

"We?"

"Yeah, Carl, Marv, and me."

"I guess so, sure."

"We won't all get in 'till sometime in the afternoon, though, if you can wait that long."

"I'll wait. No problem."

It took awhile to digest all this. So many things were happening that it was hard to take it all in. Well, first things first. I would have to walk up to the CCC Camp and get my car and then see Wade and Buckshot.

That was not going to be easy. They were so special to me, and leaving them would be especially painful.

The rain had stopped, and when I crossed the gate, Old Ned, our gentlest mule, came to me and I put my head against his warm neck and stroked him for the last time. He walked with me to the garage and stepped aside as I backed out. A lantern shone from the kitchen window when I drove to Wade's house.

"So you've come to see me with a car now," Wade said when he opened the door.

"Yes. I'll be needing it."

"George tells me you'll be leaving us."

"Afraid so."

"I don't believe I'll be around long myself."

"I hate to hear you say that Wade. How many years do you have in?"

"Twenty-one."

"How much pension will you lose?"

"At this point I don't care anymore. Ole' Buckshot and me we'll get by, won't we?" he said, putting an arm around her.

"Sure we will," she said, looking up and smiling at him. "Set yourself down and I'll put on a pot of coffee and we'll talk awhile."

Talk didn't come easy at first, knowing it was for the last time, but gradually we got to rehashing the good times and the gloom began to dissipate. The hours went by as we relived the past we'd had shared together, but at last it was time to go. I gave Buckshot a big hug and I guess we were both pretty choked up. I shook hands with Wade.

"I'll see you in the morning," he said as I walked to the car.

Alone in the bunkhouse, I spent a restless night wishing that things had not gone the way they had, but it was too late for that now. All the bridges were burned behind me.

George tried to liven things up at breakfast, but even he couldn't change the way I felt. I helped with the dishes just to kill some time and then went down to the office to take care of the necessary paperwork. Arky, the new clerk, was there alone. Ken had left for the day, not saying when he'd be back. Wade came in and we talked awhile and then I went to start a fire in the washhouse, knowing that all of us would want a shower before leaving.

Bob came in while I was packing my things followed by Carl. Just before noon Marv drifted in. None of the other boys had planned on making a career of this, so they were in a far better humor than I was. After lunch we took turns showering, packing, and filling out forms and then it was time to go.

Cameras came out and everybody took a few pictures of everybody and said their goodbys.

Wade put his big hand on my shoulder. "Good luck son, you'll come back and see Buckshot and me someday, won't you?"

"Yes, I will Wade. That's a promise."

"You've made a promise now."

"Yes, and I always keep them."

Wade, George, Arky, and Lee all waved goodby as we pulled away and after we crossed the bridge there was Buckshot standing at the gate raising her hand in farewell.

Twenty
Return to Bungalow

"Tell us a forest story, Dad."

In the evenings when the children were small and I was not working, this was their request. So, we would gather after bath time when pajamas were on and sit on my daughter Laura's bed with my son Steve at the foot and then I would dutifully tell one of the stories contained in this book. My wife always insisted, "Dad is only making all that up."

Over the course of their early childhood, they heard all the stories many times over and yet never seemed to tire of them. After hearing so much about the Bungalow and its people, it was only natural that they should want to see it firsthand, but the years went by and for one reason or another the long-awaited trip always got postponed.

Finally, in 1973, twenty-five years after I'd said my sad farewell to Bungalow and my friends, everything came together. I had sixteen days of vacation, and the kids were old enough at twelve and fifteen to make the five-mile hike up to Clarke Mountain. When the day of departure drew near, letters were written to friends in Denver and Moscow, Idaho, whom we planned to visit. Jack (Richard) Johnson now of Rathdrum, Idaho, was called and he assured me that Wade and Buckshot were alive and well. I wrote to them to let them know we were coming.

By June first, a reservation had been made at the Barkmore Kennel for our Labrador Blackie. Cameras were checked, rolls and rolls of film were purchased, suitcases came out, and the countdown began. At zero minus one Blackie was driven to the kennel. The station wagon was filled with everything and on June tenth at 0500 hours we were off and running. By 0630 we were lost in Madison, going round and round and always coming back to the state capitol building. Since it was Sunday morning there were few motorists about and even fewer pedestrians, but we finally located one who directed us out of town. That crisis past, it was clear sailing to Council Bluffs, Iowa, where we spent our first night.

Then it was up at dawn and on to Denver, where we had a delightful visit with friends we hadn't seen in years. Spectacular Rocky Mountain Park was next on the agenda and for the kids, these were the first mountains they'd ever seen. The road over Trail Ridge had only recently been opened, so we drove through a veritable tunnel of snow, with only the blue sky overhead.

We left Colorado, and after a brief look at Dinosaur National Monument and then up through Flaming Gorge, we headed out of Utah into Wyoming. Here we were in for a few surprises. At the state line the sign read PAVEMENT ENDS. Expecting the pavement to end in a quarter mile or so, I failed to slow down and to my surprise it ended right at the sign, together with a sizeable drop in the surface of the road. Everybody got bounced around and some luggage got rearranged, but otherwise no damage was done.

We had planned to spend the night in Ketchum near Sun Valley, Idaho, but the road in that direction seemed like more of the same, so Steve, the navigator, and my wife Carol got out the map and decided that Twin Falls would be a more advisable target.

As you see, we had not really intended to stay there, nor had another couple coming from the opposite direction, but we were both drawn there by fate. The day had been a scorcher, so we went straight to the Best Western where the sign said outdoor pool. There was only one room left, but just as we were about to sign in we discovered the pool was out of order. The clerk agreed to hold the room for half an hour while we went in search of another with a pool. We had scarcely left when the weather began to deteriorate and it looked like an outdoor pool would be the last thing we would need, so back we went to claim our room.

Meanwhile, another couple was driving through town only to be pulled over by a police officer.

"What's the trouble, officer?" asked the lady who was driving.

"Why no trouble at all, ma'am, we'd just like for you to be our guests tonight at the Best Western courtesy of the Chamber of Commerce," he said pulling a slip of paper from his pocket.

"Well, I don't know," she said, "we really had planned on being in Pocatello this evening."

"Would dinner for two at the Holiday Inn help make up your mind?" the office asked, pulling another slip from his pocket. That did it, perhaps if they had held out longer, he'd have given them the key to the bank, but they were satisfied.

Meanwhile, back at the motel, having showered in lieu of a swim, we agreed to have dinner down the street at the Holiday Inn. Steve and I would walk down to get a little exercise and Carol and Laura would drive down and meet us there in few moments. As we were about to start out, backing into the adjoining unit were the recipients of the town freebies. Not wanting to confuse her by stepping out, Steve and I waited for her to finish her parking and then started off across the parking lot. Just as we reached the sidewalk the rain began to come down, so we turned around to find my wife and this lady engaged in a most happy and animated conversation. It seems that the lady noticed our Wisconsin plates and asked Carol where in the state we were from.

"About thirty miles north of Milwaukee near Cedarburg," Carol answered.

"Well, isn't that something. I used to teach school in Port Washington."

"No kidding. That's my hometown."

Right about here Steve and I arrived on the scene, and one can only imagine all the "do you know this person and do you know that person" that was going on. The husband and I stood by taking in all the reminiscing and having little or nothing to contribute.

Finally he turned to me. "Where you heading?"

"Northern Idaho."

"Do you have friends there?"

"Well, yes. I used to work for the Forest Service there many years ago and I'm going back."

"What forest did you work in?"

"The Clearwater."

"Which district?"

"Bungalow."

"That's a coincidence. I surveyed the road from the Cedars into Kelly Creek in 1932."

A coincidence indeed. I doubt if there could be another couple in the world with such a combination of backgrounds, and here we were drawn together at adjoining units at this motel. Now our wives stopped talking and became interested in our conversation.

"We must surely know some people in common," I said.

"Yes," he said. "Who do you know?"

"Shorty Meneely?"

"No, can't say that I do."

"Wade Candler?"

"Wade Candler—do you know Wade?"

"I sure do, and what's more we're going to see him day after tomorrow."

We talked of Wade and old times for awhile, and then he related and incident to me that happened back in 1932 that had involved Wade.

"Just run that by him and see if he remembers me," he said.

I agreed to do this. By now we had new friends, Steve and Ardis Stevens from Bozeman, Montana. The kids were getting restless and hungry, so we agreed to meet later back at the motel, though often people make these agreements and fail to carry them out. Not so this time, though, for when we were halfway through our meal in the crowded dining room at the Holiday Inn, the hostess brought our new friends in and seated them at the table right next to us. There was no escaping it, somebody was insisting that we get together. Our friendship has been a source of great pleasure to us over the years since our first unlikely meeting.

Still sleepy, but eager to be off, we left early next morning headed north and over the heart-stopping Whitebird Grade, then on to Moscow and a joyful reunion with old friends. We went to bed that night filled with anticipation. Tomorrow we would see Wade and Buckshot and then go on to Bungalow and hike to Clarke Mountain.

Finding Wade's modest little house at Southwick was easy, and seven o'clock the next morning found us pulling into the driveway. I knocked at the door, noting Wade's old cowboy hat in the entryway. No response. I knocked again. Still nothing. I tried the door. Locked. What a disappointment. I was sure they were at home, but they must still be asleep and not be able to hear me. I left a note, and instead of going straight through from Bungalow up to Superior, Montana, as planned, we'd just have to come back again later. I hadn't come all this way to miss seeing Wade and Buckshot. No siree. After all, I had made a promise twenty-five years ago and it would be kept one way or another. I had hoped that they would enjoy going along to the Bungalow with us, but as things developed it was fortunate that they didn't accompany us, for they would have been very disappointed.

We headed straight for Bungalow. If we were going to climb Clarke Mountain and return to Wade's and then go on to Coeur d'Alene, it would be one full day. On the way, Carol repeated what she had warned me about earlier.

"I don't mind you and the kids going up to Clarke, but don't expect me to go along. That's just too far."

"I know," I said. "There'll be somebody at the office you can chat with. I'm sure they'll be glad for the company."

We drove on past Orofino and Greer with anticipation mounting as we drew nearer our destination.

I looked for the old sheet-metal-sided house near Weippe where two old gentlemen had insisted on sharing lunch with me when I'd stopped to ask directions, and sure enough there it was still standing, but it looked deserted.

We stopped for gas at Pierce. The town looked much different than when I'd last seen it. The old road to Bungalow over Shanghai Divide was no longer kept up, and I was advised not to try it. It was better to take the new one. It appeared to have been blacktopped at one time, but it too was obviously never kept up, so we bounced and jounced over potholes and washboard most of the way. At last Orogrande Creek appeared. The kids were now on the edge of their seats taking everything in. At last there was the huge boulder that I'd fished from so many times, then one more curve and there would be the bridge over the Orogrande and the barn. Yes, there it was—but why was the roof half missing and why were some of the other buildings either gone or partly torn down? The ranger station was obviously deserted.

I was devastated. The place I'd loved so much looked like a war zone. Litter filled the yard, a bunk lay on its side in front of the partially destroyed bunkhouse, and the triangle that had called us to dinner so many times was gone. If it had still been there, I'd have taken it as a remembrance and felt no guilt in doing so.

Carol was the first to break the stunned silence.

"I am not going to sit and wait here in the car for three hours while you walk up to Clarke."

I couldn't say that I blamed her. Now it was Steve's turn.

"Well, we didn't come all this way to turn around and leave. We're going up there." Laura seconded the motion.

"Hold on everybody," I said, "I'll think of something. Let's just walk out on the big bridge and have a look at the Clearwater River."

It looked like we were at an impasse. I absolutely could not allow the kids to go alone, nor would Carol stay alone. To make things worse, it was a cloudy, gloomy, damp day with rain threatening, driving our spirits even lower. We trudged to the bridge, which was new, and looked down at the swirling water, and it was keen-eyed Steve who solved our problem.

"Look over there, Dad, isn't that a Volkswagen parked at that house?"

I looked over at the old ranger's house, which hadn't been visible before, and indeed there was a car and a German Shepherd tied to a tree.

"Where there's cars and dogs there's gotta be people. Let's go over and find out."

We jumped in the car and drove over. When I knocked, there was movement inside and the door was opened by an extremely attractive blond girl in blue jeans. Surprised to say the least I managed, "Good morning, are you the ranger's wife?"

"Oh no," she answered, "this place is abandoned. I'm the traffic counter's wife."

"The traffic counter?"

"Yes. They're contemplating abandoning the road down river, and my husband counts the cars that use it."

"Must be an interesting job," I joked.

"It sure isn't," she said. "Some days there are no cars at all."

"Look," I said, getting to the point, "I used to work here a long time ago and I would like to hike up to Clarke with my kids, but my wife doesn't want to go. How would you like some company for about three hours?"

"I would be absolutely delighted," she beamed.

I waved to the family to come on in and we introduced ourselves. Our hostess said her name was Candy. She had been married just five weeks and, along with her husband, had recently graduated from the University of Idaho. Thinking this job would be a lark they had accepted it only to find themselves isolated and with no electricity or phone. The only thing to read was an old Forest Service cookbook. Even for honeymooners, this could be a bit much I suspected.

"It's ten o'clock now," I said. "You can expect us back at one."

Candy was not so sure.

"Three hours? I don't know about that. I've been up there and it took longer. After all, that's five miles each way."

"Well, that's what I used to do it in. We'll see."

With that we were off, passing the dammed up stream where Bungalow got its water supply, and starting into the switchbacking tails. Looking down at the old Bungalow from above, it looked almost like it had years ago—much better than it had close up. We stopped to take a few pictures, and then pushed on again. Steve took the lead and was soon out of sight. He would stop and wait every little while and finally he said, "Dad, why don't I go on ahead. I'll wait for you at the lookout."

"Okay, but if you come to any spots where you are the least bit uncertain about the trail just stop right there and wait for us, understand?"

"Okay."

"Remember what I said—there'll be a trail to Elk Mountain going off to the left up ahead. What's left of the phone line should go straight on to Clarke, so follow that, but if you're in doubt just stay put."

"Right, I'll see you up there."

I trusted Steve to be cautious, but you never know about fifteen-year olds. I had always believed in letting kids try their wings as I had been allowed to do, but I still worried. No doubt, my mother had worried more when I came out here to work at age sixteen. I'd see a footprint every once in awhile reassuring me that Steve had not left the trail, and after we passed the Elk Mountain cutoff and his print showed up, I was much relieved.

Laura being only twelve was beginning to slow down after three or four miles, so I put my hand on her back and began pushing, which helped her quite a bit. Eventually we came to the rocky top of Clarke Mountain, and there dead ahead stood the lookout and Steve sitting on the front step.

"What took you so long? I've been here fifteen minutes already."

"Never mind. We got here didn't we?"

"I guess you did. Boy, is it windy up here."

"It always is. Just let me look around and drink this all in. Let's see if I still remember where all the old lookouts were. Chateau should be over there, but it's hidden in the clouds," I said pointing to the north, "and Bighorn, Bear Butte, and Junction would be to the right of the river, but they're all fogged in too."

We took pictures of each other and with the movie camera I got as much scenery as I could and we started back down just as it began to snow. Halfway down the snow turned into a cold, miserable rain. Laura and I were still about a quarter of a mile up when we heard the dog bark, announcing Steve's arrival back at the house. I looked at my watch, it was exactly one o'clock. Not bad at all for two kids and the old man.

Candy and Carol had enjoyed a great visit in our absence and we were invited to bring our cooler in and have lunch at the kitchen table. Two sleeping bags hung from the oven door in an obvious attempt to dry them out. The house was cold and damp and Candy said that they had been trying unsuccessfully to light the gas space heater ever since they'd been there. Carol had assured her that I knew all about such things, so I got right to it. Looking inside, I saw literally hundreds of burnt-out matches. They had been trying all right. It took some pressure on the control rod and I got the heater going. I made sure Candy understood how to relight it, and after a hasty lunch we bid her goodbye and headed back to Wade's house.

When we arrived Buckshot came out immediately to give me a mighty hug. At the same time Wade was smothering my right hand in his huge one. It was like old times again—so much to catch up on and everybody talking at once. I introduced my family and Wade gave Steve the once over.

"You know, young fella, the first time I laid eyes on your Dad he musta been about your age, and I swear I didn't think he'd last a week, but he fooled us all and stuck it out as long as I did."

"When did you leave?" I asked.

"The day after you did. I'd had enough."

"That's awful. Did you ever go back?"

"Never. I like to remember it the way it was."

"We just came from there, and the place is abandoned."

"Yes, I'd heard that. Canyon District got some of it, Kelly Creek got some, and Pierce got the rest. The old Bungalow District is gone forever."

"Sad, isn't it. Seeing all the old buildings being torn down, really hit me. I'm glad you weren't there to see it."

"I wouldn't have gone. Remembering the old Bungalow the way she was is good enough for me."

Buckshot nodded in agreement, then turned to me, "Go get your suitcases and bring 'em in. I'll show you where to put 'em."

"Oh gosh, Buckshot, we're not going to be stayin'. We have to be in Coeur d'Alene tonight. I'm sorry, but time is so short."

Wade's face fell. "I've got the trailer all ready to go. We wanted to take you and the family up to the Selway for a few days of fishing. Couldn't you stay a little longer?"

"No. I'm really sorry but time just won't permit. I have to get back to work in about a week, and we wanted to spend sometime with Jack and his family and take in Yellowstone, the Tetons, and the Black Hills on the way home."

"Well, come on in anyway," said Buckshot. "I'll put on some coffee and at least we'll have some time to visit."

There was much to catch up on, but mostly our conversations returned again and again to the old days at Bungalow. We relived the bear incident at Chateau.

"I was as calm then as I am right now," said Wade, and you knew he was telling the truth.

The snowstorm was gone over once again, and the time Don fell off the lookout at Junction, and it was then that Wade said, "The last time I saw Shorty he still remembered about how fast you got over there. You must have run all the way."

"Not quite, but I know I was really moving."

Suddenly, Steve exclaimed, "Mom, all those stories of Dad's were true."

Wade defended me. "Yes they were true, alright, and there's plenty more."

We got around to our new friends whom we'd met in Twin Falls and I repeated the incident I'd been told about. Wade listened closely and then roared with laughter. "Why that was old Steve Stevens. I'll never forget that day."

"Would you believe I was talking to him a couple days ago?"

"You were? Where in the world did you run into him?"

I told him the bizarre story of how we happened to meet and he shook his head in disbelief.

"Strange things do happen, I guess."

I asked about Bowlander, and George and I was told they had passed away, along with old John and Bill Mitchell and so many of the

Bungalow gang. Shorty had retired and was living in Kalispel, Montana, Wade said, and he'd seen him not so long ago.

I guess we could have gone on forever, but we still had a long drive ahead of us. Before we left the cameras came out and pictures were taken, but at last we could delay no longer.

I am not given to displays of emotion, but saying goodbye to those dear people was not easy. Buckshot clung to me and Wade pressed my hand. They were in their eighties and we knew this would be for the last time.

"Drive carefully. You've a mighty precious cargo there," were Wade's last words to me as we pulled away.

It was late when we reached our motel. I called Jack in the morning. The years fell away when I heard his cheerful voice.

"I'll meet you at the store in Rathdrum and you can follow me to our house," he said.

Over the years, we had phoned each other occasionally and at Christmas time, but I'd never met Kate, his wife, nor had either of them met Carol. It was as if we'd all know each other all our lives. Then we were to meet seven of their nine children—the older two were already in college. We sat around the kitchen table and talked of the old days, the children taking it all in.

After sometime, Jack commented, "You know, I'd never have allowed my kid to do what we did. It was just too darn dangerous."

He was right. I wouldn't have either, but at the time we never thought that much about it. We had dinner together that evening and talked far into the night. "Ah, but those were the days." How fortunate we were to have been a part of them.

I plan to return again someday. Though the buildings now are gone, if I close my eyes, perhaps in the rushing of the waters I can hear once again the ring of Lee's anvil or George's dinner triangle or even Wade's hearty laugh. If I listen closely enough and give my imagination free rein, Bowlander may even sing "Back in the Saddle Again" for me as he steps up into the stirrup.

That would be great, wouldn't it?